Soul Serenade

Soul Serenade

Rhythm, Blues & Coming of Age Through Vinyl

A Memoir

RASHOD OLLISON

Beacon Press
Boston

BEACON PRESS
Boston, Massachusetts
www.beacon.org

Beacon Press books
are published under the auspices of
the Unitarian Universalist Association of Congregations.

20 19 18 17   8 7 6 5 4 3 2 1

This book is printed on acid-free paper
that meets the uncoated paper ANSI/NISO specifications
for permanence as revised in 1992.

Text design and composition by Kim Arney

Some names and other identifying characteristics of people mentioned
in this work have been changed to protect their identities.

Library of Congress Cataloging-in-Publication Data
Ollison, Rashod.
Soul serenade : rhythm, blues & coming of age through vinyl / Rashod Ollison.
pages cm
ISBN 978-0-8070-8897-5 (paperback : alk. paper)
ISBN 978-0-8070-5753-7 (ebook)
1. Ollison, Rashod, 1977– 2. Music critics—United States—Biography.
3. Journalists—United States—Biography. 4. Soul music—History
and criticism. I. Title.
ML423.O46A3 2016
781.64092—dc23
[B]
2015010975

I dedicate this book to my parents,
Royce Dianne Smith-Ollison and Raymond Ollison Jr.
Without them, I would have no story.

. . .

Contents

Part One

· · ·

. . .

THE PICTURE REVEALED THE HAPPINESS I NEVER KNEW.
On the back of the beat-up, black-and-white, wallet-size snap-shot, the names are in lovely penmanship, probably Mama's: Raymond + Dianne Ollison. The location: Juarez, Mexico, where my parents honeymooned in September of 1970.

In the picture, they sit in a café booth. Daddy's arm wraps around Mama's slim shoulders as he presses his dark, angular face next to hers. He gives the camera a seductive stare. With flipped bouffant hair, Mama looks like a member of the Marvelettes. Her smile is so wide, sweet, and radiant it melts the heart. I'm startled at how svelte she is. For as long as I can remember, Mama has battled serious weight issues.

I saw the photo nearly forty years later and its effect was like fresh air circulating through a musty room. Mama Teacake, my maternal grandmother, gave my younger sister Reagan the picture just before she died. When Reagan shared it with me, I was at her place in Little Rock. We were close to thirty and had grown up knowing only the stormy years of the marriage, which ended just as we started grade school.

"Dusty, look at this," Reagan said, handing me the photo. "Can you believe this?"

I stared at it for a long time.

"You betta not walk out of here with it," she said. "I'll get you a copy made."

Much has changed since somebody captured the budding marital bliss of the attractive couple from Malvern, Arkansas, both nineteen at the time.

Daddy's long dead. Mama steers clear of talking about the early years when their love bloomed. She will, however, go on about the drama, when Daddy left home for days, skipping out on paying the light bill to "lay up with some bitch 'cross town."

"I was always left in the dark," Mama said, the double meanings lost on no one.

The country-glam woman-child in the photograph worked two full-time jobs for years, found comfort in food, and constructed a fence around her heart that kept everybody, including my two sisters and me, at a safe distance.

As long as food was in the fridge, clothes on our backs, and a roof overhead, I guess Mama never felt compelled to offer hugs or say "I love you." The proof of that love was all around us in the comfortable homes she could barely afford to rent. The proof of that love was in every tired sigh she released before heading to a job she detested.

Growing up, I heard relatives drop intriguing bits about the early years of the marriage, and always with a tinge of sadness.

Yeah, that was back when Dianne and Raymond had just got together.

Lawd, you couldn't tell Dianne nothin' 'bout Raymond. She know she loved him and he loved her.

Uh-huh, they was silly and in love then.

Oh, that's before your time, boy, back when Raymond and Dianne used to go ev'rywhere togetha. 'Memba how they used to dance?

Whenever I asked specific questions about that time, the subject quickly changed or I was told, "Go ax ya mama." Sometimes I found the nerve to ask her how things were in the early years before Reagan and I were born. But Mama always blew me off with, "Boy, that was a long time ago. Don't even remember. Hell, think I was depressed."

She remembers. The end of that marriage, which lasted thirteen years, haunts her still. It haunts me, too. Out of the ashes, mystery and ugliness, I found music.

But music didn't bring my parents together. I believe it was sadness and intimate knowledge of childhood tragedy. They grew up in Malvern, a city smack dab in the middle of Arkansas, right outside of Hot Springs. Daddy's side was big, many aunts, uncles, and cousins.

Before Daddy made it to the fourth grade, his two older siblings had died. His mother, whom we called Big Mama, became overprotective of her oldest child left. Because his brother and sister had died so young, Daddy didn't think he'd live to see manhood, especially after he was drafted into the Vietnam War just before his nineteenth birthday.

I heard him say years later that he knew he was coming back home in a box. After a dishonorable discharge, Daddy returned to Arkansas a changed man, a time bomb, dead on the inside.

While Daddy's folks were churchgoing and discreet about their messiness, Mama's family lived out loud.

Her mother, Rosezella Cole, whom everyone called Teacake, was the indulged daughter of a bootlegger. As a teenager in the 1940s, when most of her girlfriends picked cotton or cleaned the homes of white folks, Mama Teacake rolled around town in her own car.

She inherited her mama's party spirit and a Mona Lisa smile that pulled you in and pushed you out. At fourteen, Mama Teacake married James Smith, a man seven years her senior, who built a modest white house down the hill from his parents' place just in time for their rapidly growing family.

About eleven months after Mama was born, my aunt Phyllis came, then Jannette a year later and Bonita barely a year after that. Mama Teacake, just twenty-four, was in the throes of domesticity and, from all accounts, the young couple was happy.

Then early on a Sunday morning, everything changed.

Christmas Day, 1955: James had finished a long shift and headed home in time to see the girls open their gifts. He never made it. As he drove down the highway, James fell asleep at the wheel, crashing into an oncoming truck and dying instantly. Mama, who was five, said she remembered all the toys, decorations, and food preparations. Then just before noon, as the family gathered, an officer showed up with the news.

Barely a year after James's death, Mama Teacake found a new man, Ollie Watkins, a conk-wearing young Fats Domino look-alike who moved into the house on Third Street. He was close to Mama Teacake's age and everything James was not: shiftless, unemployed, and a lover of juke joint life. James had served in the Navy, and Mama Teacake received ample benefits, plus steady money from Ma Rene, Mama Teacake's bootlegging mother, who couldn't stand Ollie.

He lived off Mama Teacake for about two years before securing a job at Acme Brick Company. They fought as hard as they drank and partied, often in front of the girls. There was an argument one unseasonably hot spring night in 1957.

Mama Teacake and Ollie had been drinking. She accused him of fooling around. He denied it.

Woman, you crazy. You gon' believe me or them lyin' eyes of yours?

You a lowdown muthafucka, Ollie Watkins, you know that?

Aw, Teacake, go'n with that shit.

Meanwhile, young Dianne, Phyl, Jannette, and Bonita sat on the couch side by side watching TV.

I'm so tired of you thinkin' you slick, Ollie, thinkin' you makin' a fool outta some damn body.

Ain't nobody makin' no fool outta nobody. You the fool, Tea-cake. You the damn fool.

Oh, I'm the fool, huh? I'm a goddamn fool?

You goddamn right you a goddamn fool. Makin' shit up and carryin' on. Sick of this!

I'm gon' show you what a fool can do. You just stay yo' ass right there, you rat-soup-eatin' muthafucka.

Where you goin'? Bring yo' ass back here.

Mama Teacake returned with her pistol. The girls stiffened. She aimed at Ollie; he grabbed her wrist. They struggled.

Let go, Ollie!

You crazy, woman!

Let go!
The gun went off.
Mama Teacake screamed. *Ollie! What you do?*
Blood flowed from the hole in Jannette's neck. Bow lips parted and baby-doll eyes flung open, the five-year-old girl died on young Dianne's lap.

The incident was ruled an accident and neither Mama Teacake nor Ollie served any time. Life went on immediately after Jannette was buried in an unmarked grave next to her father's. Pictures of her disappeared. It was as though the girl had never existed. But neighbors kept the incident alive for years through whispered conversations. Whenever they saw young Dianne and her sisters, they cast pitiful glances their way.
Them Teacake's kids.
Oh.
Uh-huh. They had another sister, 'member?
They sho did! Wasn't that awful?
Awful ain't the word. And didn't go to jail or nothin'. You can still hear Teacake and Ollie down that hill cussin' and fussin' and actin' a fool. You'd think a child gettin' killed over some mess would change they ways and they come on to Jesus.
Come on to Jesus while you still have time.
That's right.
And a child died.
A shame. Went to the funeral.
Did?
Lit' girl laid up there, pigtails and a white dress, looked like a doll.
Jesus!
And they still down that hill cussin' and carryin' on.
Don't make no sense.
That po' baby got killed.
Ain't it a shame?
My mother, who was seven, saw Jannette's blood in her dreams, staining her sundress and running like oil through her

tiny fingers. She was terrified of Ollie and Mama Teacake. Soon after her sister died on her lap, my mother moved in with her paternal grandparents, James Smith Sr. and Miss Elesta. Mama, the granddaughter with the lightest skin, was a favorite of the deep-dark, matronly woman who in pictures always looked regal and serious.

My mother lived in the quiet, protective home up the hill from her siblings until she was thirteen. During those six years, she had limited contact with Phyl, Bonita, and Ollie's three children (Kay, Stephanie, and Wayne), whom Mama Teacake bore shortly after Jannette's death.

But in 1963, after James Sr. and Miss Elesta died barely two years apart, my mother returned to the little white house her father had built. By that time, Phyl had developed a broiling resentment toward her older sister. She despised the fact that Miss Elesta removed my mother but left her in that house, where she often babysat her sisters and brother while Ollie and Mama Teacake ran the streets on the weekends.

"This ain't Big Mama's house," Phyl often told Mama. "You down here now. The bitch is dead."

Young Dianne cried herself to sleep most nights for almost a year after returning to that rough-and-tumble household, where James Brown and Bobby Bland records blared on the hi-fi. Everything Mama Teacake cooked was greasy and overseasoned, nothing like the refined meals that graced Miss Elesta's table: sautéed green beans, beef roasted with garlic cloves nestled deep in the meat, bread pudding glazed with a caramel sauce, all immaculately served on the heavy mahogany dining room table.

Mama Teacake sometimes scorched the pinto beans while she talked shit on the front porch with a neighbor who just happened by. Turnip greens cooked too long under a thick slab of fatback retained no texture and slid down the throat.

No one coddled young Dianne the way her Big Mama had. She missed being next to her, inhaling the vanilla scent of her Jergens lotion as they sat together on the couch watching *The Loretta Young Show*. Fumbling a dish or letting the toilet seat slam got her cussed out right away by Mama Teacake: "Watch it! Don't go breakin' shit 'round here. This ain't none of Miss Elesta's house. Get yo' ass beat."

Dolls, parts to board games, shoes, and copies of the *Malvern Daily Record* and *Jet* magazine were usually strewn from one end of the house to the other. Sometimes a window shade fell in the living room and stayed down for days.

On Friday nights when Ollie got paid, Mama Teacake sprayed Evening in Paris perfume on her wrists and neck and carefully drew on a pair of thin eyebrows that gave her a look of perpetual surprise. She shimmied into a dress, usually red, her favorite color, that hugged her Coke bottle figure.

Fresh from the barbershop, Ollie splashed on Old Spice, stepped into a pair of dark slacks, and slipped on a freshly pressed shirt. The musky floral air singing behind them, the couple left the kids home alone as they drove to the edge of town to a juke joint or over to somebody's rowdy house party. My mother and her sisters were always awakened in the middle of the night when Mama Teacake and Ollie stumbled in loud and drunk.

I saw you lookin' at that bitch.

Ah, you ain't see shit, Teacake.

Yeah, I did. I'm so tired of yo' ass. This is my house, muthafucka. I can put yo' ass out anytime I want. Ya heard that?

I pay the goddamn bills here now.

Why don't you go pay the bills for that raggedy bitch you was lookin' at, huh?

Teacake, dammit . . .

Lying in bed, young Dianne shut her eyes tight under the covers as the cussing and door slamming went on and on. But Mama Teacake and Ollie apparently had learned their lesson about the gun. Mama Teacake kept it in her purse.

Malvern being as small as it was, my parents always knew each other, but they lived in very different neighborhoods. Third Street, where Mama grew up, was considered "uptown," close to the busy black business district. Whatever you needed—groceries, your laundry cleaned, a portrait taken, Royal Crown hair pomade, BC headache powder, the new Brook Benton record—a black man owned and ran the shop.

East Section Line, where Daddy's family lived, was a much quieter, folksier area. Neighbors maintained gardens abundant with tomatoes, okra, corn, and mustard greens. Blackberries grew wild, and pecans fell from trees older than the city itself. Come Sunday morning, sisters in homemade pastel dresses were as glorious as Easter flowers.

Mama and Daddy attended Wilson, the all-black high school, where they became friends. They didn't date then. Mama went out with Lee Hogan, a burly football player who fathered my oldest sister, Roycelyn, whom we called Dusa. She was born during my mother's first year at Henderson State University, in spring 1969. Daddy dated a chick named Gloria. Before their senior year at Wilson, they became parents of a boy named Terrence. Daddy initially denied paternity but, as the old folks say, "Truth always comes to the light." Terry was born with Daddy's face: a wide forehead, big soulful eyes, and pouty lips.

Mama dropped out after her first year of college. She'd also broken up with Lee and waded in a deep depression. Daddy was in the pits, too. He graduated high school a year late, having flunked a grade. After receiving his diploma the same year as his younger sister Stella, Daddy dreamed of traveling. He shared this one day with Big Mama as she read through the mail.

"You're gonna be traveling, Junior," she said, handing him his draft letter, "all the way to Vietnam."

My parents' friendship deepened soon after Dusa's birth. A courtship blossomed a few months before Daddy proposed. On the morning of their wedding day, Mama went down to Miss Flossie's beauty shop and got her hair done. That afternoon, they were married in my grandparents' living room over on East Section Line. Nobody from Mama's side came, and no cake was made. Stella hastily arranged refreshments: sugary fruit punch in a blown plastic pitcher and an assortment of store-bought cookies on a silver serving platter.

The wide-eyed joy captured in the honeymoon photo faded fast. Daddy went off to Vietnam shortly afterward. I don't know much about his time there. He never discussed it in detail. Relatives say he was never the same jovial Junior afterward. He had been mild-mannered but returned forever changed, with sadness calcified in his eyes. Daddy picked up a serious heroin habit in Vietnam. He eventually managed to shake it but soon found solace in gin bottles and, later, crack pipes.

For the rest of his life, Daddy abused things: various substances and anybody who tried to love him, including the former Dianne Smith, whose smile once rivaled the sun in Mexico.

Part Two

. . .

• • •

CLARA MAE WAS DADDY'S GIRLFRIEND.

She lived in a white house with two front doors—one opened to the living room, the other to the front bedroom. The white clapboard house faced a grassy lot, where a large pool of water sat for days after a heavy rain.

Daddy and I visited Clara Mae sometimes on the weekends in Malvern, about forty-five minutes from our home in Hot Springs. He turned the white Buick onto the quiet street where Clara Mae lived alone.

"Your mama ask where we been, tell her we was at Big Mama's or Aunt Geneva's. Got that, Dus-Dus?"

I grinned when Daddy called me his variation of Dusty, my nickname. I nodded.

"I don't hear you, my man."

"OK."

Daddy turned off the car in front of Clara Mae's and reached over my legs to the glove compartment, where he kept his half pint of Seagram's gin. He stared at her high, leaning porch for a moment before clearing his throat. Then he unscrewed the cap and took a quick swig.

"Oooooweee!"

I cracked up when Daddy threw back the first taste. His reaction was always the same. In my six-year-old world, he was a big ebony clown. He tossed the bottle back into the glove compartment.

"C'mon, son."

The narrow steps to Clara Mae's porch had no railing on either side. I wondered if anybody ever fell off. I wondered how Daddy negotiated the steps without falling. At home, he was anything but graceful. He tripped over toys, skates, board game pieces—things my sisters and I left around. It also didn't help that he was usually drunk, stepping in hours after he'd left work at the Reynolds aluminum plant. Mama stood there when the door flew open—hand on hip and lips looking like a slash in her face—ready to cuss him out.

But at Clara Mae's, Daddy was gentlemanly, despite the gin coursing through his veins. He patted his hair and adjusted his clothes before knocking on the door.

Clara Mae answered with a wide smile accented with a gold-rimmed front tooth.

I'd overheard Daddy tell his buddies, "You know how I like 'em, man: light, bright, and almost white."

With her custard complexion, Mama was close enough. But Clara Mae didn't pass Daddy's brown-paper-bag test. She was the color of Big Mama's homemade sweet tea, and Clara Mae couldn't have been more than five feet tall, with features that seemed too large for her face. Her stringy, rust-colored Jheri curl was in desperate need of a few more sprays of activator.

Clara Mae may not have been a beauty queen from the neck up. But south of her collarbone, she was a petite brick house with generous hips and a have-mercy bubble ass. It was the same figure Mama had before she started to pack on pounds after Reagan and I were born.

Clara Mae's physical attributes and honeysuckle-sweet disposition, the opposite of Mama's no-nonsense ways, must've been what hooked Daddy.

"Looka there," she said, feigning surprise at the sight of me and unlocking the screen door. It was as though I were a gift she found on that raggedy-ass porch. "Just gettin' big and fine! Come on in here."

Clara Mae's ornately decorated living room couldn't have been more dissimilar to ours. Nothing was ever out of place: no stray shoes, no toys on the floor. No used dish or cup left for hours on the coffee table. At Clara Mae's, old-lady bric-a-brac adorned polished side tables. Plastic covered two wide, triangular lamp shades, and white doilies draped the arms of a faded floral couch and love seat. The stuffy décor belied Clara Mae's age. She was only in her thirties.

The scent of something savory and heavily seasoned sometimes thickened the air. Clara Mae cooked for us a few times. Her collard greens and hot-water cornbread nearly rendered Mama's irrelevant. Most times, though, her house smelled of vanilla and cigarette smoke. She and Daddy puffed on Viceroys.

Her living room was dominated by a long, handsome console stereo. Albums lined the front of it and flanked the sides. Her 45s stood in three brass racks. My eyes lit up at the sight of all that music.

"Go on, look through them records," Clara Mae said. "You know you want to."

"Don't mess 'em up, son," Daddy said, reclining on the couch as though he paid bills there.

On my knees, I flipped through the LPs, stopping at images that caught my eye: Patrice Rushen with long braids adorned with beads and feathers; Betty Wright sporting a globular 'fro, one hand on her hip, the other holding a microphone; Al Green in a dove-white suit sitting cross-legged in a wicker chair that matched his outfit.

I held up an album. "Look, Daddy, this lady got her tongue out."

Clara Mae plucked the LP out of my hand. "This ain't for you."

"Can I hear it?" I asked.

Daddy spoke up. "Who's that, Clara Mae?"

"Millie Jackson."

They laughed as if they were in on a private joke.

"Can I hear it?" I asked again.

"Boy, you don't know nothin' 'bout this," Clara Mae said.

"Go 'head and put it on."

"Raymond, this boy ain't got no business listenin' to no Millie Jackson."

"Put it on. Boy pro'ly hear worse over at Teacake's," Daddy said, referring to my profane grandmother, who sold brown liquor and homemade fried pork skins out of her house.

Clara Mae shook her head and placed the album on the automatic turntable. It fell and the needle slid into the first groove. An ominous bass line, overlaid with billowing strings and woodwinds, boomed from the speakers. Frayed around the edges, the husky female voice brought to mind the smoky, lowdown atmosphere at Mama Teacake's.

Millie sang of fires burning deep down inside, of love wheels turning that rendered one helpless and open to doing just about anything. I looked at Daddy, grinning at the sound of the record I'd picked. He smiled, nodding to the groove.

"Like that, Dus-Dus?"

I nodded my head the way he did. "Yep."

Clara Mae and Daddy laughed then looked at each other.

"Hey," Daddy said, rising off the couch. "Sit here and listen to that record, hear? Don't go touchin' nothin'. Just let the record play."

Clara Mae turned the volume up as Millie broke down the meaning of an all-the-way lover. She sounded like the free-spirited women who sat gap-legged in Mama Teacake's living room and cussed in coarse voices.

Daddy followed Clara Mae into the bedroom, which was next to the living room, and closed the door. As the album played, I heard an occasional thud on the other side of the wall. I had no idea what was going on in there—and didn't care. Millie was great company.

The needle played side A again. As Millie sang for the second time about fires burning deep down inside, Daddy emerged from the bedroom. His shirt was buttoned wrong. Clara Mae soon followed. Her dry Jheri curl was flat on one side.

Much of the down-home soul I remember hearing from my childhood explored the joys and pains of outside love. It was a popular lyrical theme in R&B in the early seventies, the newlywed period for my parents. I didn't come along until 1977, when disco thumped everywhere but not in the Ollison household. Blues-suffused soul and traditional gospel sparked good vibes and sustained us through bad times.

The come-hither croon of Eddie Kendricks and the symphonic love letters of Barry White were the soundtrack to the early years of my parents' marriage.

But by the time I was in kindergarten, their union had cracked and the songs darkened. Just about all of the records Daddy dug had something to do with cheating. And he certainly wasn't the only one listening. Just about everybody I knew had half brothers and sisters, "outside babies," as folks called them.

Clara Mae wasn't Daddy's only sidepiece, but she was the only one whose house I knew and whose food I ate. During my parents' marriage, two women bore children with strong Ollison features: thick eyebrows with high arches, full lips, and bulbous noses.

Mama, who was a few months pregnant with me, read the baby announcement for the first one in the morning paper. The baby's name, Antonio Ramon Ollison, stopped her because she had initially picked it for me. Apparently, Daddy liked the name enough to suggest it to the baby's mother, a young Malvern woman barely out of high school.

Mama forgave him after Daddy promised he'd never do it again. But he lied just as Johnnie Taylor did in "Running Out of Lies." It was "getting hard to think of an alibi."

Barely two years after my youngest sister, Reagan, was born, another woman in Malvern had another son. Mama had had enough.

Before he moved out of our house on Garden Street, Daddy spent hours playing those baby-I-didn't-mean-it songs in the living room in the dark: a cold Miller in one hand and a Viceroy burning in the other. He'd chuckle at a verse. But mostly, he stared straight ahead as an anguished voice on the stereo crooned how trying to love two sure ain't easy to do.

As the shattered pieces of the marriage settled around her, Mama knelt at the altar of Aretha.

She played *Amazing Grace*, the legend's landmark 1972 gospel double LP, seemingly every waking hour during the turbulent years of the marriage, the only years I remember. The album often played on Sunday mornings as we got ready for church.

The fiery, holy sounds of Aretha shouting the good news, shadowed by the Southern California Community Choir, sometimes filled the house well into the night.

Daddy wasn't home much during the last two years of the marriage. Some of his things (his shoes, his clothes, many of his albums) disappeared. I didn't know where he stayed. Clara Mae's? Big Mama's? Whenever he showed up, he and Mama fought.

Daddy, as usual, was drunk and the first to lay hands, shoving Mama against a wall, on the couch, on the floor. But she always fought back: kicking, scratching, and biting.

She clocked him in the head once with a phone. Her nostrils flaring, Mama set it down, carefully placing the receiver back on the base. Then she looked at us as we stood there scared and shocked.

"Y'all get somewhere and sit down," she said, stepping over Daddy, as he moaned and writhed on the floor, holding his head.

But whenever Aretha was on, order seemed restored. Her majestic voice grounded us, especially Mama. After she came home from her job at Coy's restaurant, where she prepared fancy salads all day, Mama often reached for Aretha.

The songs she played indicated her mood. If "Respect" or "(Sweet, Sweet Baby) Since You've Been Gone" rocked the house, her spirits were up; soaring ballads such as "Angel" and "(You Make Me Feel Like) A Natural Woman" meant she was reflective; moody cuts like "Ain't No Way" and "Do Right Woman, Do Right Man" meant she didn't want to be bothered. So we tiptoed around her.

Even as a child I gathered that Aretha's music, especially her classic Atlantic recordings, was an extension of church. The air changed. A sense of reverence rained down as her voice soared from the speakers. I straightened up and listened. Coupling the sky-ripping strength of Aretha's voice with Mama's warrior-woman presence, I felt protected in Daddy's absence.

So much of Mama's life was reflected and refracted in Aretha's lyrics: the longing, the loss, the hope, the faith, the perseverance. In 1967, the year of the singer's pop breakthrough, Mama turned seventeen. She entered womanhood with the Queen of Soul as a cultural guidepost.

Aretha was the natural woman/genius from down the block, world-weary and accessible, nappy edges and all on full display. She mingled the muddy funk of the Delta with the cosmopolitan sleekness of the North. And in her music, Mama seemed to always find a home. She admired other dynamic black female singers of her generation and played their music often. Diana Ross and Gladys Knight come to mind. But her reaction to their songs wasn't the same as when Aretha sang. Mama swayed and rocked. She waved her hand in the air, the way she did in church. Sometimes she cried. In 1983, her marriage fell in sharp glittering pieces all around her. My oldest sister, Dusa, was fourteen; Reagan, the youngest, was five; and I was six. Garden Street was bleak, save for the aural sunbeam of Aretha singing through the surface noise of well-worn vinyl, assuring us that God would take care of everything.

In the summer of '83, a few months before my parents' divorce was final, we moved into the housing projects over on Omega Street.

The apartment felt like a step up from our place on Garden. That house, a small white one with three bedrooms, had been built sometime in the 1920s, with a wide front porch and not much of a yard in the front or the back. It faced the old National Baptist Hotel, at that time an abandoned building my sisters and I thought was haunted. Decades before, the majestic red-brick hotel attracted every major black performer who came to Hot Springs. The building, which took up a block, included a bathhouse, a performance venue, a conference center, a gym, and a beauty parlor.

The neighborhood surrounding the National Baptist Hotel had been a glorious one in the years before integration. Black doctors, lawyers, teachers, and other professionals lived in the stately homes, some of which were teetering on dilapidation just before we moved out. Reagan and I rode our Big Wheels up and down the hill in front of our house. Drunks staggering out of the dives and liquor stores on Malvern Avenue, the main drag that ran perpendicular to Garden Street, were mostly nice. Some were even parental, telling us to be careful on our Big Wheels and to stay out of the street.

We were all happy to leave that old white house, which was also home to mice and roaches. I remember once going into the kitchen and seeing a mouse swimming around in the cold, greasy dishwater left overnight in the sink. I almost pissed myself.

Daddy's absence hung over everything. I missed our clandestine trips to Clara Mae's; to the liquor store on the street directly behind the house, where he bought me Guy's potato chips and Dr. Pepper; to the homes of his drinking buddies, where I was treated like one of the fellas. I wasn't given beer to drink, though occasionally Daddy gave me a quick sip of his and laughed his wheezing laugh as I frowned and gagged at the acrid taste.

I sat among his ragtag friends and absorbed their tall tales peppered with "bitch" this and "muthafucka" that. For the longest time, I thought my name was "Lil' Mafucka." As I followed Daddy into smoky backrooms, a grinning drunk man with a beer in his hand knelt down to rub my head and say, "Hey there, lil' mafucka."

I remember the last time Daddy darkened our front door on Garden Street.

It was a Saturday morning, and Mama was at work. Dusa was in charge, sitting on the couch talking on the phone, as usual. Reagan and I were glued to the TV, eating cereal and watching *The Smurfs*, when the door opened and in walked Daddy.

We rushed him, hugging his legs. I couldn't remember the last time he had been home.

He hugged us and went into the bedroom he shared with Mama. We followed him, pelting him with questions: "You come home, Daddy? You stayin', Daddy?"

"Y'all go on back in the living room now," he said. "Go on."

We went back into the living room, giddy that he was home at last. After he was in the room for a while, I snuck in. He sat on the edge of the bed crying, something Daddy often did when he was drunk. So this wasn't an unusual sight.

He looked up, saw me, and sobbed.

"Your mama don't love me no more," he said.

I saw the luggage at the foot of the bed.

"I wanna go," I whined.

"Nah, you can't," he said, lifting himself off the bed.

He picked up his suitcases and headed out of the room. As he walked through the living room, Reagan jumped from her spot in front of the TV.

"Daddy, where you goin'?" She was in tears.

"I'll be back," he said, hugging us both. He looked over at Dusa, who was still on the phone. Daddy had been a father to her longer than he had been to us, and yet she seemed indifferent to his departure.

"Tell your mama I'll call later," Daddy said to Dusa, who just nodded and said, "Okay."

"Y'all be good," Daddy said as he closed the door.

We didn't realize that Uncle Alvin, the husband of Daddy's sister Stella, had been outside the entire time waiting in the car. From the living room window, I saw Daddy load his things and get in. He and Alvin sat there for what seemed like a long time before leaving.

Daddy haunted every room on Garden Street. He lived barely an hour away in Malvern. But he may as well have been across two oceans because he didn't come around. In the new room I shared with Reagan on Omega Street, I kept a stack of 45s he'd bought me—music that connected us.

The projects were designed like townhomes. Our three bedrooms and bathroom were upstairs. A kitchen with washer and dryer hookups was to the left as you entered the front door. Each unit had a small front porch; some had a small back porch, too. The grounds were well kept.

Barely a block away, there was a park with a tennis court, a basketball court, swing sets, a merry-go-round, and a large pavilion, where DJs in the summer spun the latest in R&B and hip-hop.

The music in the air during the summer or whenever the weather was warm and mild enlivened Omega Street. Neighbors dragged their stereo speakers out on porches or perched them in windows, and the gritty sounds of Z. Z. Hill, Lakeside, or the latest punk funk by Rick James complemented the sun-kissed weather and the aroma of ribs sizzling on a grill.

You identified the neighbors by the music they played. Next to us, Betty played the blues first thing Saturday morning—the slick Southern kind, Denise LaSalle, Latimore, and Johnnie Taylor. Sherry, who sometimes lived with her grandmother Miss Wyrick across from us, played Luther Vandross all day. And from Sharon's unit three doors down, the effervescent funk of Shalamar and the sleek romantic duets of Alexander O'Neal and Cherrelle blared routinely.

No men were around, save for somebody's no 'count boyfriend or a creeping married man breezing in and out. The block was dominated by single women, all black, raising their kids and everybody else's. Some were elderly and retired, like Miss Wyrick. A matronly, gossipy woman, she and Mama became fast friends.

Loud Miss Wells, who policed the grounds ("Child, you betta pick that candy wrapper up!"), lived two doors down. Betty next door to us was one of Miss Wells's daughters and a projects diva. Svelte and stylish with no job, Betty smoked cigarettes and in the summer squeezed her cantaloupe breasts into tube tops. She threw loud card parties that went on well past midnight, which pissed off Mama, the only woman on the block who got up every morning and went to work. Everybody else waited for the welfare checks to come the first and the middle of every month, which is usually when their boyfriends showed up.

Betty's sister Dot lived a few doors down across from her. She was also a tube top–wearing projects diva, who strutted around like a peacock with nails painted shades of purple, yellow, or blue. Her voice was loud, like her mama's. When she wasn't strutting from door to door, she was cussin' and fussin' at her badass boys, T.J. and Prince, who were about the same age as Reagan and I.

My sisters immediately took to our new neighborhood, spending hours on the porch and chatting with folks. I was glad to be in a place free of mice and roaches and the sight of the creepy Baptist Hotel. But I withdrew.

It seemed I mourned the breakup of my parents' marriage more than anybody else in the house. Daddy could be stormy when he was home, usually as gin streamed through his system. But there were calmer times I relished.

We used to eat sardines with yellow mustard and saltine crackers at the kitchen table, just us two, because nobody else in the house liked them. When he wasn't working the graveyard shift at Reynolds, Daddy was up during the early part of the afternoon. In the summer, he took us to the park or out for a ride. He watched old westerns and cartoons with us on the couch.

Sometimes on Fridays after he picked me up from my kindergarten class at Langston Elementary, we stopped by the Dairy Queen for a cherry slush, then went on to the dusty record shop downtown that sold new and used music. Daddy bought himself albums and picked 45s he thought I needed to hear.

"This here is music you should know 'bout," he said.

I showed off my records to Mama when we got home.

She shook her head. "Why you buy this boy all these old-ass records? What the hell he know about Johnnie Taylor?"

Daddy laughed as I spun the blues on my Mickey Mouse record player.

But over on Omega Street, I felt as though I were standing in a river. Everything just kept moving as though Daddy never existed. Mama had a new job at a hospital, and her hours were long. Dusa, who turned fifteen just before we moved, had a part-time job after school at Taco Bell. Well developed and pretty, with Mama's creamy skin, keen features, and lush dark hair, she kept herself busy with the boys in the neighborhood when she wasn't in school or behind the counter for a few hours at Taco Bell.

Some of those boys regularly snuck in the house through the back door when Mama was at work. They couldn't come through the front, not with Miss Wyrick perched at her kitchen or bedroom window, both of which faced the front of our unit. She'd surely let Mama know that So-and-So's mannish boy was over there.

We never told Mama about Dusa keeping company. Reagan did anything she said, so she wasn't going to tell. I kept quiet, because Dusa was bigger and threatened me with force: a punch in the shoulder, a kick in the leg, a slap upside the head.

An only child for nearly nine years, Dusa never got over the fact that I was born. She was the creamy-skinned dream child relatives adored, with long hair, a living doll with Shirley Temple vibrancy. The girl danced and sang for anybody who paid attention, and Dusa loved attention. Mama Teacake's attachment to her bordered on possessive.

According to family legend, Dusa strongly resembled Jannette. My grandmother had her favorites and made no qualms about it. In her eyes, I guess, Dusa was her second chance with Jannette. Mama Teacake rarely smiled, but her face brightened whenever Dusa appeared. When the bubbly girl left her sight, Mama Teacake's face fell back to its usual fuck-you expression.

Dusa had no relationship with her biological father, who moved to California soon after she was born. She was barely two when Daddy and Mama married, and he spoiled her as though she were his own. That changed when I was born. Then Reagan came a year and five days later. Dusa had to share attention in the house, and this fucked with her for years.

By the time we were on Omega Street, Dusa had been saddled with more responsibilities than her age and emotionally fragile nature could handle. But she played the part of the steely womanchild, fumbling new liberties and exploring her sexuality with boys from around the way.

I didn't care about what she did on the couch or in her bedroom with those knuckleheads. But I don't think anybody had to tell Mama a thing. That year, she put Dusa on birth control.

With Mama working all the time and Dusa busy with school, Taco Bell, and fucking, Reagan and I were forced to be independent. At six and seven years old, we let ourselves in the house after school and fixed sandwiches or bowls of cereal if Mama hadn't left something cooked in the oven. Dusa usually got home a few hours later and ran everything. If Mama hadn't cooked, Dusa handled the pots and pans. Her fried chicken was red at the bone, and the frozen Banquet potpies were still cold in the middle when she took them out of the oven. Dusa checked our homework and put us to bed. Sometimes the entire day passed without us ever seeing Mama.

I escaped into my records.

The swirling shades of purple mesmerized me. The hallelujah voice trapped inside the wax sang about losing her mind over something she heard through the grapevine.

Reagan played outside with the neighborhood kids, but I preferred to sit in our room next to my record player. The rest of the world disappeared while I stared at the 45s spinning. The colors of the labels attracted me first. Purple and yellow were favorites. When Daddy and I were in the record shop, I picked 45s with those colors.

"Daddy, this one."

He plucked it from the row and read it. "Oh, yeah. You gonna like this."

"It's yellow," I said, grinning.

Daddy bent down to show me the label. "Can you read this? That's the Staple Singers."

I pointed to another row. "That's a purple one."

"Hold on. Let me see," Daddy said, plucking the record. "Oh, yeah. Gladys Knight & the Pips."

As the music played, I thought about Daddy and ached for him. Whenever I asked Mama about his whereabouts, her face tightened: "Boy, go somewhere. You ain't got no daddy."

I felt a sting inside each time she said that, which was often.

I changed records. The label was lemon-yellow with a black rectangular box on the left. Inside, slender brown fingers froze in a snap. The voice, as earthy as turnip greens, sang of a place where "ain't nobody cryin'" and "ain't nobody worried."

She sure wasn't singing about No. 1 Omega Street.

A new thing called MTV took my mind off Daddy for a while.

Watching it became the only pastime I shared with my sisters. We did our homework lying on the living room floor as videos by Madonna, Pat Benatar, and the Police dazzled the screen. The only time it was turned off was when Mama came home and changed the channel to the evening news. By that time, we were on our way to bed anyway.

Just about all the acts on MTV were white with colossal hair, but we didn't care. It was thrilling to see music with visuals. Some of the early videos stood out, like "You Might Think" by the Cars. Geeky-looking lead singer Ric Ocasek stalks a pretty blond model in bizarre computer-generated scenes. In one, the band plays its instruments floating on a bar of soap in the woman's bubble bath. In another, Ric's head is superimposed on a fly.

I loved the video for a-ha's "Take On Me," which came on seemingly every hour. In pencil-sketched animation, a woman and the lead singer run hand in hand while two bad guys, one wielding a big wrench, chase them down several corridors.

But one video wrecked my seven-year-old world and convinced me that its star was divine.

I had heard the song "Billie Jean" on the radio, over the loud speakers at K-Mart, seemingly everywhere. But seeing Michael Jackson in the video, stylish in a black leather suit, a strawberry-ice-cream-pink shirt, red bow tie, and two-toned shoes, amazed me. When the video came on, Dusa shrieked and leapt off the couch, pushing me out the way to turn the volume up. We all stood there, frozen in front of the TV.

Michael strolled along a littered sidewalk as the ground lit up under his feet. He leaned against a post, which also glowed. How *did* he do that?

He spun around like a top then stopped on the tips of his toes, the sidewalk ablaze under him. He sang and danced with one hand in his pocket.

There was something street but chic about Michael in that video. With his juiced-up curl, honey-brown skin, and love-me eyes, he melted us. The way he moved and sang, Michael Jackson was not of the same realm as humankind.

He was the possessor of some divine power. The "Billie Jean" video revealed it. Only he could make me happy now that Daddy was a memory.

I later developed a Michael Jackson fantasy and replayed it over and over.

Michael came on a Saturday morning in a pearl stretch limo. Everybody on the block—Dot, Betty, Miss Wells, Miss Wyrick, wishbone-thin Sharon, who had three small children and moved in about the same time we did—stepped out onto their porches to point and gawk.

A chauffeur opened the back door. Michael stepped out wearing dark aviator shades, his famous red-leather jacket with studs and zippers, and signature glittery socks and one glove. Nobody rushed him because the glow around him, a celestial force field, stopped everybody in his tracks.

He walked up onto our porch and knocked on the door. I answered. His smile was wide, his glow almost blinding.

"Come with me," he said, extending the gloved hand. Slowly, I took it. On our way to the limo, I waved good-bye to the neighbors standing around with dropped jaws.

We disappeared into the vehicle. It rocketed into the sky after pulling out of the parking lot. I never developed the fantasy beyond that. Just the thought of leaving Omega Street with Michael Jackson was enough.

A few weeks after the "Billie Jean" video froze my sisters and me in front of the old Magnavox console, Mama surprised me with the *Thriller* album. It wasn't a special occasion, wasn't my birthday or anything. I hadn't even asked her for it, because she was perpetually broke.

"Dusty!" Mama's voice had the clarion tone of a trumpet. Had she had the inclination and training, she probably could've been a singer.

I ran down the stairs and into the living room. She put her purse down on the couch and pulled the album from under her arm.

"Here," she said, handing it to me, a smile stretching across her face. "I know you want this."

My face felt warm when I pulled the LP out of the bag. I could've passed out right there.

"Michael Jackson!"

"I know you tired of playin' those old records. What you supposed to say?"

"Thank you."

I bound up the stairs.

"Stop that runnin' 'fore you fall and break yourself and that record," Mama shouted.

In the room, I removed the plastic and slowly opened the gatefold. Michael reclined in an ivory suit, a tiger cub on his knee. I pulled out the record and studied the denim-blue label with "Epic" sprawled across the top in curly script.

I placed the record on my tiny white turntable, clicked it on, and jumped as the first notes of "Wanna Be Startin' Somethin'" sounded like Alvin and the Chipmunks. Wrong speed. Once I changed it, I let the music play and stared at Michael on the LP jacket enveloped in that glow.

Weeks later, I took the album to my first-grade class at Garden Elementary for show and tell. I was the invisible black boy before that day. I sat near the back of the class and stayed to myself and kind of preferred it that way. Mrs. Mathis, my teacher, noticed. On one of my report cards, she wrote a note about my being reluctant to interact with classmates. Mama read it, glared at me, and said, "Boy, what's your problem? You better get in that class and act like you got some sense."

My grades were OK. I just never made much of an effort to connect with my classmates, not even the three other blacks, who also ignored me. Most of the class was white and from the nearby suburbs. Some looked at me as if my face was upside down. I returned the look. They were just as strange to me as I was to them, because white folks didn't live on or ever come around my part of town. I was my own best friend since Daddy was gone. On the large playground encircled by sky-high pines, I raced to a swing and swung as high as my little legs could propel me. I sat under a tree if the swings were taken and daydreamed about possessing superhuman powers. I could fly in the sky, doing all kinds of dips and spins, or zap you with a thunderbolt from the palm of my hand.

The day I brought in *Thriller* for show and tell, everybody knew my name. Classmates smiled and pointed when I walked in with the LP tucked under my arm. "Hey, he's got Michael Jackson." Even Stephanie, the rude brunette who always tossed papers at me when she had to pass them back, flashed a smile. She turned around.

"I love Michael Jackson." Her voice was high and pinched. I just stared at her. "He's cool." I said nothing. Her smile fell away and she mumbled, "You're weird," then turned around.

Later, in front of the class, I showed off the LP's gatefold picture as "ooos" and "ahs" rippled through the room. This was *my* Michael Jackson. I showed off the LP jacket photos as if I had taken them myself. Mrs. Mathis played the album, and for a moment the class became an elementary disco. I watched my classmates wiggle and dance way off the beat to the music of *my* Michael Jackson. But when it got too rowdy, Mrs. Mathis lifted the needle.

"Settle down," she said.

She slid the record back into the jacket and handed it to me. The class gave Michael and me a round of applause. As we filed out at the end of the day, several classmates commended my contribution to show and tell: "That record was fun."

I met Reagan in front of her kindergarten class, and we climbed onto the school bus for the long ride back to Omega Street. We let ourselves into the house, made sloppy peanut butter and jelly sandwiches, and watched MTV 'til Dusa came home.

Daddy called Mama and said he'd be by to pick us up for the weekend. Something jumped inside and remained suspended. Mama told us on a rare Friday evening she didn't have to work.

"He's supposed to be by here to get y'all sometime Saturday," she said, doubt coating her words. "He said he was coming, so y'all be ready."

Mama wouldn't be there because, of course, she had to work. Dusa, who was off that weekend, would go with us. But Daddy would drop her off at Mama Teacake's.

Reagan and I would stay with Daddy. After the divorce, he'd moved back home with Big Mama and Paw Paw. I couldn't remember the last time we had seen our paternal grandparents.

We were excited to get away from the projects and see family members who gave a damn about us. Dusa usually worked on the weekend, which meant Reagan and I were often home alone. We mostly stayed in the house and watched TV. No neighborhood kids were ever allowed in, and we couldn't go to their homes.

We sometimes played on the porch, but we were never far from the phone. Mama called at two- or three-hour intervals to check on us, but Miss Wyrick was her main lookout. We could see her peeping from her window.

One day, she knocked on the door. "How y'all doin' over here? Y'all eat?"

We stood in the doorway and looked at each other not knowing what to say. We'd had pressed ham sandwiches, potato chips, and Jungle Juice, a syrupy fruit drink that turned your mouth bright red. But we had devoured all of that soon after Dusa left. By midday, we were hungry again.

"Y'all hungry over here?" Miss Wyrick's voice was high and direct.

Our eyes genuflected.

"Y'all c'mon. I'll call Dianne and tell her where y'all at."

We followed Miss Wyrick to her fastidiously clean place. She fixed us heaping plates of collard greens and pork neck bones.

"Eat up now," she said. "Y'all should be good and full 'fore Dianne gets off work."

Mama was livid when she got home.

"Y'all had food in here. Why y'all over there eatin' up Miss Wyrick's food?"

We said nothing.

"Y'all hear me?" Mama glared down at us. Her lips were tight and eyes on fire, the same look she gave Daddy when he stumbled in smelling of gin, Clara Mae, or some other bitch 'cross town.

I looked at Reagan, then up at Mama. "We was hungry."

"It's not 'we was,' Dusty; it's 'we were,' and y'all were not hungry." Mama crossed her arms.

Reagan and I looked at each in the awkward silence.

"Y'all stay y'all asses in this house and stop eatin' other folks' food, hear?"

We harmonized: "Yeah."

"Now get on upstairs and don't come down 'til I tell ya."

Reagan followed me to our room. She slumped on her bed. I sat across from her on mine and looked at the floor.

"What we do?" Reagan asked. "I like neck bones."

After that, Mama became more consistent about leaving cooked meals for us: heavy casseroles or stews that slow-cooked all night in an avocado-green crock pot.

The Saturday morning before Daddy came, we made ourselves bowls of cornflakes, and Dusa made us take a bath—Reagan was first, then I was next. Dusa morphed into a barbed-tongued projects diva when Mama was away. She seemed to mimic Dot's slinky walk around the house, and she cussed at us: "Dusty and Reagan, y'all come pick this shit up!"

Frying chicken too fast, wearing jeans too tight, mothering us when she wasn't at school or at work, Dusa started to look much older than fifteen.

She packed her bag, then ours. She sprayed Reagan's Jheri curl with TCB activator and picked it out. With her perpetual scowl, tomboy ways, and that greasy curl, folks always mistook Reagan for our little brother. Put a dress on her and clip a frilly bow in her hair, and old church members with thick glasses still asked, "Is that Dianne's lit' boy?"

Dusa brushed my hair so hard I cried. She popped my shoulder with the back of the brush. "Stop crying! This shit is nappy. Told you to start brushin' yo' own damn head. Be still!"

About midafternoon, after *Soul Train* went off, my stomach kept twisting into knots worrying that Daddy wouldn't show. I'd heard Mama tell Dusa that he was supposed to be there by "late mornin'." I figured that was before *Soul Train* came on at 11. We were packed, dressed, and ready as Don Cornelius introduced songs and guests on the "hippest trip in America." But I was anxious by the end of the show as Don wished viewers peace and *soooooul.*

When his white Buick pulled up in the parking lot at last, I screamed, "Daddy!"

He may as well have been Michael Jackson in the rocket limo. Reagan and I nearly tripped and scrapped our knees as we ran out the door. Daddy stepped out of the car. We hugged his legs.

"Hey now," he said.

"Pick me up," Reagan chirped in that annoying baby voice she used only around Daddy. Any other time, she sounded like a gruff-voiced midget. Daddy lifted her and rubbed my head, still tender from Dusa's abusive brushing.

"Y'all ready to go?" he asked.

Lord knows I was. Still carrying Reagan, he walked into our apartment, which was presentable, a rarity. Mama told Dusa to have the place spotless before Daddy got there.

"Hey, Dusa," Daddy said. "Dianne said you workin' now."

"Yes." Dusa's answer had icicles.

"How you doin' in school?"

"Good. We ready to go. I called Mama already."

Dusa was an ice cube as she rode shotgun on our way to Malvern. It was a futile effort to try to converse with her. So Daddy ignored her and talked to Reagan and me as we sat in the backseat and watched Hot Springs pass us by.

"Hey, Dus-Dus,"

"Yep."

"How's my main man?" Daddy looked at me in the rearview.

"I'm fine."

"You got a girlfriend?"

I looked at Reagan and we giggled.

Dusa sucked her teeth. "He got too much sugar in his tank."

"Hey," Daddy said, "don't say that 'bout your brother."

"Well, it's true," she shot back. "He sit up and listen to records, go around switchin'."

"No, I don't!" Waves crashed in my stomach and my face felt flushed.

"Won't even go outside and play." Dusa looked over her shoulder at me. "Act like a lit' ol' girl."

"No, I don't!" Tears stung my eyes as I slumped back feeling defeated by a teenage bitch who couldn't even make a decent frozen potpie.

"Dusa, that's enough," Daddy said. "Don't talk 'bout your brother like that, I said."

He looked back at me in the rearview mirror and softened his tone. "Hey, Dus-Dus. Hey, lit' man. Don't cry. Your sister didn't mean it, hear?"

I glared at Dusa, then looked out the window as I wiped the tears. I wanted to turn my palms toward her, release my superhuman thunderbolts, and zap her head clean off her shoulders.

We pulled up to the black-and-beige brick house where Mama Teacake lived. After raising his kids in the house on Third Street, Ollie built a more spacious one on Happy Street. It had to be one of the most ironically named streets in the world, because nobody was happy on Happy Street.

Next door to Mama Teacake's busy house, where she lived with Ollie and my shiftless Uncle Wayne, pitiful Miss Beadie lived in a rundown white house.

Kind as she was, toothless smile and all, she seemed to stay drunk sunup to sundown. She bought her liquor from Mama Teacake. Miss Beadie's daughter, Linda, lived with her along with Linda's three kids: Sugar Plum, the oldest, was an overdeveloped girl, couldn't have been more than thirteen, with full breasts and wide hips; Shady, Linda's son, was about my age, with freckles and knotty, cinnamon-colored hair; and Taletha, the youngest, was about Reagan's age and seemed dimwitted.

Visiting Mama Teacake during the summer was like doing a stint in jail. She woke us up early, fixed us a heavy breakfast, made us clean up her house, and then banished us to the yard in the punishing heat.

"Y'all ain't gon' be runnin' in and out my house," she'd say. "I don't know what Dianne play, but I don't play that shit here. Y'all get thirsty, get cha some water out the hose."

Dusa could stay in the air conditioning and watch TV. She parroted Mama Teacake: "Y'all go'n outside!"

We often went next door to Miss Beadie's and played with Shady and Taletha in her backyard. There was a rusty swing set and a plum tree heavy with fruit. Miss Beadie gave us Kool-Aid in jelly jars. If Linda was around and in a good mood, she'd make us all hot dogs. She was prone to fight and sometimes got drunk and pushed Miss Beadie around.

Linda was the first person I ever saw fire a gun. It was the summer I turned five and Reagan four. Mama threw us a birthday party in Mama Teacake's big front yard. All of my cousins, who were about the same age and all lived in Malvern, were there. We saw Linda marching down Happy Street, her blouse ripped open and her bra exposed.

Mama Teacake called out to Linda from the porch. "Linda, you all right?"

"I'm gon' kill him!" Linda screamed.

She disappeared into Miss Beadie's house. Moments later, she emerged carrying a pistol.

Miss Beadie trailed her. "Linda, come back here," she pleaded.

As Linda passed Mama Teacake's front yard, where all of us kids sat around a picnic table eating cake and ice cream, she pointed the gun into the air and fired. Reagan cried for Mama, who rushed out on the porch.

My aunt Kay, Mama's gusty younger sister who at the time was about six months pregnant with my cousin Ryan, jumped from her chair on the porch: "Bitch, are you crazy? These kids are over here!"

Mama Teacake ordered Kay to sit down. Meanwhile, Linda kept marching down the street, her hair a wooly explosion, and the gun pointed to the ground. I never knew if she shot anybody that day. But a few years after that, Linda went to jail for a while.

The grown folks never talked about it, and I missed Linda's kindness. When she wasn't getting her ass kicked by men she tried to love or marching down the street shooting her pistol through the air, Linda's smile was wide and her voice baby-doll sweet when she asked me, "Dusty, you want ketchup or mustard on yo' hot dog?"

Daddy turned off the car.

"We goin' to Big Mama's?" I asked.

"Yeah, we gonna stop in here and say hi to Teacake real quick."

I did not want to go inside.

"C'mon," Daddy said.

Mama Teacake was a molasses-brown, wide-hipped woman who commanded everything around her, especially the kitchen. She was queen there. Folks entered her house through the side door, which opened to the kitchen, and she was usually seated at the head of the table.

A mess of fried pork skins was in front of her, and she stuffed handfuls into plastic baggies.

Daddy greeted her and Mama Teacake answered with a lifeless, "Hey there."

Dusa went over and hugged her neck. I never got close enough to touch Mama Teacake for fear she'd bite my head off. She spoke to Reagan: "Hey there, Reagan."

Still in baby mode, she was attached to Daddy's hip.

"She too big for you to carry, Raymond," Mama Teacake said, echoing exactly what I thought.

Then she looked at me. "Hey, Dusty."

I frowned and said nothing.

"Speak to your grandma," Daddy said. "Don't be like that."

"Ain't nobody stud'n his lit' red ass," Mama Teacake said, waving her hand as if shooing away a fly. "He got them funny ways. Dusa the only one stayin'. You takin' Dusty and Reagan out there with you and your mama and nem, right?"

"Yeah, Teacake, they goin' with me."

Daddy looked down at me. "Ready to go?"

"Yes!" My answer was damn near emphatic.

Daddy chuckled.

Mama Teacake huffed. "I don't care. I don't want you over here, anyway, Dusty. He gotta lotta damn nerve."

"All right, Teacake. I'll see you later. C'mon, Dus-Dus."

I almost tripped over myself escaping the evil kitchen queen.

· · ·

East Section Line was much more inviting than the overwhelming funkiness of Happy Street.

Big Mama and Paw Paw's house was like the others around it: modest, boxy, well-kept symbols of the owners' pride. Robins pecked at water in ceramic birdbaths on lawns that looked like plush green carpet squares. Elephant ear plants bobbed next to porch steps; azaleas bloomed in clay pots next to screen doors. Deep-green bushes snowed with honeysuckle spilled over chain-link fences and sweetened the air.

Behind several homes, proud gardens were abundant with turnip greens, squash, tomatoes, cucumbers, and okra. Neighbors shared the bounty.

Paw Paw, who loved to fish, caught enough catfish for So-and-So next door and Miss What's-Her-Name down the street. On Sundays, sisters headed to church in wide-brimmed hats and homemade dresses that put to shame anything hanging in Dillard's.

Big Mama's house enfolded me. She worked for years as a domestic, and her place was exemplary, not a speck of dust anywhere. The scent in the house was a distinctive combination of vanilla, wood, and laundry soap.

We followed Daddy into the living room. The chestnut-brown and burnt-orange furniture looked as though it had just left the store's showroom.

Big Mama was happy to see us. She was a slip of a woman with gleaming, deep-brown skin and a pronounced but charming overbite. She wore her ebony-dyed hair in marcel waves and had an approachable Queen Mother–like bearing. All of the adults, even the senior citizens, called her "Miss Ollison."

"Look at you. Give Big Mama a hug." She may have been a petite woman but her hugs were strong.

Our cousin Cuda came down the hall.

"Hey, DustyandReagan." She always said our names together, never one or the other. She was in her early twenties, attractive and shapely with a sprightly, bell-like voice. "Y'all haven't seen your new cousin."

New cousin? Since the last time we saw Cuda, she'd had a baby.

We followed her to her bedroom and there lying fast asleep in the middle of her bed was our cousin Patrick: chunky and mahogany-brown with thick hair and an adorable cleft in his chin.

At Big Mama's, everything had an orderliness that felt right and complete. We all sat around the table for dinner. We never did that on Omega Street. Of course, Mama was away at work, and my sisters and I ate our meals in front of the TV.

Big Mama and Cuda set the table with white plates trimmed with tiny blue flowers that matched the bowls and serving platters. Garden-fresh green beans in a savory broth surrounded a smoked ham hock. Lemon slices floated in a brown plastic pitcher of dark, sweet tea. Baked low and slow for hours, a beef roast had rested in its own gravy. Buttered cornbread had been flipped out of a cast iron skillet and onto a plate. Big Mama made us wash our hands before coming to the table, another ritual foreign to Reagan and me.

"Why we gotta wash our hands?" Reagan asked as I turned on the sink faucet in the bathroom.

We all sat at the long oval table: Paw Paw at the head, Big Mama to his left, and Cuda to his right. Daddy was at the opposite end as Reagan and I sat to his left and right. Paw Paw mumbled a quick blessing over the food. He was a slim man who looked like an older, grayer version of Daddy. His ocean roar of a voice seemed to resonate from the very core of him. I only understood, "Amen."

Over dinner, Big Mama asked us about life at home. "Where y'all livin' at now?"

"In the projects," I said, stuffing my face with the best fried corn on Earth.

"Slow down, Dusty," Big Mama said, touching my arm. "The projects?"

"Yep."

"Junior," Big Mama looked at Daddy, "you didn't say Dianne had moved into the projects."

Daddy looked annoyed. "Ma, I told you that."

"I don't like it," I said.

"You don't?" Big Mama asked.

"Why come?" Cuda wanted to know.

"Mama work all the time and Dusa mean."

"Dianne leave y'all there with Dusa?" Big Mama asked.

"Yep. But Dusa be at work."

"Dusa work? You and Reagan there by y'all selves?" Big Mama sounded shocked.

I suddenly felt like I had said something I wasn't supposed to say.

Daddy looked at me. "Why y'all at home by y'all selves?"

I looked down at my plate. "I don't know."

Big Mama sighed. "They babies, Junior. Anythang can happen. They shouldn't be at home by theyselves. Dianne know better than that."

Daddy looked down at his plate. "Nah, they shouldn't."

After dinner, Daddy wanted to take a ride. Reagan whined that she wanted to go with us, but Daddy persuaded her to hang out with Cuda.

"Don't you wanna play with the baby, Puddin'?"

Reagan looked over at Pat, cooing in Big Mama's lap.

"I'll bring you something back. Want some candy?"

Reagan nodded, Daddy kissed her on the cheek, and he and I slipped out the front door.

Before Daddy started the car, he retrieved the gin in the glove compartment and threw back a taste. "Ooooowee!"

I giggled.

"Listen at you," he said, tossing the bottle back into the glove compartment. "That still tickles you. Hey, lit' man, wanna hear some music?"

He looked through a few cassettes in the space below the tape deck.

"I like Michael Jackson!"

"Michael Jackson?"

"Yep. Mama got me the record."

"She did, huh? Here."

Daddy slipped in a cassette. A whiskey-and-cigarette voice rode a swaggering synthesized groove.

Daddy pulled out of the yard. "Yessir! That's Bobby Womack, man."

We drove down East Section Line as Bobby sang about wanting to fuck his best friend's wife.

"We goin' to Clara Mae's?" I asked.

Daddy shook his head and chuckled. "Oh, no."

"Why?"

"Never mind. You know Dickie?"

"Uh-uh."

"You know Dickie, man. Cousin Dickie? He 'member you. We goin' out there."

"He got records?"

Daddy laughed. "You a music freak, you know that?"

I grinned. What's a freak? Is this a good or bad thing?

Dickie lived in a sprawling house way out on the edge of town. There was a deck right off the den with a patio table shaded by a huge umbrella.

Dickie opened the patio doors for us, and he and Daddy hugged. Then Dickie looked down at me: "Hey there, Dusty."

This man obviously knew me, but I hadn't seen him before.

We stood in the airy den with its plush carpet and woodsy smell.

"You done got big, gettin' tall," Dickie said. "Last time I seen you, man, you was this high."

He stooped and held his hand about two feet above the carpet. Dickie was ebony-skinned like Daddy with broad shoulders, a handsome guy. They were about the same age and looked like brothers. Dickie was the son of Big Mama's sister, Aunt Ruby.

"Y'all sit down, man," he said, leaving the room and heading up the two steps that led to the kitchen.

I sat down and looked around the room. Family pictures lined the wood-paneled walls. A Holly Hobbie kitchen set stood in a corner. It must've belonged to the unsmiling girl in the eight-by-ten frame near the patio door. She wore two shoulder-dusting pigtails tied with ribbons red as candied apples.

Dickie came back with a beer for him and Daddy and an opened Little Debbie oatmeal cream pie for me. This cousin had endeared himself to me already. How did he know I lived for oatmeal cream pies? I scooted back on the couch and damn near inhaled it.

Dickie sat down in the easy chair opposite us on the couch. "How things goin', man?"

"You know, man. Nothin'." Daddy sighed.

As he and Dickie made small talk, my eyes fixated on a shelf that was packed with albums. A complicated-looking stereo system was encased in a glass-and-stained-wood stand.

"Daddy, he got records," I said, interrupting his conversation.

"You 'spose to say, 'Excuse me,' lit' man," Daddy said. "Forgot to tell ya, Dickie: this boy here is a music freak."

Dickie laughed. "Ain't nobody here but us. Wife and kids over at Mama's. Hell, we can turn this sucka up."

Dickie went over to the stereo, pushed open the glass door, and touched a button. Dots of orange light flashed on the components.

He scanned the shelf and selected an album. He dropped the needle and cranked up the volume as a sassy guitar line filled the room. Then the bass and drums kicked in, laying down the relentless groove of "Call Me" by Skyy.

"Hell, yeah," Daddy said.

"Ain't that bad?" Dickie asked.

Daddy nodded his head and snapped his fingers. "Hey, lit' man. Can you dance?"

I smiled and buried my face in the couch.

"C'mon, man. Get up and show me and Dickie some moves. We old men."

I looked up. "I don't know how to dance."

"Yeah you do," Daddy said, rising off the couch.

"Man, I know you ain't gon' dance," Dickie chuckled.

"Hey, I still got it. C'mon, Dus-Dus."

I stood up. Daddy bent his knees and sucked in his bottom lip. He jerked, popped his fingers, and swung his hips, dancing off beat. Dickie and I laughed.

"Show Daddy what they do on *Soul Train*, Dus-Dus."

I tried to approximate the robotic pop-locking moves I'd seen on the show.

"Go 'head, lit' man," Dickie said.

Daddy danced as if he had ants in his pants, and I didn't want to be anywhere else.

We spent a few hours at Dickie's listening to albums. His taste leaned toward the jazzier and pop sides of soul, with several albums by George Benson and Donald Byrd. He played Al Jarreau's "We're in This Love Together" twice.

"Man, this is my jam," he said, cueing the record.

While Daddy and Dickie drank beer and talked in low voices away from the music, I studied the album covers: Stephanie Mills smiling with one leg up; Minnie Riperton with a crown of baby's breath seated next to a lion; Rick James in braids and painted-on jeans leaning against a street lamp.

When it was time to go, Dickie stooped down, gave me a warm hug, and said Daddy needed to bring me by more often.

"You a cool lit' man," he said.

He patted Daddy on the shoulder. "Ev'rything'll be all right. Hang in there."

The roads were dark as we made our way to East Section Line. I dozed off while Daddy sang along to Bobby Womack's tortured croon.

I woke up when the interior lights popped on. We were back at Big Mama's.

Daddy opened my door. "C'mon, Dus-Dus. You was out the whole time."

I followed him into the house, where Reagan, who was swimming in a nightgown Big Mama had found for her, was watching TV with Cuda.

Reagan sprang off the couch as Daddy shut the door.

"Where my candy?" she wanted to know.

We woke up to Big Mama cooking Sunday breakfast—scrambled eggs, biscuits, and hand-patted sausage—while the Clara Ward Singers wailed "Surely God Is Able" on the stereo.

Big Mama, Cuda, and Pat left for church soon after the dishes were cleared. Big Mama had washed our clothes the night before, tightly folded them, and packed them in our bag.

Dressed in a mauve skirt suit and matching hat, she gave us a hug before leaving.

"Big Mama love y'all, hear? Be good."

Daddy wanted to swing by Aunt Stella's before we were due back in Hot Springs that afternoon, but we didn't make it. I was pissed, because I adored Aunt Stella, her inviting home and abundant snacks. But we had to go back over to Happy Street to get Dusa. It was lovely to take a break from her, and I'm sure she felt the same way. She wasn't even packed when we arrived at Mama Teacake's.

Her house, as usual, was abuzz with folks. Three old men I didn't know sat in foldout chairs under the carport. Ollie sat on the porch on his way to being drunk, his shirt unbuttoned to his navel. Daddy stood under the carport and chatted with the men. He sent us in for Dusa.

Mama Teacake held court at the head of the kitchen table. Edlee, an obese neighbor with the saddest eyes I'd ever seen, sat at the table, along with my aunts Nita and Kay. Dusa sat among them.

"Daddy outside," I announced.

"So!" Dusa said.

"You gon' walk up in here and ain't gon' speak?" Mama Teacake said.

"Hi, y'all."

Mama Teacake looked at Reagan, who stood beside me. "I guess you ain't gon' speak, either? Come back from old Miss Ollison's with ya nose all in the air, like her shit don't stank."

Everybody around the table laughed as Reagan mumbled, "Hi, y'all."

"Y'all see Cuda's baby?" Kay asked.

"Yep," I said.

"Who's the daddy?" Dusa asked Kay.

"Somebody she was messin' with," Nita said. "He in the pen, I heard."

Edlee looked shocked. "In the pen?"

"I heard that too," Kay said. "I saw her out with Miss Ollison and that baby down at the Food Center. Cute lit' thang, but he must look like his daddy 'cause he don't look nothin' like Cuda and nem."

Their personal lives were always in shreds, yet my aunts and Mama Teacake gossiped endlessly about everybody else in town, especially Daddy's side of the family. I wondered if others sat around talking about how fucked up their lives were.

Kay was something of a firecracker and had become a mother twice before her sixteenth birthday. Before she was thirty, she had five kids. Nobody was really sure who their fathers were, save for the last one, Ryan, who was the spitting image of Kay's volatile husband, Reggie.

Nita lived down the street and around the corner from Mama Teacake. She didn't work, but her husband, my uncle Henry, had a good job at the gas company. Nita was moody and an agitator. She was known to fan the flames around family fights and seemed to get a kick out of getting shit started and keeping it up.

Outside the family, her friends were few. When Nita wasn't lying around her house snacking in front of the TV, she spoiled her two children, my cousins Rodney and Ralanda, whom everybody called Wee-Wee. Both were obnoxious, especially Rodney, who like his mama kept shit up. He always laughed at our clothes and talked about how poor we were.

"What Miss Ollison cook today?" Mama Teacake asked.

I shrugged. "She went to church."

"She didn't feed y'all?" Kay asked.

"We ate breakfast."

Mama Teacake huffed. "Well, I guess y'all eat when y'all get to Dianne's, 'cause you ain't eatin' here."

And that was fine with me—didn't want any of her greasy food anyway.

Nita chimed in. "You know Miss Ollison pro'ly cooked the same thang she always cook on Sundays: a roast, some greens or green beans."

"Yeah, and some cornbread," Mama Teacake added. "She like clockwork."

Daddy knocked on and opened the side door. "How y'all doin' in here?"

"We makin' it. How's Miss Ollison, Cuda, and nem?" Mama Teacake quickly switched to a friendly tone.

"They doin' just fine." Daddy looked at Dusa. "You ready to go? Dianne told me to have y'all back 'fore dark."

"I need to get my stuff ready," Dusa said without looking at him.

"Don't you think you need to do that now?" Daddy asked.

Mama Teacake looked at Dusa. "Go on, now. Don't keep him waitin'."

Dusa rolled her eyes and left the kitchen in a huff.

Daddy took Dusa's seat at the table. While she collected her things, he made small talk about the weather and Cuda's baby. I stood beside him, and Reagan sat on his lap. The air was pungent with the smell of the mustard greens simmering on the stove.

The women sat around Mama Teacake's table talking and talking, their voices knotting together in a dissonant blues. I looked at them and surveyed the kitchen. Grease coated the wall behind the stove. Old liquor bottles cluttered the countertops. I wanted to be back at Big Mama's.

The heaviness floating around inside started to throb the closer we got to Hot Springs. As Daddy made the turn onto Omega Street, tears filled my eyes and rolled down my face.

Dusa turned around in the front seat as Daddy parked the car.

"God, he's crying," she said.

Daddy opened his door and let me out.

"C'mon, lit' man. What you cryin' for?"

He knelt down and gave me a hug.

"I wanna go with you."

"Stop that, Dus-Dus. See, Puddin' ain't cryin'."

"So!"

"Hey, now," Daddy's tone was sharp. "Cut it out."

My tears continued to flow as we walked to our unit. The door was open; Mama was home. She was in the kitchen cooking dinner in an old pink housedress with rollers in her hair.

"Look who's back," Mama sounded like she was in a good mood. When she saw me, she frowned. "What's wrong with you, Dusty?"

"Cryin' like a girl, as he always do," Dusa said.

"Shut up!" I felt empowered. She wouldn't hit me as long as Mama and Daddy were around.

"Don't start that!" Mama told us.

"Hey, Dianne." Daddy's voice was low.

"Hey, Raymond." Mama's voice had spikes.

"I need to holla at you for a minute, need to talk to you 'bout somethin'."

"What is it?"

"Not in front of the kids."

Mama sighed. "Y'all take ya stuff upstairs. Go."

We all went upstairs but left our doors open. I couldn't hear much of what Daddy said, but Mama's trumpet voice rang through the air.

What the hell am I supposed to do, Raymond? I gotta work.

Shit, you sho ain't sendin' no money.

They ain't babies!

Well, why don't you come by here more often 'stead of when you feel like it and see yo' kids, huh?

Daddy's baritone sax voice rose: "Soon as I get my own place, Dianne, they can come and stay sometimes. But they ain't got no business in this house by theyselves."

Raymond, you ain't runnin' shit in here.

Send some money, and maybe I can afford a damn babysitter.

"Nothin' bet' not happen to them babies," Daddy said.

They ain't no babies, Raymond!

Daddy said something I couldn't hear, to which Mama responded: "I don't wanna hear it."

Then the door slammed. Reagan and I looked at each other. I sprang off the bed and ran downstairs. "Where Daddy?"

Mama stood in the kitchen archway, hand on hip. "Dusty!"

I paused at the bottom of the steps.

"Come here right now." Mama pointed to the floor.

"Where?"

"Boy, bring yo' lit' yella ass here."

Slowly, I left the steps, made my way to Mama, and braced myself for a slap upside the head.

"Boy, open yo' eyes!"

I peeked out of one. "Yeah?"

"What you tell yo' daddy, 'cause I know you said somethin.' You the only one go runnin' yo' damn mouth."

"I ain't say nothin.'"

"You bet' not stand here and lie to me, Dusty. You tell him you and Reagan be home by y'all selves?"

"Yeah."

"Why?"

"I don't know."

"Yeah, you know."

I looked at the floor.

"Look at me, Dusty."

I looked up at the small mole on Mama's chin.

"Let me tell you somethin': What goes on in this house is my business, you hear me?"

"Yeah."

"Yo' Daddy ain't sendin' y'all a damn dime, so he don't control shit in this house. You hear me?"

"Yeah."

"And don't you ever run yo' mouth over at Miss Ollison's 'bout what I do over here. Am I makin' myself clear?"

"Yeah."

"Do you understand what I'm tellin' you?"

"Yeah."

"Now get yo' ass upstairs and don't come down 'til I tell ya it's time to eat. And don't you put on that damn record player, either."

My eyes filled with tears.

"And stop all that damn cryin'!"

I stomped upstairs. When I entered the room, I threw myself on my bed and buried my face in the pillow. Reagan asked, "You in trouble?"

I ignored her.

Why couldn't Michael Jackson hurry up and take me away from this shit?

Months after realizing Michael Jackson was never coming in a rocket limo, Jason, my cousin, arrived on our doorstep with a suicide note.

The youngest son of Aunt Phyl, Jason was five, with eyes as big as half dollars and a quick smile that suggested he knew much more than you. He came on a chilly Sunday afternoon when Mama was off work. We were all in the living room watching TV when he knocked on the door. Mama answered.

"Where'd you come from?" she asked as Jason welcomed himself inside.

Reagan and I lit up; finally, a playmate to break the monotony.

"Where Phyl?" Mama asked.

"She gone," Jason said, sounding like a little old man.

"Gone where? Where's your coat?"

Jason shrugged. We rarely saw him. Phyl, who worked as a nurse, often moved around Hot Springs. Nobody knew where she lived from one month to the next. For years, she maintained a demanding job and a sloppy personal life peppered with recreational drugs and no-good men she sometimes fought brutally.

Phyl had three kids, the first two with her husband, Doug, whom she divorced after a mostly abusive marriage. Jason's father was a man named Bobby, whom Phyl courted soon after she divorced Doug. She dumped all three of her children on relatives when they were five years old. Kim, the oldest, was a few months older than Dusa and was raised by Mama Teacake. Kevin, whom I hardly knew, was in his father's care. Then Jason showed up at our door with ill-fitting clothes, no coat in winter, hair that looked as though it hadn't been brushed in days, and a smile that was stupid and smart all at once.

"He look like he hungry," said Dusa, who was curled up on the couch. "Phyl feed you?"

"Nope." Jason said, joining Reagan and me in front of the TV.

Mama looked confused. "So she just dropped yo' ass off, no nothing? I'll be damned."

"What's that sticking out your pocket, Jason?" Dusa asked.

A small white envelope poked out of his back pocket when he sat down.

"Give that here, Jason," Mama said.

He handed her the envelope. Mama sat on the love seat and read the note inside, which had been torn out of a spiral notebook. She furrowed her brow and whispered, "Lord."

"What, Mama?" Dusa asked.

"Dusty, Reagan, Jason, y'all go'n upstairs and play."

Reagan and Jason bounded up the stairs. I acted as though I hadn't heard my name called. I wanted to know what Phyl had to say in the letter.

Mama glared at me. "Dusty? Upstairs."

I pouted and climbed the stairs, crouching at the top to eavesdrop.

"This bitch is crazy," Mama said.

"What she do?"

Mama read from the letter, "'Big Sis, I can't take this any-more. It's become too much to bear. I've been thinking about killing myself. Please take Jason.'"

Dusa's voice rose. "Take Jason? What, is he supposed to stay here? Where is his daddy? Mama, she gonna kill herself?"

"Please! Phyl ain't killin' herself. She would've done that a long time ago."

"She said she is."

"Phyl ain't gon' do shit. I don't know what her problem is, but she got one. Look at how she dropped that boy off here, like he's trash. Lord, like I can afford another mouth to feed 'round here."

I couldn't see her but I imagined Dusa crossing her arms and pushing herself back on the couch when she said, "Dang!"

Jason got my hand-me-downs and Phyl managed to drop off a few things—wrinkled clothes and too-little shoes in a brown paper bag. All of a sudden, he lived with us. Jason now slept in Reagan's bed across from mine, and Reagan was in Dusa's room down the hall near the bathroom. Jason and I never developed much of a relationship. I was eight; he was five. In my mind, Jason was just a baby. What could we possibly talk about? He was always touching things, asking, "What's this?"

I made it very clear to him that my records and record player were holy.

"You touch 'em, I will kill you," I said, meaning every word.

"I'll tell Aunt Dianne."

"How you gon' tell if you dead, stupid?"

"I'm gon' tell anyway."

"You so dumb."

"No I ain't."

"Nappy head."

"Doo-doo head."

"I hate you."

"I hate you too."

"Bet' not touch my records."

Jason and Reagan were closer in age, barely a year apart, and played well together but only for so long. Ultimately, Jason did something to piss Reagan off, which didn't take much since she'd clearly inherited Daddy's post-Vietnam temper. If they played a game and Jason broke a rule or did anything Reagan deemed unfair, she slapped him upside the head. He'd hold the throbbing spot and wail like a fire alarm, tears streaming. Then suddenly, Jason's face would tighten, and the fight was on. Dusa constantly pulled them apart. I stood back, amused. Once, just to be an asshole, I started the fight.

"Bet you can't beat up Reagan. She can kick yo' butt."

"No, she can't."

"You a boy, gettin' beat up by a girl."

"She can't beat me up."

"Yes she will."

To prove he was no punk, Jason smacked Reagan on the arm.

"Boy! You crazy," Reagan said before pouncing on him.

Reagan tornado-slapped Jason's head, beating it so fast her hands were all a blur.

"Dusa! They fightin' again," I yelled, grinning and moving away from the brawl.

Dusa separated them and hissed her words into their faces, "If y'all don't stop, I'm gon' kill ya both."

Before Jason arrived on our doorstep, he had already known horrific beatings at the hands of Phyl. His back was marked with welts and scars. He once woke up in the middle of the night weeping.

I raised my head off the pillow. "Jason? What's wrong with you?"

"Leave me alone."

"Go back to bed, boy, 'fore you wake Mama up."

"Where my mama?"

The ache in his voice stung and made me think of Daddy. I wanted to leave my bed to pat him on the head, but I didn't move. I softened my tone.

"Go back to sleep, Jason. It'll be OK. OK?"

He sniffed. "OK."

When Jason set the kitchen trash on fire, he had to go.

That happened in the third and final year he lived with us. Phyl's sporadic visits always set him on edge. Most times she came bearing a gift, usually an outfit that was either too big or too small for Jason.

Phyl knocked on the door out the blue one Saturday morning just after Mama and Dusa had left for work. I answered.

Phyl sashayed past me. "Where Dianne?"

Dark-skinned with a short Jheri curl and drawn-on, pencil-thin eyebrows, Phyl was a commanding presence, like Mama Teacake.

She wore a perpetual scowl. Phyl carried no purse, only a red-leather cigarette case and a can of Coke.

"She at work," I said, closing the door.

"Where Bossman?" Phyl said, calling Jason by his nickname. She shouted, "Bossman!"

Jason and Reagan bolted down the stairs. Jason's old-man eyes lit up, and he rushed to Phyl, hugging her around the waist. She looked down at him and frowned.

"Why yo' hair ain't brushed?" Phyl shot a look at me. "Where Dusa at?"

"She at work."

"Why the hell y'all here by y'all selves? Let go, Bossman."

Jason released his mother's hips, and she sat on the couch. She pulled out a cigarette and lit it.

"Mama don't like smokin' in here," I said.

"Shut up, Dusty!" Phyl snapped, smoke escaping her plum-dark lips.

Jason sat close to her. "Scoot over," she said, grimacing. "Damn! All up under me."

Phyl picked up the phone on the side table.

"Mama said we can't use the phone," I said.

"Dusty, if you don't shut the fuck up!" Phyl's voice boomed.

She dialed and stared me down as she waited for whomever to pick up.

"Hey," she said. "I'm at my sister's. Where you at?"

For a moment she listened intensely. Then finally she nodded and said, "You know where she stay. Hurry up."

She hung up and surveyed the living room. "Y'all asses need to be cleanin' up in here."

Jason looked at her. "Mama, where we goin'?"

"'We' ain't goin' nowhere," Phyl said frowning. "You stayin' here."

Reagan and I sat on the floor and stared at them. She glanced at me. We knew this wasn't going to be good. Jason wrapped his arm around Phyl's small waist.

"I wanna go with you."

Phyl looked at the ceiling and rolled her eyes. She took one last drag off her cigarette and dropped it in the Coke can.

"You ain't goin' with me," Phyl said, her tone prickly. "I'll bring you somethin' back next time. I was just in the neighborhood."

Jason began to cry, and Phyl pushed him away, then smacked the side of his head. Reagan and I winced.

"You gon' stop all that cryin' like a lit' bitch!" Phyl's voice seemed to rock the room. Jason held the side of his head and wailed.

Phyl smacked his arm. "Stop it!"

His mouth was open, tears trailed his face, but no sound escaped. He buried his face into the couch. Phyl waved her hand as if shooing a gnat away. Just then, a car horn honked outside.

"Tell Dianne I stopped by here." She rose and held the Coke can out to me. "Dusty, throw this away."

I sprang off the floor and retrieved the can. Phyl looked at Jason, whose face was still buried in the couch cushion, muffling his sobs.

"Bossman, if you don't stop all that cryin' I'm gon' break yo' neck. Look at me!"

Jason looked at her, his old-man eyes drained of all hope and magic.

"I'll bring you somethin' next time, hear?"

"OK," Jason whimpered.

The car horn honked again. Phyl slinked toward the door, her hips moving to an undulating rhythm, the projects diva stroll. She remembered to lock us in before pulling the door shut.

Late that night, I awoke to a scream.

It was Dusa. My head shot up from the pillow, and I noticed Jason wasn't in his bed. I left the room just as Mama and Reagan emerged from theirs. We rushed downstairs and into the kitchen, where Dusa dumped a pot of water on a fire blazing in the brown plastic trash bin. The top of it looked like melted fudge.

"Dusa! What the hell is goin' on?" Mama shouted.

Dusa tossed the sauce pot into the sink. "I smelled somethin' burnin' and thought I left somethin' on down here."

"What? How the damn trash get on fire?" Mama looked inside the bin.

"Jason ain't in his bed," I said.

Mama and Dusa looked at me with the same shocked eyes.

"Lawd, let me call . . ." Mama rushed out of the kitchen.

We followed her into the dark living room. When she grabbed the phone and turned on the lamp, we all jumped. Jason sat in the spot where Phyl had been hours earlier. He held his knees to his chin and looked straight ahead as though we weren't there.

Mama Teacake took Jason in soon afterward. When we dropped him off, I felt sorry for him. I couldn't imagine living with the evil kitchen queen.

During the next seven years with Mama Teacake and Ollie, Jason only got worse, especially after Phyl suddenly moved to California when he was about nine. For a long time, nobody knew exactly where she was out there. Her calls to Mama Teacake were erratic and always explosive. "She out there on that crack," Mama Teacake said. "I know she is. Ain't done nothin' for her kids."

At fourteen, Jason stood six feet. He often fought at school. The bane of his existence, it seemed, was Phyl. She called once promising to be on her way back to Arkansas to get him. She was coming on a Friday, she told him. And he waited. Of course, she didn't show.

It set off another domestic fit. After an argument with Mama Teacake, he spray-painted obscenities on the back of the house. After he threatened to kill them, Jason was shipped to a home for disturbed youth and then to a caring foster family, where he thrived for a while.

But his emotional progress stalled the next time he saw Phyl. None of us had seen her for eight years when she came home for Kay's funeral. Jason towered over Phyl, who looked gaunt and weathered. She didn't know who he was.

Her mean eyes squinting, Phyl looked into his handsome face. "Bossman?"

Jason fell to his knees before her, sobbing the way he did the day she slapped him over on Omega Street.

The trumpet in Mama's throat could be sharp and piercing.

It often cut through the music spinning on my record player, knocking me off my cloud and back to Omega Street.

"Dusty! Turn that shit down, or turn it off."

I always wondered if she had a problem with the music itself. These were Daddy's records, after all. And Lord knows she never had a kind word to say about him. Something in Gladys Knight's anguished belting and Bobby Womack's testifying growls made me feel wise. Maybe they unsettled Mama. I don't know. It probably wasn't even that deep.

Sometimes, though, her face unknotted when she walked by my bedroom door and a song stopped her. This sudden change in her mood always surprised me. One day, it was "The Rubberband Man" by the Spinners. Mama pushed opened the door. Her hair was in rollers, her feet were in slippers, and her old housedress hugged her hips.

"Oh, that was the jam," she said, a smile brightening her face. I smiled too. "Turn that up."

Mama snapped her fingers and bounced her shoulders. She wasn't in the room. She seemed transported well beyond our apartment as she shuffled her feet, the Spinners harmonizing through the scratchy vinyl. She shouted, "Hey!" and rolled her hips.

I wanted Daddy to appear. And suddenly, there he was: sober, groomed, and handsome. He grabbed Mama, their smiles met, and the room became a bright and infinite place in the sky. Daddy released her and she dipped. "Get it, baby," he shouted. He pulled her from behind and whispered something in her ear. Mama threw her head back, flashing the smile she wore in Mexico all those years ago. A silly song about a rubberband man had lassoed joy and made all well again. Then the record went off, Mama stopped dancing, and the ghost of Daddy vanished.

Mama's smile faded and she pulled her housedress down.

I didn't want her to leave. "You want me to play it again, Mama?"

"No," she said, heading toward the door. She stopped and furrowed her brow, her face back to a tense mask. "Turn that music off, anyhow. Come down here and sweep this kitchen up."

In the summer of 1986, we left the projects.

Mama held down two jobs at the main hospitals in Hot Springs. By day, she delivered food trays to patients at one, and she worked by night as a monitor technician at the other.

We moved into a quaint ivory house on Baker Street, just off Grand, the main drag. The porch was wide and screened in. The living room had a brick fireplace. French doors led to a dining room with large windows, and sunlight flooded the space. Push past the swing door and the kitchen was bright, with a window over the sink and several in the breakfast nook.

There were three spacious bedrooms. Reagan and I bunked again. Just behind the house was a tiny, two-room maid's quarters attached to the garage, with a toilet that didn't work. Reagan and I converted it into a playhouse, where we entertained ourselves with Monopoly and other games—until we inevitably got on each other's nerves and started fighting.

Decades before, well-to-do white folks filled the neighborhood. The Colonial- and Victorian-style homes were still nice and stately by the time we moved in. Our neighbors, whom we never knew, were mostly retired, standoffish, and white. The block had an antiseptic feel and looked like the set of a TV sitcom. No funk. No badass kids running up and down the street. No projects divas strolling around in tube tops and denim cutoffs or screaming out of windows and doors. I was relieved.

Dusa still worked at Taco Bell, and her commute by bus to Hot Springs High School was shorter. Reagan and I transferred to Jones Elementary, which was about three short blocks away, and we walked to school. It also was around this time I wanted to exit my cocoon and interact with other kids, but nothing changed at Jones. Aside from multiplication tables, I learned a new word: faggot.

On the playground one day I found the nerve to approach a group of four black boys.

"What y'all doing?" I asked.

They looked at one another and laughed. The tall one, whom I recognized from the class across the hall from mine, glared at me.

"Listen at you. 'What y'all doing?'" he said in a voice pitched a few octaves higher as he batted his eyes and put his hand on his hip.

"I don't talk like that," I shot back.

"Yeah, you do," said the tall muthafucka.

Another guy, scowling, spat his words: "You act like a faggot."

The boys all laughed and walked off. One shouted back, "Stay away."

I stood there, my face flushed and a cyclone whirling inside my stomach. Later that evening I went into Dusa's room, where she lay across the bed doing her homework. She looked up. "What you want? Get out."

"What's a faggot?"

"Uh-uh."

"What?"

"Where you hear that?"

"At school. These boys called me a faggot."

"Well. That's what you get."

"I didn't do nothin'."

"Dusty, I been tellin' yo' ass for the longest. Boys who act like girls? That's a faggot. Got it?"

I was confused and tried to hold back the tears but was unsuccessful.

Dusa rolled her eyes. "See? That's what I'm talking about. You so need to get that together, Dusty. Get out."

"I didn't do nothin'."

"Get out!"

I turned around. Maybe she was right. I needed to find an edge from somewhere, but I wasn't tipping out of my cocoon for it.

Dusa told Mama about the faggot incident, and she called me into her room a few nights after Dusa kicked me out of hers. Mama didn't look at me as she clipped foam rollers into her hair.

"Yeah?"

"You havin' problems at school?"

"No."

"You lyin'?"

"No."

"Why Dusa tell me boys are callin' you a faggot then?"

I looked at the floor and didn't answer.

"Huh?"

I mumbled, "I don't know."

"Yeah, you know." Mama's tone was accusatory.

I said nothing, and the tension pulsed for several seconds.

"Dusty, I'm talkin' to you."

"Don't cry," I told myself. I concentrated on the hardwood floor. Maybe if I looked at it long enough, hard enough, I would melt into it. Or magically crumble like unbleached flour, leaving a mess that somebody else (maybe Dusa) would have to clean up. Or maybe I could just close my eyes and escape somewhere with Michael Jackson. I could—

"Dusty!" Mama's voice blared. "Look at me."

She put the comb down and turned toward me, half of her hair wrapped in tiny tissue paper and pink foam rollers.

"When you were born, the doctors brought me you and said, 'You have a boy.' I didn't have a girl. I want you to start actin' like a boy. You hear me?"

All I knew was something—a defect that Mama, Dusa, and those nappy-headed boys on the playground could clearly see— made me feel lonely and deeply disliked. Tears streamed.

"What did I do?"

Mama rolled her eyes. "You go 'round here actin' like a woman. Reagan act more like a boy than you. You wanna be a girl?"

The floor blurred through the tears.

"Dusty!"

"Huh?"

"I said you wanna be a girl?"

"No."

"Then start actin' like a boy and folks at school won't be callin' you no faggot. You ain't no faggot. You hear me?"

Liquid fire stirred in my chest and coursed through my body.

"Dusty!"

I wanted to be invisible.

"Dusty!"

Mama's trumpet sputtered sharp, ragged notes that spiraled round and round inside my head.

Maybe she carried the moon in her pocketbook and lions slept in her backyard, because her voice suggested a strength and comeliness of an otherworldly queen. There was a liberating fuck-you in every primal wail on a Chaka Khan record—and I started to gather my strength from there.

I saw her on Solid Gold *and* Soul Train. *She was a few years past her artistic prime in the mid-eighties, her voice clashing against trendy synthesizers, her massive, purplish hair obscuring her face.*

I found a younger Chaka in the records Daddy left, the shapely chick with the mysterious eyes in leather and feathers, sitting gap-legged on a couch shaped like a pair of big red lips.

I watched, as I always did, the label spinning on the turntable. The sun-yellow outer rings with the red-and-violet core worked like a hypnotic spiral as Chaka's brassy voice pulled me into a "Fool's Paradise." I had no idea what she sang about. I didn't absorb lyrics then. The voice was all that mattered, and I wanted to be the sound: free and powerful, bold and assured.

This was not the sound of a faggot. This was not the sound of a lonely and disliked person. Now that I had headphones, I could plug in and blast her defiant voice. I could close my eyes and become nothing. I could exhale and surrender to a woman who tamed lions in her backyard and kept a full moon somewhere in her purse.

Over on Baker Street, it wasn't unusual for us to come home from school and find the lights shut off.

Reagan always became irate—stomping her feet, throwing something across the room and pouting. She rushed home to see *Zoobilee Zoo*, the kids' show with Ben Vereen dressed as a leopard. I dug it sometimes but often found refuge in my records. With no electricity, neither of us could escape.

"I hate we even moved here," Reagan said and slumped on the couch. I called Mama at work.

"We ain't got no lights."

Mama sighed.

I repeated, "We ain't got no lights."

"I heard you," she snapped.

"What you want us to do?"

"What y'all got to eat in there?"

"Nothin'."

"Dusty, there's something in there."

"Peanut butter, I guess."

"Eat that 'til I come home. Dusa home yet?"

"Nah."

"Well, I don't get paid 'til next week. When Dusa get home, tell her I'm gon' have to get the money from her."

I rolled my eyes. Mama always appointed me to do this shit. She knew damn well that Dusa hated my guts and would misdirect her frustration at me.

"She gon' get mad at me," I whined.

"No, she won't."

"She always do."

"Just tell her I'm gon' need the money, and y'all stay in that house."

"Ain't no lights; ain't nothin' to do."

"Don't y'all have homework? Do that before it gets dark up in there."

Mama hung up.

By the time Dusa walked through the door, the sun had slid down the sky. Reagan, still pissed, stared at the TV screen as though she could turn it on with her mind. I had just finished my math homework.

Dressed in her brown-and-orange Taco Bell uniform, Dusa smelled of meat and onions. "Why y'all sittin' in the dark?"

"No lights," I said.

Dusa threw her purse and book bag down. "Damn!"

"Mama said she gon' need to borrow the money from you," I blurted.

"What? I'm so sick of this shit! Borrow? She never pay me back. She work two goddamn jobs. Why can't she keep the lights on in here?"

Dusa was almost in tears.

"You askin' me?" I said.

Dusa stomped down the hall to her room. She slammed the door so hard Reagan and I flinched.

Mama's bones weren't always made of steel.

She softened early in the morning soon after the sun rose, when we were asleep. I'd hear her stirring around, and I'd smell the coffee brewing. Lying in bed, I felt comforted by her morning noises, which sometimes lulled me back to sleep.

Early on a Saturday before she was due at her first job, I heard her in the kitchen, which was next to the bedroom I shared with Reagan. I wanted to see her before she left.

When I heard her leave the kitchen, I slid out of my bed, walked through the kitchen, pushed past the swing door, and slipped through the dining room and into the living room.

Mama sat out on the screened-in porch in a shapeless house-dress in the cool morning air. I didn't want to disturb her, so I watched her through the gauzy curtains on the window above the couch. I crouched down so she wouldn't see me.

She sat in a lawn chair, sipped her coffee, and placed it on the small table next to her. She opened the dog-eared Bible on her lap and scanned the pages.

All was quiet. Steam rose from her mug. Her face was relaxed but not peaceful. She nodded at the pages for a while then closed the Bible. She sipped her coffee, closed her eyes, and bowed her head.

Mama started to rock and nod. Her eyes were shut tight and her lips moved fast with no sound escaping. I wanted to go out and rub her shoulder, ask her if everything was OK, offer to clean up, do something.

She looked so private. There was no place for me between her and God.

No prayers kept the lights on at Baker Street. So after about a year, we moved. The new house, across town on Audubon Street, was just around the corner from Dusa's high school. Reagan and I transferred to Oaklawn Elementary, which was two or three short blocks away. The neighborhood was another quiet one where standoffish whites dominated. Maple and magnolia trees shaded fastidiously neat homes, where plastic pink flamingos bent their necks in fresh-cut grass and ceramic gnomes nestled under chrysanthemums.

Our house was moss-green and smaller and much less stately than the one on Baker. It felt like a cottage, with wood-paneled walls and stingy windows that didn't let in much light. The kitchen was large with ugly floral-print carpet. The bathroom, tiny as it was, must have been an afterthought.

Soon after we moved in, Mama started wearing more makeup, Fashion Fair Glam Girl, and her smile was dazzling. She still worked two full-time jobs, but she wasn't home much the few days she had off.

She'd met a man.

We'd walked home from school one day, excited to see Mama's bug-eyed, sky-blue Chevette under the carport. But whose boxy white sedan was parked in front? Reagan and I ran inside and found an ebony-skinned man in a burgundy sweater with black geometric leather patches sitting on the couch, his arm thrown over the back. We froze at the door.

Aglow with a made-up face, Mama strolled in from the kitchen. "There's something to eat on the stove," she said. "Y'all fix your plate and go in your room."

We exchanged looks. Who was gonna ask about this mutha-fucka on the couch?

I looked directly at him. "Who are you?"

"Dusty!" Mama hissed my name through tight lips. "You don't pay no bills in here."

The man chuckled and rubbed his knees. "That's OK, Dianne. I'm Dennis, lit' man."

His smoked-out baritone caressed Mama's name with a sly affection that made me bristle. I could smell his pungent, gag-inducing cologne all the way at the door. I hadn't known this Dennis cat for one whole minute and already I detested him—the way he sat on our brown-and-burnt-orange couch gap-legged as though he'd bought it; the way he rubbed his knees as though he was satisfied and expected someone to bring him something.

I hated Reagan's juiced-up Jheri curl, and so did she. Now here was this Dennis, greasy and shining with a stringy curl—short on the sides and long in the back. Did Mama think he was cool? Gold chains hanging from his neck, a gold-nugget pinky ring gleaming on his broad, dark hand—who the hell did he think he was, Rick James?

Mama snapped her fingers and pointed to the kitchen. "Dusty and Reagan, y'all go fix ya something to eat and get back in that room and do your homework now."

We slowly made our way to the kitchen, dragging our coats and book bags while looking back at Dennis.

Later that night, Mama went out with him. Dusa didn't have to work and, as always, was pissed about having to stay home with us. We were in the living room watching *Alf* when I asked Dusa about Dennis.

"Who is he?"

"Mama's new boyfriend."

"He ain't my daddy," Reagan said.

"Nobody said he was," Dusa shot back.

"Where she meet him at?" I wanted to know.

"Who you askin'? I don't know." Dusa pouted. "And she gon' go out with him and leave me here, like I don't wanna go out on my night off."

"Where you gonna go?" Reagan asked.

Dusa continued, ignoring her. "And we don't know nothin' about him. He was in here the other day, before y'all got home from school. I'd missed the bus and needed Mama to take me to work, and she gon' fuss me out. They were getting ready go somewhere, and I had to be at work."

Dusa sighed.

"She take you to work?" I asked, suddenly feeling like her equal.

"She finally did, and I was late." Dusa rolled her eyes.

We turned back to the TV. After *Alf* went off, Reagan turned to us and affirmed what she'd said before: "He ain't my daddy."

His love caged him and set him free, and I didn't understand how both could be possible. Pain seared David Ruffin's voice as he walked away from love. The cha-cha rhythm and celebratory horns leavened the sorrow. Gritty and commanding, then airy and silken, his voice was sunlight and shadow.

All of the men in Daddy's records sang of love with drastically imbalanced emotion. In the span of three minutes, they begged for it and kicked it to the curb. They turned to anybody, even to God, with a perpetual request: Please send me someone to love.

But once they got it, love scrambled them.

Love'll make you do right; love'll make you do wrong. Make you come home early; make you stay out all night long. I don't love you anymore; it's just that simple. I want you so, babe, can't even get mad at you. If you want this love I'm giving, you better put something down on it. I'm leaving, yes I am. This time I'm playing it smart. I'm gonna walk away from love before love breaks my heart.

David sounded relieved as the song faded, and I thought about Daddy. I couldn't remember the last time I saw him. He never came to visit after we left the projects. No calls. No letters. Was he avoiding us? Had he, like David, just walked away before love could break his heart? Mine already was shattered.

Mama's affair with Dennis snatched from us what little time she had between jobs. When she was home, Dennis was usually around or on his way over. Once, in the middle of the night, I awoke to use the bathroom and noticed Mama's bedroom door closed. She never slept with the door closed. Dennis' musky cologne sang in the air as it always did when he was around. I wanted to bust into the room and tell him to get the fuck out. The fantasy was delicious: Dusty, the pint-sized, shit-talking hero in Superman pajamas.

I would snatch Dennis's curl shag and pull him through the living room and onto the front porch. I'd stomp his leg and say, "Split! Before I kick yo' dog ass up and down this block."

He'd struggle to his feet, looking at me all bug-eyed, and scurry to his raggedy car and peel away. I'd stand on the front steps with my fists on my hips and send a deadly beam from my eyes, zeroing in on the back of his car, and blow the muthafucka up to the sky. Afterward, I'd strut back into the house, like Sherman Hemsley as George Jefferson, and slam the door.

But Dennis brought out Mama's sunshine smile, which she beautified with cranberry-colored lipstick. But he remained a stranger to me, a hologram with stank-ass cologne, whose presence made me deeply resent the fact that I could neither vanish nor fly.

Mama's affair made Dusa defiant. Her relationship with Mama, especially after Dusa started working when we were over on Omega Street, became a partnership. Mama leaned on Dusa a lot—to help with the bills, to mother Reagan and me while she held down two jobs to make ends at least wave at each other if not fully meet. Sometimes Dusa seemed to relish the responsibility. By the time we'd moved to Audubon, her cooking had improved. She'd make easy recipes from the old, tattered cookbooks Mama had. She'd stand at the stove hand on hip as she stirred the pots. Her grown-woman affectations had become less awkward.

Like Mama, she wore her invisible suit of armor, her voice often a whip snapping at us for every offense no matter how small. But from time to time, the insecure seventeen-year-old playing the weary grown woman revealed herself.

"Y'all come eat," Dusa ordered.

Reagan and I exchanged glances as if to say, "Lord, what did she cook now?"

Dusa had fixed our plates. Anytime she tried a new recipe she insisted we all sit at the table.

"This is tuna casserole," she said.

I examined it and noticed the melted cheddar on top; didn't look bad.

Reagan asked, "What's this green stuff in it?"

"Peas," Dusa snapped. "You eat peas."

Reagan frowned. "Not like this, though."

"Eat!" Dusa commanded.

We all picked up our forks and dug in. I felt Dusa's eyes on us. When I turned to her, the armor was temporarily gone and her eyes searched for approval. Her face softened.

Slowly, I chewed. I had a feeling that if I said the casserole was disgusting, it would crush her. But it really wasn't bad; needed less salt, but pretty tasty. Tell the truth and shame the devil, as Mama would say.

"It's good," I said.

Reagan nodded her approval and said in between forkfuls, "Uh-huh. I like it."

A half-smile almost crept across Dusa's face, but she stopped it and put on the armor.

"Y'all gon' wash these dishes after y'all get finished."

Snap!

With Dennis's regular visits, Dusa's affronts to Mama went from sly to bold. Whenever he came by, we all gave him a limp "hello"

and disappeared into our rooms. He and Mama stayed in the living room, watching TV, talking, or listening to the stereo. Dennis sometimes brought over cassettes—mostly Quiet Storm cuts by Freddie Jackson or Peabo Bryson. I thought his taste in music was lame.

When Dusa arrived home from school or work and saw Dennis, she'd roll her eyes, go to her room, and slam the door. She'd sometimes interrupt Mama's time with him by busting into the living room and abruptly asking for the keys to the car. Mama sometimes gave her the keys, just to get her out, I guess. But whenever she told her no, Dusa stomped back to her room, slammed the door, and got on the phone.

Once while Dennis was over, Dusa strolled through the living room dressed in panties and a painted-on T-shirt. Reagan and I sat in the adjacent area, playing Uno at the dining room table. Dusa's half-nakedness didn't shock us. She always strolled around in her bra and panties—but never in front of Dennis. Reagan whispered, "Look at her."

Mama sat straight up on the couch. Dennis glanced at Dusa and quickly turned his head to the TV.

"Dusa! What the hell you doin'?" Mama said. "Get the hell outta here and put some clothes on."

"I'm looking for something," Dusa said, shuffling through *Jet* magazines on the coffee table.

Mama's eyes flashed fire. "Girl, I'm gon' tell you one more time to go put some damn clothes on."

Dusa plucked a *Jet* from the stack. "Found it," she said and sauntered back to her room, slamming the door.

Dennis left shortly afterward, and Mama rushed to Dusa's room. Reagan and I followed to catch all the drama.

Mama opened the door and ordered Dusa off the phone.

"What was that shit you tried to pull?"

Reagan stood close to me in the doorway. Dusa sat up in her bed, looked at us and shouted, "Y'all go somewhere."

"Never mind them," Mama said. "I'm talkin' to you."

Dusa folded her arms, rolled her eyes, and turned toward the Prince poster on the wall.

Mama put her hands on her hips. "Heffa, you roll your eyes at me one more time, I'm gon' knock them clean out yo' head."

She stood over Dusa. "Look at me!"

Dusa's jaw tightened and she didn't move.

Mama snatched Dusa's hair and jerked her toward her. Reagan and I flinched as Dusa's face scrunched up and tears fell.

Mama's voice had spikes. "Girl, don't you ever pull no shit like that again, disrespectin' me in my damn house. You hear what I'm tellin' you?"

Dusa whimpered, "Yeah."

"You are still a child in here. There's only one damn queen. You hear me?"

"Yeah."

Mama pushed Dusa's head away, and Dusa buried her face into a pillow, the way Jason did that day Phyl slapped him over on Omega Street.

Mama turned toward the door. "Dusty and Reagan, y'all get somewhere and sit down."

We scurried across the hall to our room and shut the door. I slid onto my bed, and Reagan sat on hers facing me. We exchanged wide-eyed stares.

"Mama sho was mad," Reagan said.

I didn't blink. "She sho was."

A few months after Mama snatched Dusa's hair, she felt strange pains in her abdomen. She went to the doctor and had several tests done. After she got the results, she called us into the living room and delivered the news in her usual straight-no-chaser style.

"I got cancer, y'all."

When Dusa put her hand to her mouth, I sensed this was not good. I had no idea what cancer was. I looked at Reagan and knew damn well she didn't know.

"You got what?" I asked.

"Cancer, Dusty," Mama said, rolling her eyes. "I'm gonna have to go into the hospital for a while, and they gon' have to do a hysterectomy."

I was confused. "A what?"

Dusa sighed. "Mama's gonna have to have a surgery, Dusty."

"Where we gon' go?" Reagan asked, on the verge of tears.

"Well," Mama said. "First thing, we gotta move again."

Dusa and I slumped back on the couch.

"Shoot!" Dusa said.

After just a year, the rent on Audubon had become too high. We never knew our neighbors. Like Baker Street, the area hardly had any color (literally) and definitely no funk. I was glad to leave Omega Street but sometimes missed the wooliness over there.

"We gon' be all right," Mama said. "I'm just gonna have to go into the hospital for a while, and Dusa, you gon' have to look over things. Doctors said it shouldn't be too serious, that I should be fine after this hysterectomy. Caught it in time, they said."

"You talk to Dad?" Dusa asked.

"Raymond? Nah."

"Where's Daddy?" Reagan asked.

"Shit, I don't know," Mama said, curling her lips. "Over in Malvern somewhere. Ain't sent no child support. That much I do know."

"He needs to know what's going on," Dusa said.

Mama looked away as though her thoughts were reflected on the wood-paneled wall. After a moment, she said, "He don't need to know shit. It's just us. Always been just us."

He was blind. Yet his music brimmed with vivid imagery and joy abounded even when the song was sad.

Stevie Wonder wasn't like the other hard-knock men in Daddy's collection, fools for love in dogged pursuit of a woman's affection. Enamored and struck dumb by her sexy ways. Haunted by her absence. Despondent without the love he'd taken for granted, sung in a voice ragged with regret.

Stevie's love seemed all encompassing. Even as he sang about his lust, his heart, open like a magnolia blossom, was ready to surrender. There was a man-child smile behind every note stretched liked taffy. A drop of honey in the melody eased the bite of vinegar in the lyric.

Wavy memory: The windows are down in Mama's old midnight-blue Electra 225, and the summer breeze is a hot rush across my face. It's a Saturday afternoon and we're all happy that Mama's off work. We're going to Malvern to see the kinfolk.

In a rare good mood, Mama Teacake had called early that morning and said she had picked turnip greens from her garden a few days before. She'd parboiled and frozen them and had plenty to send back.

Neither Mama nor Dusa wears her armor as Reagan and I sit in the couch-like backseat of that old deuce and a quarter, watching Hot Springs zoom by. Mama looks in the rearview from time to time, and her eyes smile. Dusa turns up the radio when the DJ announces Stevie's latest hit, "That Girl."

"I like this song," Dusa says, as the terse beat fills the car.

"Stevie be jammin'," Mama says.

There's something loving and golden about his voice, and he's bewitched by that girl, who turns his tears to joy from sad. I melt into the leather seat, warmed by the day and the music.

Not knowing how to process Mama's illness, I turn to Stevie's openhearted voice, and I'm transported away from the fear.

The new place, a three-bedroom white Colonial on Garland Street, held no cheer.

We were two blocks away from Baker Street, back in the same lifeless neighborhood that looked like a Kodak shot. The living room had a fireplace and generous windows. The long hallway seemed to stretch a mile, and at the end of it, a mirror covered the storage closet door. Two full baths. One was across the hall from Dusa's room, and she designated it as her own, and "Stay out," she told Reagan and me.

The other was between Mama's bedroom and the one I shared with Reagan. Mama's closet was linked to ours, and you could walk through our clothes and hers and open the door into her bedroom.

Soon after we settled in, Mama got ready to go into the hospital. She gave Dusa her checkbook and went over what bills to pay and when to pay them. At seventeen, Dusa had complete run of the house and keys to the car, in addition to going to school and working at Taco Bell.

Reagan and I had transferred back to Jones Elementary, barely two blocks away, where our third- and fourth-grade classes were mostly white. And we had no friends.

The day Mama left for the hospital, she called us into the living room. She was beautiful—her thick amber hair nicely coiffed, as always, her makeup expertly applied. If she felt any fear, it must've been concealed by the Fashion Fair or buried so deep that no trace revealed itself in her steady gaze.

"Y'all give me a hug," she said.

We threw our arms around her. A lump rose in my throat, and I tried to hold it together.

"Dusty, don't start cryin' now," Mama said. "You too big for that. I'm gon' be OK. Y'all be good and mind what Dusa say. Hear me?"

Mama left and I refused to look up for what seemed like a long time. I could have turned to stone in that spot and would not have cared—head bowed, my tears dotting the chestnut carpet.

Dusa ran the house and made sure we didn't forget it. In the mornings, her cigarette smoke wafted through the air. She didn't hide her new habit anymore as she strolled through the house, puffing away, her armor on, her projects-diva affectations on full blast.

The morning after Mama went into the hospital, she barged into our room.

"Dusty! Reagan! Y'all get up and get ready to go to school. Get up!"

I glared at her from my pillow. Did she have to do all that yelling? I was ten, almost as tall as she was, and thought I needed to start asserting myself.

All that time absorbing the no-nonsense wails of Chaka Khan had stoked a fire inside. I felt defiant and just wasn't up for Dusa's shit—not this morning, anyway.

The night before, I'd cried myself to sleep. Mama was in the hospital with cancer and needed a surgery whose name I couldn't even pronounce. Nobody explained what was going on or what could happen to her. And now Dusa, blowing cigarette smoke, burst into my room, yelling like she'd gone damn crazy.

I didn't move after she left the door. Reagan got up.

"Dusty, Dusa said get up."

"So!" I rolled over.

Reagan left the room and I heard her tell Dusa I was still in bed.

Almost in an instant, I felt Dusa standing over me.

"Dusty! I said get up."

My head remained under the cover.

"Get your punk ass up!"

She snatched the sheet back and pushed my shoulder. I sprang up and slapped her arm. Dusa looked at her arm then at me and smacked my head so hard I thought I saw the Smurfs. I pushed her chest, and the fight was on.

She pulled me out of bed and we tussled on the floor. I tried to snatch her hair, the way Mama had done. But she was stronger than I thought. She slapped me a few times and pinned me down.

"Boy, you better stop fuckin' with me."

"I hate you, Dusa! Get yo' big ass offa me."

Her grip hurt as I tried to squirm free.

"Be still!"

"Get offa me!"

"I'm gon' let you go and you better get ready for school. I don't want no shit outta you. And the next time you hit me, you die. You hear me?"

"I hate yo' guts."

"You can hate me all you want, but I'm running this shit 'til Mama gets back. And you gon' do what I say."

"I ain't gon' do shit."

She smacked my head again.

"I ain't playin' with you, Dusty."

I lay still, defeated. My face and head burned from Dusa's powerful slaps. She finally released me and left the room.

Reagan stood over me, scowling as usual. Her arms folded, she said, "Told you to get up."

Felix Hunter, Dusa's boyfriend, didn't live far from us. He was out of high school, about two or three years older than Dusa, and lived with his parents in a comfortable house encircled by a chain-link fence. They were the king and queen of fast food: He worked long hours at McDonald's and Dusa was down the street at Taco Bell.

She sometimes took us along to his house. Tall, burly, and surly with a perpetual smirk, Felix never greeted us. We'd sit in his mama's cozy living room, whose décor reminded me of Clara Mae's. Family pictures covered the blond-wood-paneled walls. While Dusa and Felix disappeared into his room in the back of the rambling house, we watched TV.

"And don't y'all touch shit," Dusa said.

The Hunters had cable, something we didn't have at home. Movies on HBO transfixed us while Dusa and Felix stayed in his room for what seemed like three days.

"I bet they back there doin' it," Reagan whispered.

"Probably. Dusa's a skeeza."

"How long they gon' be back there? I'm hungry."

"You askin' me?"

"You see anybody else in here?"

"I don't know."

Reagan chuckled.

"What?"

"You said Dusa's a skeeza."

I'd heard Dusa use that slang once when she was on the phone with her friend Stephanie, and the word dripped with venom. Whatever it meant, Dusa was that.

When we weren't at the Hunters' waiting on Dusa to emerge from the room with her hair flat in the back, Felix was knocking on our front door. Dusa had long ignored one of Mama's top rules: No company. She'd been sneaking boys in the house forever. But it was always quick: They'd hit it and quit it and the boy would escape through the back door.

Over on Garland, we didn't have to worry about a neighbor like Miss Wyrick calling Mama at work to report sightings of a knucklehead. And nobody on the block was going to ever knock on the door and invite us over for neck bones and collard greens.

With Mama in the hospital, Felix stayed for hours, lounging on the couch watching TV while Dusa curled next to him. I always had an attitude when he came over. Dusa would send us to our room, the way Mama did when Dennis visited. I'd act just as obnoxious as she did with Mama's company. I rolled my eyes when Felix plopped down onto the couch, stomped to my room, and slammed the door.

When Felix was around, Dusa wore makeup, like Mama. She preferred a lighter shade of red lipstick, though. Dusa had always been boy crazy and cried loudly in her room whenever one broke up with her. She seemed especially devoted to Felix, hanging onto every word he mumbled through that ever-present smirk, smiling Mama's sunshine smile whenever he showed up.

But he never returned it.

Going to sleep was hard without Mama in the next room snoring. I missed the familiar comfort of her early morning noises: her house shoes scrapping across the bathroom floor, the news playing on the TV in the living room, coffee brewing in the kitchen. I missed the floral scent of Beautiful, her perfume, lingering after she left. The nearly two weeks she was in the hospital felt like a year. Every time I asked Dusa for an update, she said, "She's fine."

"Can we go see her?"

"No."

"Why not?"

Dusa softened her tone. "She's OK, Dusty. Stop worrying. And, Lord, please don't start cryin' up in here. You know how you do."

The radio near my bed was always tuned to Power 92, the urban station. At night, the DJ mixed new and old soul. A song struck me one night. The lyrics were about a woman, a "sweet and gentle flower growing wild" whose freedom only comes as she sleeps. The wrenching emotion imbuing the song, shadowed by ebbing horns, washed over me as I lay with my headphones on. New Birth seemed to sing Mama's story.

She was always tired. And everything was a struggle: paying the bills, keeping us fed, maintaining a house she could barely afford to rent, in neighborhoods where we were invisible.

She always told us, "I got to work like this. Who else gonna pay these bills and take care of y'all?" Working two full-time jobs also meant Mama wasn't home much and didn't have to look into our faces and see the loneliness hanging there; she didn't have to feel the cold absence of a husband, either. Often, when she came home between jobs, we were still at school, and she had time to take a nap, take a bath, and change into her uniform before heading to her evening job, job number two.

When we got home, her perfume still lingered and maybe a casserole was wrapped in foil on top of the stove, if she'd had time to whip one up. I just wanted her to be there in the living room smiling her sunshine glamour smile when we walked through the door. Sometimes I'd go into Mama's room to watch TV after school. She always told us to stay out of her room, but I just wanted to be where she had been, to wrap myself in the comforter where just a few hours before she had fallen into much-needed sleep inside a quiet house.

New Birth's lead singer crooned of a weary flower, the horns echoing his sympathy, and I wondered if things would've been easier for Mama had I not been born.

Dusa was her partner, and Reagan was the baby, seemingly in constant need of attention. I was needy, too, but I hid it—or tried to. I always felt pressured to be a "big boy," stoic and unaffected. But I always felt what I felt intensely, and that seemed to annoy everybody in the house.

Daddy sometimes made cameos in my dreams, and those old records remained an aural lifeline to him. I was his friend, his running buddy, his Dus-Dus. Now he never came around.

What was I to Mama? I looked for her smile whenever I entered the room but seldom found it. Most times, it was the severe, critical face—lips tight, eyes stern—making sure my hair was combed and my clothes were neat, policing my mannerisms and correcting my speech. I often left the room gathering pieces of myself.

But life became magically coherent—storm clouds parted, blossoms opened, rainbows arced in a turquoise sky—when Mama beamed her *Ebony* magazine smile.

The thought of her never coming home made my stomach twist and turn. She's coming home, I told myself, sometimes aloud. And when she finally arrives, healed and picture-pretty, I'm going to be a very good son. I'm going to clean up more, study more, and make myself indispensable. Maybe I'll learn to cook. Maybe I won't eat so much.

"Damn, Dusty, you finish your food that fast?" Mama said a few times. "Did you even taste it?"

Mama will direct her Fashion Fair smile at me and say, "You're a very good son." She'll rub my head and I will float. Whatever it takes, whatever I need to do, I'm going to find a way to make Mama happy. She'll come home from work and will be glad to see me, beaming the smile she gave a greasy-haired Rick James wannabe who smoked cigarettes and wore a pinky ring.

"There you are," Mama will say, "my baby, my honey, my very good son."

On our way home from school on a brisk day, Reagan and I stopped a few yards away from the house when we noticed Dennis's car was parked out front.

"What he doing here?" Reagan asked.

As we approached the house, we noticed the front door open and the sounds of Luther Vandross on the stereo. Inside, Dennis reclined on the couch, a Coke in his hand.

"Hey, look how big y'all getting," he said, grinning.

"Where my mama?" I asked with all the attitude I could muster.

Mama floated out of the kitchen, through the dining room, and into the living room, looking slimmer and rested in a white cotton housedress.

We rushed her and hugged her around the waist.

"Ain't this a helluva greeting," Mama said. "Y'all must've missed somebody."

"You better?" I asked, almost on the verge of tears.

"Yeah, Dusty, a little sore, but I'm better. Y'all go in the kitchen and fix ya something to eat. There's some chicken on the stove. Go 'head now."

Mama crossed the room and slid next to Dennis, glowing, as Luther Vandross sang softly about the night he fell in love.

I stared at them for a moment. What was I to Mama?

"Dusty," she snapped. "Why you standin' there? What's wrong with you? Go fix you something to eat, and you and Reagan go back in that room."

After Mama returned to work, Dusa was hardly ever home. Reagan and I were often left with nothing cooked. So I, the very good son, started taking over the pots and pans.

While Reagan watched her beloved *Zoobilee Zoo* in the living room, I carefully read the instructions on the back of Hamburger Helper boxes.

"You want chili mac or cheeseburger?" I shouted from the kitchen.

"Cheeseburger, fool!"

Brown the ground beef.

The meat sizzled in the screamingly hot pan.

Drain the grease. Add the sauce mix and water.

As the orangey liquid spilled over, flames leapt and hissed at the sides of the skillet.

Add the noodles, cover and simmer until noodles are soft. Sauce will thicken to standing.

"Come eat, Reagan!"

We sat at the table across from each other and looked up as we chewed the first bite.

"It's good," I said.

Reagan nodded her approval. "I like it."

"It's better than Dusa's," I said. "She can't cook, anyway."

Reagan swallowed and chuckled. "She a ho."

I almost choked on my food.

When Dusa finally made it home, Mama was often still at work. She'd strip off her Taco Bell uniform, reeking of onions, shower, and get dressed.

I stood in her bathroom doorway one night, watching her curl her hair. "Where you goin'?"

"You don't ask grown folks where they going."

"You ain't grown, though."

"Dusty, don't start with me."

"Mama know where you goin'?"

"Ain't none of Mama's business where I go."

"Bet you won't say that shit to her face."

"Watch yo' mouth."

"You watch yo' mouth."

"Dusty, really, I so don't have time for your shit. Why don't you go cry to some records?"

"I hate you."

"Good."

"Where you goin'?"

"Didn't I say none of your business?"

"Somewhere with Felix?"

"None of your business."

"Mama gon' beat yo' ass."

Dusa snatched the curling iron plug out of the wall, held it aloft like a wand, and lurched at me. I sprinted down the hall as Dusa yelled, "Scared ass! Get somewhere and sit down."

. . .

Dusa usually made it home just before Mama arrived from one job, slept a few hours, then headed to the other. I'd leave my bed sometimes in the middle of the night and peek inside Mama's room to make sure she was there, that her presence wasn't a dream.

Although she seemed to work all the time, Mama wasn't oblivious to everything. She knew Dusa was messing around with Felix, and she had long ago put her on birth control. Early on, she administered the pills to Dusa, to make sure she took them. But by the time we were over on Garland, Mama had given Dusa the pills and fully expected her to take them on her own.

I often learned what was going on via Mama's phone conversations with her girlfriends: Miss Lurene, Maxine, Ida Mae, and Loretta. I don't remember who she was talking to one day in the kitchen, but she was pissed.

"Uh-huh. I went in her room to check to see if she's been takin' her pills. And it don't look like any of 'em been touched. . . . Calm down? Girl, I ain't tryin' to hear that. She ain't bringin' no baby up in here. . . . What? I don't know what she doin,' but I wanna know why she ain't been takin' her pills. I left a whole supply in here before I went into the hospital, and ain't none of those pills been punched out."

I wasn't around when Mama confronted Dusa about the birth control pills, but I later heard Dusa's reaction on the phone with one of her friends.

"She got a lotta nerve to ask me about what I'm doing with my pills."

Whoever was on the other line cut her off, and Dusa was quiet for a moment. Then she said, "I know that's right. I'm grown."

Christmas 1987 rolled around soon afterward, and Mama was going to miss it. She pulled long hours at both jobs to catch up on bills that piled up during her stay in the hospital. So for Christmas, she had to work. Before she left on Christmas Eve, we opened our gifts: We all received new outfits—jeans and sweaters and board games to share, including Monopoly, Connect 4, and Operation, which required keen hand-and-eye coordination that I didn't seem to have. Dusa got some makeup and Reagan a new doll whose hair she soon cut off or mangled somehow. I got a copy of Anita Baker's *Rapture* album, which was already about a year old then, but I was glad to finally get it.

Mama never indulged any Santa Claus fantasy. "Ain't no white man dropping off gifts in here," she once said. "Hell, I wish."

After we opened all the presents, Mama said, "What y'all supposed to say?"

We harmonized, "Thank you."

She let Dusa drive us to Malvern that afternoon, and we had dinner at Mama Teacake's. I wanted to go to East Section Line, but Mama's rule was if Daddy didn't come get us nobody was to take us over there. If Big Mama had any gifts for us, Cuda or somebody dropped them off at Mama Teacake's. That Christmas, we received no gifts from East Section Line.

We were holed up over on Happy Street, or Misery Lane for me. As usual, Mama Teacake's house was red with noise, and folks streamed in and out. The kitchen was the epicenter. Aluminum foil–covered dishes, cakes, and pies packed the counters. Mama Teacake was the eye of the funky storm, ruling from the kitchen table with a cup of Seagram's VO nearby.

"Dianne let you drive down here?" she asked Dusa. "That's a shock."

Mama Teacake glanced over at Reagan and me. "Merry Christmas," she said flatly. "Santa Claus bring y'all a buncha shit?"

"Mama bought it," I said defensively.

"Oh, really, Dusty? I guess you too big for Santa Claus?"

"Mama said it ain't no Santa Claus."

Mama Teacake rolled her eyes. "Lord, I guess she tell y'all that 'cause y'all Daddy ain't there."

I glared at her.

"Betcha ya Daddy didn't bring y'all nothin,'" Mama Teacake said, chuckling. "Shit, Santa Claus will bring you somethin' 'fore Raymond's sorry ass will."

"Ain't that the truth," Dusa said.

"Shut up!" I told Dusa, wishing I could sling the sentiment toward the evil kitchen queen making judgments about the ghost I called Daddy.

"You shut up!" Dusa shot back.

"You think you so grown. You make me sick."

"Punk!"

"Skeeza!"

My cousins standing around howled at my insult. Dusa's lips tightened and she turned to Mama Teacake. "See what I have to put up with? See?"

Mama Teacake looked at Dusa and maybe she saw the pained face of the daughter she'd killed all those years ago. When she directed her eyes toward me, her contempt blazed.

"You lit' red fucka, you ain't gon' be talkin' to her like that long as you up in here. This ain't Miss Ollison's house, and it ain't Dianne's, either. I don't play that shit."

How sad, how terribly sad and cruel that I didn't have the ability to zap Mama Teacake with thunderbolts, like a villain in an Atari game, and turn her into a smoking pile of ash. I rolled my eyes.

Mama Teacake slammed her hand on the table. "Cut yo' eyes at me again, boy, and I'll knock 'em clean out yo' goddamn head."

During Christmas break, a rare snow storm hit Hot Springs. We were out of school for three or four extra days, and the roads were treacherous. Mama didn't dare risk driving in her unreliable Chevette.

The city was socked in one Thursday morning, and no cabs were running. Mama called in, which excited everybody but Dusa, who had an attitude most of the morning. Mama cooked one of her super brunches: home fries with onions, scrambled eggs, Hungry Jack biscuits, and fried chicken.

After the dishes were cleared and washed, Reagan and I played our new Connect 4 game on the living room floor. Mama lounged on the couch and gossiped loudly on the phone with her good friend Ida Mae, the volume on the TV nearly muted.

Dusa had been in her bedroom most of the morning, talking on her separate phone line. When she came out, her armor was on. She'd roll her eyes at Mama and snap at Reagan and me.

"Dusa, what's the hell wrong with you?" Mama asked.

She just ignored her and disappeared into her room.

Reagan had beat me in a second round of Connect 4 and Ida Mae said something so funny Mama put the phone down for a moment to catch her breath.

"Ida, girl, you a trip!"

Just then, Dusa, dressed in khakis and a jacket, appeared in the living room. Mama stopped Dusa just before she opened the front door. "Ida, hold on real quick. Dusa, where you think you goin'?"

"Out."

"Out, where?"

"Felix comin' to get me. I'm gon' meet him down the hill."

"No, you ain't. You ain't goin' nowhere with all that snow and ice on the ground."

Dusa rolled her eyes. "Felix is on his way."

Mama sat up. "I don't give a damn, Dusa. You ain't goin' nowhere in this snow and ice. I couldn't even get outta here to go to work today, and you gonna get in a car with some nigga and go slippin' and slidin' down these streets? Oh, I don't think so."

Dusa stared Mama down, and Mama returned the look.

"Did you hear me?" Mama said. "You ain't goin' nowhere."

The air chilled. Mama put the phone back to her ear and didn't take her eyes off of Dusa, who stood at the door slashing Mama with the meanest look I'd ever seen from her.

"Ida Mae, girl? I'm back. Yeah. This child thinks she's goin' out in this weather. Must be crazy."

Dusa turned away from the door and stomped down the hall. Just before she made it to her room, she yelled, "Bitch!"

I froze. Reagan dropped one of her red plastic discs. Our mouths in the shape of O's, we looked at Mama. Ida Mae kept talking, but Mama certainly wasn't listening at that point.

Her words came out staccato. "Ida, girl. Let. Me. Call. You. Back."

Mama slammed the phone on the receiver and left the couch. Reagan and I trailed her down the hallway. Mama barged into Dusa's room and stood toe to toe with her, her hardened eyes locking into Dusa's. "What you call me?"

Dusa's breath quickened, but she didn't back down.

"I'm gon' ask you one mo' time, Dusa. What you call me?"

Dusa pushed Mama. "Get offa me!" she screamed.

Mama's back slammed against Dusa's chest of drawers, and her eyes widened with shock, then narrowed. She tucked in her bottom lip and grabbed a handful of Dusa's hair. Dusa fought back, and they fell to the floor. Reagan's scream was like a fire alarm as I tried to pry them apart. But mother and daughter were too entangled, biting, scratching, and pulling hair.

Mama straddled Dusa's back and beat her shoulders with her fists. She pulled her hair as Dusa kicked and clawed the carpet, her cry high and piercing. Mama's face was tight with rage. A tiny raspberry tattooed her cheek where Dusa had bitten her. I tugged Mama's arm and pleaded.

"Mama, stop! Mama, stop!"

She released Dusa's hair and stood up. Dusa sprang to her feet. Bruised and panting, they faced each other, the pain and anger crackling in their eyes. For a moment, all was quiet, save for their heavy breathing and Reagan's soft whimpers. Then finally Mama pointed to the door. "Get out! Get out of my house."

"I'm goin'," Dusa said, sobbing.

"Get out!" Mama roared.

Dusa slipped on her shoes and snatched her jacket off of the bed, all in one swoop. Then she ran down the hall and out of the door. Through all of that snow. Going who knew where.

When Michael Jackson stopped smiling and declared himself "bad," all the color and magic drained from my fantasies. Jason's arrival with the suicide note killed the rocket limo dream. But Michael's music, especially the tender yearning of his ad-libs in "Human Nature," continued to fuel my hopes for an escape. And even without the rocket limo, it all seemed tangible.

In that infinitely bright place free of toxic words and down-cast eyes, the music gleamed. Michael floated around with a universe-shifting smile that said, "I understand." No pain, no tears allowed. He took my hand in that glittery glove and we left the ground, laughing and circling clouds.

But about the time Dusa ran through all that snow, bruised and weeping, Michael danced in subway stations with thugs. In the video for "Bad," he grimaced as hoodlums surrounded him. His eyes were darts. "Who's bad?" he asked, his voice a switchblade.

After Dusa ran out the door, Mama frowned and rubbed her hands together as loose strands of her daughter's hair floated to the floor. Who's bad? Dusa thought she was. And despite our differences, I worried about her. I worried about Mama, too, who didn't sleep that night. Nobody did.

Headphones on, I tried to conjure the smiling Michael to take me away. But all I saw was the new intense one who bristled and danced with thugs. I felt adrift and hollow, orbiting nothing. I looked at the glowing Michael on the Thriller LP cover.

I remembered Dusa applying rosy-pink lipstick in the bathroom mirror, her eyes searching her reflection. I pulled off my headphones and lifted the needle. Weary from wondering where my sister had gone, I turned the record off.

Part Three

. . .

SOON AFTER MICHAEL JACKSON TURNED BAD AND DUSA MADE
tracks in the snow, Mama's affair with Dennis ended. There had
been a fight involving another woman, but not his wife.

Wait.

He had a wife? The details I gathered from Mama's phone
conversations with her girlfriends.

*And I went over there and she was there . . . Uh-huh. And he
gon' tell me, "This ain't none of yo' business." Right. I said, "The
hell it is." That's when he hit me.*

He'd hit Mama?

*He ain't gotta worry 'bout me no mo.' Yeah, girl. Before I left, I
threw a damn brick through the window. Yeah. Driver's side. Oh,
girl, he was pissed, cussin' and showin' out. He bet' not bring his
ass by here.*

Worrying about Dusa's whereabouts, Mama's fights with a
wannabe pimp, and Michael Jackson's turn from angelic thriller
to grimacing badass, I couldn't concentrate in school, and my
grades started to slip. Every Friday, Mrs. McHenry sent home a
packet of the class work we'd done that week. We were supposed
to bring it back the following Monday with a parent's signature. Mama never saw the D's and a few F's I'd gotten. Reagan's
grades, which usually hovered around average and below, were
falling, too.

I'd always had excellent penmanship, with curlicues and flour-
ishes, and could easily forge Mama's flowery signature. I'd also
signed her name on our field trip permission slips. Mama was so
busy working, courting, and fighting Dennis that I guess she'd
forgotten to ask about our report cards. Dusa usually signed them
and got onto us if our grades were low.

And now we had no idea where she was. We didn't dare ask Mama, who was bitchy whenever she was home.

"Y'all get y'all asses up and clean up! I work all the time to keep a damn roof over ya heads—no help from that sorry-ass Raymond. The least y'all can do is keep the damn house clean. I swear! One of these days, I'm just gon' keep on drivin' when I get off work, just drive right past this house and leave y'all nappy heads up in here."

Reagan mumbled, "Well, go'n then."

I chuckled.

Mama swung around and bucked her eyes. "What was that?"

We harmonized: "Nothin'."

We were relieved when Mama was at work. We watched our favorite shows and I mastered all the flavors of Hamburger Helper. I even started experimenting with them, adding chopped onion to the cheeseburger kind.

"Don't do that again," Reagan said, frowning at her plate. "That shit's nasty."

If Mama had to pull an all-nighter at St. Joseph Hospital, she took us with her. Reagan and I spent the night in the small waiting room down the hall from where Mama watched monitors of patients all night. Sitting in plush leather recliners, we watched the TV mounted high on a wall. I never liked the antiseptic feel of hospitals. Sometimes I heard the tortured moan of a patient or saw a decrepit-looking man or woman being pushed around in a wheelchair by an indifferent nurse. We did our homework and stayed quiet. Reagan always dozed off, but I never got much sleep. Dressed in her white lab coat, Mama peeked in on us throughout the night.

"Y'all ain't in here fighting, are you?"

"No. Reagan's 'sleep."

"Oh. You go on to sleep, too. I'll be getting off soon."

Mama slipped back down the hall, and I sank into the chair, wishing I were someplace else.

Nearly a month or so after Dusa left, Mama abruptly informed us that we were moving—again. This time, we were going "up to

Little Rock." We had no family there, and the city, which was barely an hour away, seemed so big and fast.

"Where we gon' stay?" Reagan asked.

"I got a job up there, at St. Vincent's."

"What's that?" I asked.

"A hospital, Dusty."

"Oh."

"Where we gon' stay?" Reagan asked again.

Mama rolled her eyes. "Gotta figure that out. Y'all might have to stay here until I get settled up there."

I looked at Reagan then at Mama, thinking maybe she was finally delivering on her threat to leave our "nappy heads on Garland Street." My stomach sank. "You leavin' us here?"

"No, Dusty. I gotta find a place first."

"We can stay with Daddy," Reagan suggested, her voice going up an octave.

Mama shot down that hope with, "Hell, no."

"Is he comin'?" I don't know what made me ask that. Mama must've wondered the same thing, because she just glared at me and didn't answer.

"What about Dusa?" Reagan asked.

"What about her?" Mama was annoyed.

"Is she comin'?" I asked.

Then Reagan pelted her with questions: "Yeah, where is she? Can she come back and live with us in Little Rock?"

Mama's lips tightened. "I don't know where she is, and she ain't comin'. And if y'all keep asking all these damn questions, y'all won't be comin'."

Loretta Jordan and her teenage daughter, Dee, lived in a small, neat house across town. Concrete squares led to the tabletop-like porch, and the tiny yard was impeccably manicured.

Inside, porcelain unicorns, dozens of them, stood captive in a curio cabinet and adorned side tables in the living room. Baby pictures of a cherub-faced Dee hung on the wood-paneled walls, and the air always smelled of lemon Lysol.

Tall, thin, and the color of molasses, Loretta wore a neat Jheri curl and so did Dee, who was also thin but butterscotch-brown and didn't look much like her mother. Loretta worked at AMI Hospital with Mama, and they were good friends. Loretta and Dee had lived in the projects in a unit two streets over from where we stayed. Now they lived in a neighborhood thick with trees where the old folks nearby kept wicker lawn furniture on the porch and potted plants on the steps.

After Mama packed up the house on Garland Street, she dropped us off at Loretta's. She told us to "be good" and to "mind what Loretta and Dee say." A month passed before we saw her again.

Loretta's smile was easy, her tone usually soft. She didn't bark her orders like Dusa and Mama. She assigned chores as though she were issuing a kind reminder.

"Now you know, Dusty, you're supposed to sweep the kitchen," Loretta would say with a knowing smile.

"I am?"

"Uh-huh."

"Oh." I was confused trying to recall if she'd actually told me that earlier. Her smile and tone were so warm it seemed I was hypnotized as I grabbed the broom and dustpan.

Loretta's house cast an orderly spell. Reagan and I didn't fight or cuss at each other. The neatness of everything, the preciousness of the unicorns with their heads forever bowed in the curio cabinet, the lemony scent in the air that permeated our clothes—it all made us straighten up without making a conscious effort to do so. Dee wasn't as needy or hellishly selfish as I'd expected from an only child.

At fourteen, she cooked and cleaned like a grown woman, but she also watched cartoons with us. She didn't try to "act grown" and often engaged us and helped us with our homework. Sometimes Dee seemed to crawl into herself, reading a Judy Blume novel or listening to her Madonna or Janet Jackson cassettes.

Loretta signed my class work packets every Sunday night before we went to bed. She noticed our grades improving. "See, Dusty, you doin' better," she said. "You need to keep that up."

We were all cramped in Dee's tiny room—Reagan in the bed with Dee, and I on a pullout. Loretta's room was just across the way, and she played Power 92, the urban radio station, low on her clock radio at night, the house still and dark. One night "Wildflower" by New Birth came on.

I heard the horns ebb and flow. I felt the sadness about the lady in tears. I thought about Mama. I thought about Daddy, whom I hadn't seen in probably a year. Where was Dusa? What was Little Rock like? Will Mama really come get us? I pulled the covers over my head and shut my eyes tight. I buried my face in the pillow to stop the tears.

But they came anyway.

One Friday after the month-long stay at Loretta's, she came home from work and told us to pack up our things. Reagan and I looked at each other.

"Mama comin'?" I asked Loretta.

"Oh, I talked to her this morning. She asked how y'all was doin', and I said y'all been good."

"We goin' to Little Rock?" Reagan asked.

"I gotta go up to the school and let 'em know y'all movin'. Think Dianne told me to do that, or she was gon' call or somethin'." Loretta rubbed her chin. "Yeah, I need to check to see if Dianne wanted me to do that for her."

Reagan looked at me then back at Loretta and asked again, "We goin' to Little Rock?"

Loretta shook her head and smiled. "Oh, yeah, you did ask that, didn't you? Yeah. Y'all Aunt Phyl supposed to take y'all."

My stomach sank, and Reagan must've had the same reaction, because her eyes widened.

"We goin' over to Phyl's?" I asked.

Loretta smiled. "Yep."

Loretta didn't have a car, so her mother came by to take us to Phyl's house, which was two or three miles from our old place on Garland. Mama sometimes stopped by there, but the rest of us avoided Phyl's place. Even on sunny days a dark cloud seemed to hang over that mud-colored house with the wide red porch.

Jason briefly lived with Phyl that year, and we didn't see him, either. After he set the trash on fire over on Omega Street, Mama banned him from our home. Phyl answered the door with her usual scowl. Her mean eyes didn't leave us as she tossed Loretta a dry "Hey, girl."

"Hey there, Phyl. How you been?"

"Was doin' just fine 'fore you dragged these muthafuckas over here," Phyl said staring us down. "Y'all say bye to Loretta and c'mon in the house."

Loretta's hug was tight. After she let Reagan go, she scurried back to the car with her mama. I wanted to watch the car pull off—and run behind it.

"Dusty, get yo' ass in here!" Phyl shouted.

With all the trees and bushes encircling the house and the thick beige drapes covering the windows, hardly any sunlight beamed through the living room. Oppression floated through the place like a haze, clinging to the walls and hovering over the sand-colored couch and love seat. Even the potted fern near the TV seemed to bow and weep.

Jason rushed into the living room, his old-man face lighting up. "Hey, y'all."

A cherry-sized hickey dotted his wide forehead. I was certain it wasn't from a fall or a run-in with a door.

"Y'all put ya shit back there in Jason's room," Phyl said. "Loretta feed y'all?"

"No," I answered.

"I know you lyin', Dusty."

"Her mama came and got us when got home from school. We didn't get a chance to eat nothin'."

Phyl rolled her eyes. "That bitch. The least she could've done is feed y'all before she dragged y'all asses over here. I guess y'all hungry?"

"Well, we didn't eat nothin', so yeah," I said.

Phyl's penciled eyebrows arched. "You gettin' smart, Dusty?"

"No."

"'Cause I know you ain't tryin' to get smart with me. I'll beat the black off yo' ass."

Jason snickered.

"I know you ain't laughin'," Phyl sneered. "Y'all get on in that room somewhere. Gotta cook somethin' for you hungry mutha-fuckas. Y'all only stayin' tonight. I'm takin' y'all asses to Dianne first thang tomorrow. Shit, y'all ain't gon' be stayin' here, eatin' me outta house and home."

This was the same woman who had dumped her five-year-old son on our doorstep without a coat for winter, his uncombed hair looking like dried-out taco meat, and a maudlin suicide note stuffed in his back pocket. He lived with us for three years and ate damn near everything in the kitchen, when he wasn't going around breaking shit. He almost set the house on fire in a crazy-ass response to her contempt for him.

And now Phyl was raising hell about doing Mama this one favor?

I didn't understand her and all the venom coursing through her veins. It seemed that life and everyone in it had fucked her over. Her drawn-on eyebrows were always furrowed, ready to combat the world, including those who dared to love her—especially those who dared to love her. It must've taken a lot of energy to be that loud, gruff, and hateful. Or maybe that venom coursing through her veins gave her strength. I don't know. But this was certain: She drained the life out of everything around her, including that poor potted fern weeping near the TV.

Phyl's food was pointless. The hamburger steak was dry, the gravy too thin and salty. The whole kernel corn had just been warmed through and tasted like the can. She stood over the table as we ate, dragging on a cigarette and barking orders as though she were a prison warden.

"Bossman," her nickname for Jason, "stop eatin' so goddamn fast, like you ain't ate in all yo' life."

"Blue," that's what she called Reagan, "wipe yo' mouth."

I felt her mean eyes on me. "I thought you was hungry, Dusty."

I picked at the hamburger steak and wondered if I could stand another bite. I said nothing.

"You betta eat all that damn food. You ain't wastin' shit in here."

Reagan, Jason, and I were all piled into Jason's full-sized bed later that night. He had a million questions for us, most of which I answered.

"Where y'all been?"

"Over Loretta's."

"Who that?"

"You don't know her."

"Why y'all ain't come over here?"

"We over here now," Reagan said.

"Y'all movin' to Little Rock?"

"Mama up there," I said.

"Y'all gon' like it?"

"I don't know."

"Can I move with y'all?"

"No!" Reagan and I answered together.

"I'm movin' anyway."

"No, you ain't," Reagan said.

"Yes, I am."

"Where you get that thang on yo' head?" Reagan asked.

"Phyl probably," I said.

Reagan, who was in the middle, shifted her weight. "You always doin' somethin' bad, Jason."

"No, I don't."

I lifted myself on my elbows. "Yeah, like setting trash on fire. That's why you can't come with us."

Jason shot up. "I will!"

"You won't," I said.

"I will!"

Phyl's voice roared from down the hall. "Y'all betta take y'all asses to bed 'fore I come in there and start kickin' ass all over the place."

Jason dropped back onto his pillow and pulled the comforter over his head. We all giggled. After the laughter faded, Jason's voice, slightly muffled by the pillow, rippled with sadness. "I wanna go with y'all."

Loretta and Mama had notified the school that we were moving. Reagan and I cleaned out our desks and felt excited about never returning to dull Jones Elementary again. To get to Phyl's house, we had to walk down Garland past our old place, which was still vacant. I wanted to keep walking but Reagan stopped.

"C'mon, girl."

Reagan's stared at the house, her lips poked out as though she were in deep thought. "Where you think we gon' live in Little Rock?"

"How I'm supposed to know?"

"What if Dusa come back here? She ain't gonna know where we at."

"We don't know where she at."

"Hold up."

Reagan dropped to her knees and searched her backpack. She pulled out a notebook and pencil.

"What you doin,' girl? C'mon."

"I'm gon' leave her a note."

I rolled my eyes. "We ain't got all day. We gotta meet Jason. Phyl gave me the key."

Reagan ignored me and sat on the sidewalk.

"What you writin'?"

Reagan wrote quickly then handed me the note. It read, "Dusa, me and Mama and Dusty in Little Rock. Come if you get this."

I handed it back. "How she gon' know where to find us, stupid?"

Reagan snatched the note and folded it in half. "She gon' know, dumb ass."

She ran up on the porch and stuffed the note into the mailbox then fled.

"C'mon!"

Reagan snatched her backpack off the ground. "Shut up!"

As we entered the doom-and-gloom force field swirling around Phyl's house, Jason's bus pulled up. I unlocked the door and thought I heard a heavy sigh from the oppressive spirit haunting the place. Jason turned on the TV, and we went into the kitchen to find something to eat. We made Spam sandwiches and parked ourselves in front of the TV.

Phyl would be home before dark and planned to take us to Little Rock that night. "Have y'all shit ready, too," she had said and punctuated her command by slamming the door on her way out.

Reagan and Jason were enraptured by *Zoobilee Zoo* and I had to use the bathroom. On my way out I noticed that the door to Phyl's bedroom was ajar, and I couldn't resist slipping in and snooping around.

What little light that entered the house mostly spilled through the windows in Phyl's big bedroom. Stale cigarette smoke and her musky perfume hung in the air. An old dog-eared Bible, much like the one Mama had, sat next to the lamp on the nightstand.

Her bed wasn't made but everything else in the room was neat. The lid of her dark wood jewelry box was up. I looked at myself in the dresser mirror then down into the top drawer, which was slightly pulled out. I tugged it open and carefully sorted through the miscellany: loose buttons and ink pens, scattered nickels and dimes, several envelopes of bills and letters. Empty orange prescription bottles rolled around.

Tucked into a corner was a small black box that may have once held a necklace or a pair of earrings. I took the top off and found a tiny brown vial with a black cap. I plucked it out and held it up, studying the whitish kernel inside. I didn't know what it was, but the chill that stroked the back of my neck made me hurriedly return the vial to the box. I pushed the drawer back the way it had been and slipped out of the room.

When Phyl came home later that evening, she changed out of her nurse's uniform and told us to get our shit. We threw our things into the trunk of her beat-up white Corolla, and she pulled away. My stomach flipped and flopped. I missed Mama and wondered what our new place looked like. Would I like the new school? Would the kids call me a faggot?

Hot Springs zoomed by in the darkness, and a wave of sadness swept over me. I wondered if Dusa would step onto the porch of the house on Garland. Maybe she'd think to look in the mailbox and find Reagan's ridiculous note. She'd show up on our new doorstep in Little Rock and everything would be fine. Maybe she was already there, helping Mama get settled. Or maybe not. Wherever she was, I hoped she wasn't scared. I hoped she was safe.

Phyl turned up the radio when a new singer, Keith Sweat, came on. She popped her fingers to "Something Just Ain't Right." Reagan and Jason dozed off in the backseat.

"Hold the stirring wheel real quick, Dusty," Phyl said.

Nervously, I gripped the wheel as Phyl quickly lit a cigarette. Then she brushed my hand away. She cracked the window and stared ahead as Keith whined about his woman cheating behind his back. I closed my eyes.

Daddy's slippery smile suggested he knew something but wasn't going to share it.

His feet didn't touch the ground, which spooked me out. And no matter how hard I tried to run to him, something kept pulling me back. We were in the living room at our old place on Garden Street. Holding a cigarette and handsomely dressed in slacks and a buttoned-down shirt, Daddy floated near the stereo by the front door, and I stood in the entrance of the dining room.

"Where you been?" I asked.

He didn't answer; his smile made me nervous.

"Daddy, come get me." I tried to rush to him but couldn't move.

Daddy shook his head. "You hear the music? You need to listen more."

"Ain't no music."

"There's always music, son. You know that."

"Come get me."

"I ain't left you."

I was angry now. "Yeah, you did."

"No, I didn't."

"Yeah, you did!"

Daddy's slick smile dropped and he pointed at me, holding the cigarette between two fingers. "Don't raise your voice at me, boy."

My face felt flushed and my voice wavered. "I don't know why you don't come get me."

Daddy took a drag on the cigarette and his secretive smile returned.

"C'mon over here."

"I can't."

"C'mon, Dusty."

When I was finally able to leave my spot, he vanished and so did all the furniture in the room. Darkness replaced daylight in a snap as though someone had turned the lights off all over the world. I was scared and couldn't breathe.

Phyl's dark, commanding voice pulled me back. "Dusty, wake the hell up. You jumpin' in yo' sleep. You pee on yo'self?"

"No!"

Reagan and Jason, now wide awake, laughed. We were driving down an illuminated stretch, Asher Avenue in Little Rock. Car dealerships and fast food restaurants lined both sides of the wide street. I rubbed my eyes and sat up. Asher looked busy in the darkness. There were more cars on the road than what I usually saw in Hot Springs. Abuzz with movement and dazzled with lights, Little Rock felt like a real city.

Phyl made a right into a complex of townhouses. The sign out front read "Chateau DeVille" in huge Old English script.

"This is nice," Reagan said.

"I'm coming up here to stay," Jason said.

Phyl parked in front of a cluster of townhouses. "Y'all c'mon," she said, opening her door. Our place was at the end of the row. Phyl knocked, and Mama answered, smile aglow. "Hey, y'all."

We rushed in. Our old living room furniture—the overstuffed burnt-orange-and-brown couch and the wicker chair with a huge, fanlike back that nearly took up a wall—looked brand new in this clean, inviting space. A gray box sat atop the old Magnavox.

"We got cable?" Reagan asked as though it were a Christmas gift.

"Yep," Mama said.

"Scared of you, girl. This place is nice, Dianne," Phyl said, strolling through the living room, peeking into the full bath adjacent to it and on into the bright and spacious kitchen.

The sliding doors next to the fridge led to a small patio with a privacy fence. The oak cabinets gleamed. The stove was electric, something we'd never had in our Hot Springs homes.

We all followed Mama upstairs. There was another bathroom at the top and two bedrooms to the right. I was hoping for three, because I was tired of bunking with grouchy Reagan. Our dark-wood bunk beds were new and neatly made with matching burgundy comforters. My record player sat on a small table between the beds. A box of my records was underneath. I claimed the bed near the window.

"You doin' it, Big Sis," Phyl said, smiling faintly. The biting edge of her voice was gone. Standing side by side, the sisters were mirror opposites: Mama, a creamy-skinned picture of inviting down-home elegance; Phyl, a deep, dark beauty, but her stubborn scowl masked it. She talked to Mama with a sisterly affection that seemed deeply felt.

"Girl, I'm just trying to make a dollar out of fifteen cents up in here," Mama said.

Phyl chuckled. "I know that's right. Oh, girl, I know it's late, but you gon' have to feed yo' kids. I didn't have a chance to fix 'em no dinner. They shouldn't be that damn hungry, though. Hell, they ate up my Spam when they got home from school."

After Phyl and Jason left, Mama cooked us Hamburger Helper. We ate at the kitchen table, something we hardly ever did together in Hot Springs.

"We gonna keep this place clean," Mama said.

She chewed like a queen. A bit of sauce dotted Reagan's bottom lip as she shoveled her food. I forked the tender noodles and smiled inside.

The kids looked like they could've been my cousins. My eyes surely revealed traces of the fear I felt as I entered Mrs. James's fourth-grade class at Fair Park Elementary near central Little Rock. But I also felt excitement, as though I were meeting family for the first time. None of my classes in Hot Springs had had so many black faces. Mrs. James stood beside me in front of the blackboard.

"Class, this is our new student, Rashod."

I looked up at her and said nothing. Rashod? I knew that was my name but nobody ever called me that. I always went by Dusty, even in school. But this was a new school and these black faces were all my new cousins. Here, I would be Rashod, the boy who'd fit in. Dusty was the faggot nobody liked. He could never show up here.

The desks were arranged in groups of four. I was seated near Mrs. James's desk in a cluster that included two wishbone-thin boys and a chunky girl: Robert had a long, narrow face, saucer-sized eyes, and an ashy mouth; Dennis, jug ears and a sneaky grin; and Tamika wore long pigtails that kissed her shoulders. Her mouth, like Reagan's, seemed to be in a perpetual pout. She spoke first.

"Hey."

"Hi."

"You say your name's Rashod?"

"Yeah."

"I gotta cousin named Rashod."

I smiled.

She frowned as though I'd offended her. "You smart?"

"Yeah."

"Shut up, Tamika," Robert said. "She always be talkin'."

Dennis chuckled while Tamika stared daggers at the side of Robert's head.

"You shut up, boy."

"That's his girlfriend," Dennis said, nudging me with his elbow. The touch made me feel welcomed.

Tamika rolled her eyes at Dennis. "You shut up."

Robert pouted. "She ain't my girlfriend. She talk too much."

Dennis and I snickered. Mrs. James stood over us.

"Y'all get quiet over here," she said, peering over her glasses. "Rashod hasn't been here a hot minute and already y'all starting a mess."

With her tight curls and string of pearls, Mrs. James looked like a matronly member of somebody's Baptist choir.

Holding a large stack of papers in the crook of her arm, she turned to me. "Rashod, it's Black History Month." She handed me one of the thick packets with Xeroxed bios of people I'd never heard of: Daisy Bates, Benjamin Banneker, Malcolm X, Ralph Bunche, and others.

"I don't know if you all celebrated Black History Month at your old school but we do here," Mrs. James said. Near the large bulletin board of crude artwork by the class, I'd noticed the colorfully illustrated posters of African kings and queens.

Mrs. James stood in front of the blackboard. "Turn to page five, class. Today, we're going to read about a woman called Moses, Harriet Tubman, who brought many, many slaves to the shores of freedom."

Slaves? My mind sailed back to a conversation I didn't understand, a drunken chat Daddy had with his buddy Coleman. It was shortly before Daddy moved out, and we were visiting Coleman's dark apartment. Low on the stereo, Tyrone Davis crooned about making a woman melt like ice cream.

Miller beer cans that Daddy and Coleman had sucked dry stood like golden soldiers on the coffee table. Daddy sat on the edge of the chair, leaning forward, a cigarette burning between his fingers. Coleman sat on the edge of the couch, his knee touching Daddy's. His wide, sleepy eyes stared ahead as he listened to Daddy go on and on. Both seemingly had forgotten I was in the room.

"Can't trust no white man as far as you can see him," Daddy said, slurring his words. "Hear me, man? Let there be a wagon, let there be a goddamn wagon coming to take away all the niggas like they did the Jews, man, and as sure as you born, as sure as you born, them cracka muthafuckas will throw yo' black ass right on it."

I sat in the chair opposite Daddy, smiling at his profanity, the way the word "muthafucka" glinted. He only cussed around his friends when he was good and juiced.

"Listen," Daddy continued. "The white man ain't never meant the black man no good."

Coleman frowned. "C'mon, man. Been plenty niggas done fucked us over, too. Who shot Larry dead soon as he come back from 'Nam, huh? A nigga, that's who."

Who was Larry? I wanted to know but didn't dare ask.

Daddy took a drag off his cigarette. "But who sent Larry over to 'Nam? Who sent me over there, barely eighteen years old, scared out my goddamn mind? Who sent me over there to fight some chink muthafuckas who ain't done shit to me? A white man, that's who."

Coleman shook his head. Daddy took a long drag off his cigarette before dropping the butt into one of the beer cans. He looked up then, his soulful eyes holding the beginning and the end of everything. They were fixed on me as if he was trying to figure something out. He stared at me for what seemed like a long time as Tyrone Davis begged for a woman's affection and Coleman sat back on the couch, his eyes closed. Then Daddy's lips slipped into a dark grin, and his words drowned out the music.

"Son, the white man brought us over here as slaves," he said, his tone direct and serious. "He made your Paw Paw a slave. He made your Big Mama a slave. He made your Mama a slave, and he made me a slave. Don't you let no white man, don't you ever let no white man make you a slave. You hear me?"

I had no idea what Daddy was talking about. What was a slave? Who did what to Paw Paw and Big Mama? What did he do to Mama? My six-year-old brain could process only so much.

But somebody, whoever this white man was, had hurt them. And I couldn't let him hurt me.

Daddy's eyes flashed a rage that scared me. "You hear me, boy?"

"Yes."

The needle lifted itself off the record. I was relieved when Daddy turned his eyes away and shook a few cans on the coffee table. Coleman had begun to snore when Daddy smacked his knee. Coleman jumped, his leg bumping the table and knocking over the gleaming cans.

"Get up, man!" Daddy said, grinning. "We ain't got no beer."

Mrs. James walked between the desks, a packet in hand and peering over her glasses.

"Not every slave wanted to be free," she said. "But Harriet Tubman carried a shotgun. There was no turning back."

A bucktoothed girl raised her hand and Mrs. James called on her. "Paula?"

"Why didn't the slaves want to go with Harriet Tubman?"

"It was scary running away from all you knew," Mrs. James said. "If they got caught, well, they could have been beaten or even killed. Harriet Tubman once said she would have freed more slaves had they known they were slaves."

I looked at Mrs. James and tried to connect what she was saying with what Daddy had said about slaves, the rage flaring in his eyes.

A jug-eared boy had elbowed me in the side as we laughed at a pouting girl sitting across from us. A woman who looked as though she could sing "His Eye Is on the Sparrow" in a sunlit soprano transfixed a class of black kids with a story about a woman called Moses, who, armed with a shotgun, led slaves to freedom. Warmth I hadn't felt before in a classroom enveloped me.

Mama had been nodding off on the couch when Reagan and I rushed in from school. She worked late nights as a monitor tech at St. Vincent Hospital. It was nice finding her home after we'd gotten out of school.

Mama was at work when it was time for us to get up in the morning. She would put the phone in our room before leaving at midnight. At 6:45, she called us. Since the phone was close to Reagan's bed, she answered. I could hear Mama's trumpet voice on the phone all the way on my side of the room. "Y'all get up!"

We washed up, dressed ourselves, poured us some cornflakes, and watched cartoons before catching our 7:30 bus in front of the apartment complex. I was responsible for making sure everything was off before we left and that both locks on the front door were secure. I carried the key on a shoestring, which I wore under my shirt.

And apparently Mama didn't like my blue shirt with the yellow stripes worn with my green camouflage pants with the deep cargo pockets, my favorite pair.

Before I could share with her that Mrs. James said my handwriting was pretty and that we learned about Daisy Bates, who'd in 1957 helped nine black kids integrate Central High School, that big stately building that took up a block over on S. Park Street, Mama frowned.

"You wore that to school?"

I looked down at my clothes. "Yeah."

"That doesn't even go together."

"I like these pants."

"They're too tight, Dusty!"

Reagan snickered and Mama shot her a glance. "Shut up!"

Mama's lips were tight. Was she that pissed off at my clothes?

"Why didn't you wear those khakis I laid out with that shirt?"

I looked down at the carpet.

"Dusty?"

"I don't know," I mumbled, my eyes fixed on the snaking beige pattern in the coffee-colored carpet.

"You do know. I guess you like wearing those pants 'cause they tight on your butt."

I looked up. "Huh?"

"You like that, don't you? Going around switchin' in some tight pants. Get upstairs and take those damn pants off. I'm throwin' 'em away."

I stomped up the stairs, eyes burning.

"And you better stop stompin' up those steps!"

I crashed across my bed.

She was suspended in the sky, glowing and singing in a voice so warm and soothing I melted in the cool grass. I was stretched out in a field somewhere encircled by trees. And everything was bathed in a milky light. A butterfly floated past my nose and made graceful loops and arcs, leaving behind a faint, shimmering rainbow.

The music—a dramatic sweep of strings and a cascade of Fender Rhodes—came from the trees. I couldn't make out the face of the woman suspended over me in the milky light but her voice was reassuring.

In this enchanted place with a faceless sky woman singing only to me, I don't feel the sting of Mama's words. Sometimes it seemed I didn't have to do anything but show up and all the frustrations from her day, all the bitterness from a marriage that died, all the heartache from a terrible childhood hit me on the one, like the forceful beat from a James Brown record. The terse, sharp criticisms she trumpeted always sent me scurrying for an escape. With nowhere to run, my mind took flight.

The mental transport came via a Tamla 45, a disco number by Thelma Houston called "Saturday Night, Sunday Morning." But "Come to Me," the song on its flip side, evoked the light, the trees, the butterfly trailing rainbow dust. I could stay here forever, never leaving the ground, smiling in the light, eyes closed.

Suddenly I felt someone looming over me. My eyes flung open and I was back on my bunk bed, Reagan's pouting face over mine.

"Mama want you in the kitchen."

I had taken off the camouflage pants she hated so much and was in a pair of shorts. Mama stood at the counter dicing onions.

"I'm making spaghetti." The thorns in her voice earlier were gone. "Come over here and watch so you can know how to make it yourself."

I stood next to her as she sliced a large, green bell pepper into half-inch slivers, lined them up, and diced them. The onions were in a neat, small heap.

"You like your new school?" Her voice wasn't exactly warm, but I figured this was her way of starting conversation.

"Yeah. Mrs. James said she liked my handwriting, said I write real pretty."

"She did?"

"Uh-huh. And we learned about Daisy Bates."

"Daisy Bates?"

"And she helped the Little Rock Nine get into Central High School. That's over there on Park Street, Mrs. James said. And . . ."

Mama's eyebrows furrowed. "Why you got to talk with your hands?"

I looked at them. "What I do?"

Mama rolled her eyes. "Never mind."

My insides sank, and I shut up. Mama scooped up the onions and peppers and tossed them into a pan of sizzling butter.

"What else you learn?"

I didn't feel like talking anymore. "Nothin'."

She stirred the vegetables until the peppers were soft and slick and the onions translucent. Then she added the ground beef, breaking it up with a wooden spoon and seasoning it with garlic salt. We were silent during this until Mama abruptly picked up the conversation she had interrupted minutes before.

"So Daisy Bates helped some black kids get into Central, huh?"

"Yeah."

"Uh-huh. I was a little girl when all that happened."

"Really?"

"Uh-huh. I remember being at Big Mama's and seeing that on the news."

"Y'all had a TV?"

Mama frowned at me. "Yes, Dusty, we had a TV. It was in black and white. Saw that crowd behind that girl, being so hateful."

"That happened right here in Little Rock."

"Uh-huh."

As she stirred the beef and vegetables and added more garlic salt, my mouth watered.

"Get me that big pot from down there and fill it with water."

I reached into the cabinet near the stove and went to the sink with it.

"Don't fill it all the way, just about half way."

I carefully placed the half-filled stew pot on the stove. Mama sprinkled salt in the water.

"Reach down there and get me the lid."

Mama placed it on the pot and turned the burner on.

"Why you do that?"

"The salt gives the spaghetti flavor, and you put the top on to bring the water to a boil faster."

"Oh."

"You think you gonna like your new school?"

"I already do."

"Well, don't you be out there showin' out."

"I don't."

"Uh-huh. And don't be talkin' with your hands the way you do. Watch that. Don't have nobody callin' you a faggot."

That word always stung.

"You hear me?"

"Yeah."

I hated having to edit and rearrange everything I did. Some-body found fault in every mannerism. Dusa used to; the boys at Jones Elementary used to. And Mama did, which stung the most. I missed her sunshine smile, the one Dennis used to bring out. I wanted to feel it beaming down on me. I studied her intense pro-file as she stirred the tomato sauce into the meat, careful not to splatter it. She was so pretty and so distant.

Mama looked at me. "You payin' attention?"

"Yeah."

"Well, don't look like it. You look like you in another world."

Mama opened the box of spaghetti and slid the contents into the boiling salted water.

You look like you in another world.

I sure wanted to be.

The hallelujah voice sang my desire.

This time, Gladys Knight wasn't torn up about something she'd heard through the grapevine. She belted about the possibilities of being invisible, the Pips echoing her sorrow. The fat-bellied Buddha on the label slowly spun around, his face frozen in a knowing grin as if mocking the pain Gladys sang.

Mama had a way of making me wish I were invisible. Even standing next to her at the stove while she was stirring dinner, it seemed as though she didn't want to be there. And neither did I. Everything was hard for her. She had become so tense since moving to Little Rock, more so than usual. Any flub or dropped object turned her eyes to lasers and her tongue into a whip.

Why you have to say 'uh' so many times when you talk? Do you hear yourself? Dusty, don't stand like that. Dusty, don't walk like that. Turn off that music and clean up the kitchen. If that room ain't cleaned up, I'm gonna throw those damn records in the garbage. No, Dusty, you don't do it like this. Don't let me have to get up to show you. I swear, you and Reagan are on my last nerve. I'm gon' send y'all to Raymond and let him deal with y'all.

Word was Daddy was living pillow to post, off and on with Big Mama or with a girlfriend who let him stay a while before she got tired of his ass and put him out. Then he was back at East Section Line, sleeping on cool, fresh-smelling sheets Big Mama hung out to dry on the clothesline out back.

The child support came sporadically. When Mama was upset, she'd call somebody official. I knew she was talking to somebody official and white, because her voice went up an octave and she enunciated every word. No "uh-huh" but a very crisp "yes."

Then she'd call a girlfriend immediately afterward and switch back to soul sister mode. "Uh-huh, girl. They gon' have to put Raymond in jail. His dog ass is behind on child support—again!"

One warm spring day, Mama came to school just before lunchtime and checked us out. She was dressed as though she were on her way to church—navy-blue coat dress hugging her generous curves; Fashion Fair applied as though she were the spokesperson for the brand; her honey-blond hair full and loosely curled. Whenever she was looking good, Mama affected haughtiness—her nose in the air, her expression fierce like the models in *Ebony* magazine.

"Get in the car," she told us.

"Where we goin'?" Reagan asked.

"To Hot Springs."

"Hot Springs?" I said.

"Is there a parrot in here? Yeah, Dusty, Hot Springs."

"For what?" I asked.

"We goin' to court."

Reagan stuck her head between the two front seats. "We goin' to jail?"

"Reagan, sit back," Mama said, looking in the rearview mirror. "No, we're not going to jail, but ya daddy is."

We were silent during the forty-five-minute ride. On our way into the courthouse, Mama said, "Y'all, don't get in here actin' a fool or I'll have the judge throw y'all asses in jail with Raymond."

Inside the old, depressing courtroom, Daddy and Paw Paw sat near the front. Mama instructed us to sit near the back. Daddy looked bloated in a fisherman's foam-and-net cap and a tight button-down shirt. He didn't look like the confident, swaggering man whose feet floated a few inches off the ground in my dreams. Sitting beside him, Paw Paw was an older mirror image, thinner and also wearing a fisherman's cap.

They both looked up at the same time when we entered the room. Daddy looked shocked to see us trailing Mama. He turned to Paw Paw, whispered something, and shook his head.

He rose from his seat and strolled past Mama without looking at her or uttering a word. We remained seated as he squatted in the aisle.

"Hey, Dus-Dus; hey, Puddin'," he whispered. "Ain't y'all supposed to be in school?"

"Mama took us out," Reagan said loudly, her voice echoing in the room. Mama snapped her fingers and narrowed her eyes from the front where she sat. "Be quiet," she hissed.

"Y'all shouldn't be here, but I'm glad to see you," Daddy said.

His bushy hair stuck out on the sides and he needed to shave. I was embarrassed. Why didn't he look like the man in my dreams or the man who stood on Clara Mae's raggedy porch, patting his hair and smoothing his shirt before he knocked on the door?

"Dus-Dus, you OK, man?"

I didn't answer. I stared at my hands. If I looked at him, I was going to throw my arms around his neck, rub my chin against his Brillo pad–like stubble, and refuse to let go. Or, I was going to smash my fists into his face, kick him, and bite him for leaving me with a distant woman who looked fabulous, although there was more lint in her purse than dollar bills.

And she worked hard and hated it. I hated it, too. And she had cancer, Daddy, Mama fuckin' had cancer, and where were you when Dusa pushed Mama into a chest of drawers, and Mama threw her to the floor like a rag doll, and they fought like coldhearted bitches in a honky-tonk? And I had to break them up. Where were you, Daddy, when we had to stay with Loretta and Dee in their tiny house where unicorns bowed forever behind glass that I had to spray with Windex and wipe until no streaks were visible? And why, Daddy, tell me why in the hell did Michael Jackson decide to dance with thugs and grimace and declare himself bad?

Everything inside churned and I didn't want to look into his bloodshot, half dollar–sized eyes and see the melancholy living there.

"Dus-Dus?"

Reagan touched my arm and I snatched it away, eyes fixed on my hands.

"OK, lit' man."

I kept my eyes mostly on my hands during the brief time Mama and Daddy stood before the judge, an old white man whose voice boomed as he admonished Daddy. His questions dripped with condescension.

"Is there a reason you haven't paid your child support as ordered by the court, Mr. Ollison? Speak up now. I can't hear you."

Daddy had an excuse. Whatever he muttered, it didn't matter anyway, because the judge ordered him to go with the bailiff. The image of Daddy's defeated shoulders as he was escorted to a room behind the judge seared into my brain.

Lying in bed with my headphones on, I looked at the wall as Gladys sang about the desire to be invisible, to not have to explain a thing or even "be on the scene." Her voice bore witness and carried a strength I hoped to know one day. But in the meantime, the desire to be invisible throbbed like a fever.

Dusty showed up at school one day and ruined everything.

Rashod was in the good graces of his classmates—or so it seemed. Shy, without an athletic bone in his body, Rashod didn't usually participate in the basketball games at recess. Instead, he shadowed the boys, staying a few paces behind, and laughed along with everyone else whenever Robert, the leader of the pack, made a stupid quip. Rashod kept his hands still as he talked, and he affected the slightly lumbering walk of the other boys.

But Rashod didn't show up one day, and Dusty, the faggot, came in his place.

One day at recess, Dusty, whom everybody else thought was Rashod, was asked to join in the basketball game. Rashod would have found a way to avoid playing, but Dusty, who like Rashod knew nothing about basketball, said, "OK."

Kevin, who was also tall like Robert and in Mrs. Williams's fourth-grade class down the hall, picked Dusty for his team.

Dusty ran and stumbled all over the place, confused about what to do. Then somebody threw Dusty the ball and he froze.

"Shoot it! Shoot it!" his teammates shouted.

Dusty tried to make a basket and the ball sailed well below the hoop. He found it all amusing, put his hand to his mouth and giggled. The boys on his team stomped and howled; they were pissed. Robert and a few others glared at him. Dusty recognized that look: mild shock quickly twisting into disgust. It was the same look Dusty got when Dusa caught him standing with his hand on his hip or when he talked with his hands or when he cried.

Then a rail-thin, ashy-lipped boy from Robert's team said aloud what everybody else must've thought while Dusty stood there giggling at himself.

"Faggot!"

Concentric circles of laughter swirled around Dusty, threatening to envelop him. One boy sneered and shooed him away; another doubled over laughing. Like a foul scent, word of Dusty's faggot behavior soon spread all over the school. The boys avoided him after that day, elbowing each other whenever Dusty walked into the restroom. In the hallway, girls snickered.

They all didn't seem to remember Rashod, the shy boy who was "normal," just like them. There, giggling at himself on the basketball court, was the object of everyone's disgust, with mannerisms boys weren't supposed to have. Giggling under your hand? The fuck wrong with you?

Faggot.

Mrs. James tapped my shoulder and whispered in my ear one day as my classmates lined up to go outside for recess, "Stay in your seat." After the others left the room, she pulled up a chair to my desk and looked at me over her glasses.

"You're one of my smartest students, Rashod. But I've noticed you seem to kind of pull into yourself—not participating in class much. You seem really withdrawn. This has been going on for the past—what?—week, maybe? Doesn't seem like you. Is everything OK?"

I looked down as if the answer lay in my palms.

"Rashod?"

"Yes?"

"Well, what's going on? You were like a light in here and now you seem so sad all the time. Look at me."

My face met her concerned eyes.

"If there's anything going on I need you to tell me. You haven't been yourself."

Maybe it was the motherly warmth of Mrs. James's voice, a tone I wish Mama had, that made me cry.

"Nobody likes me here."

Mrs. James went to her desk and snatched a tissue from her Kleenex box. Handing it to me, she kept her voice warm. "Rashod, let me tell you now: Not everybody's going to like you. And don't you worry about that. How someone feels about you is none of your business. We all want to be liked, but you got to like yourself first. That's most important. Child, you are very smart, got a lot of sense. Some people may be jealous, and who cares? Folks used to make fun of me when I was in school."

"What you do?"

"It used to hurt my feelings, too, and I'd cry. And my mama"— Mrs. James paused for a moment and smiled to herself—"Mama told me what I'm telling you: that it's none of your business how they feel about you, because people are gonna talk about you if you do and they sure gonna talk about you if you don't. They talked about Martin Luther King; they talked about Harriet Tubman. All those folks we talk about in black history, they were talked about, spat on, beat up. And they were good people. But you know what you need to do?"

"What?"

"You just keep on steppin' like you somebody. Those same folks making fun of you now will try to be your friend when you're doing very well years from now."

Mrs. James stuck her chest out, turned her nose up in faux haughtiness, and smiled. I smiled, too.

"There's a song we sing in church called 'This Little Light of Mine.' You know that?"

"Yes."

"Remember that. Don't let anybody take it and don't you hide it, either."

· · ·

Shortly afterward, Mrs. James recommended me for the school's new "TAG" program for students deemed "talented and gifted." She sent a letter home for Mama to sign. After Mama read it over, she looked at me. "Guess they think you special, huh?" Smirking, she scribbled her flowery signature.

I was given an IQ test and was soon pulled out of Mrs. James's class two or three times a week to go to a trailer on the west side of the small campus. Inside, Mrs. Lambert, a large woman who rocked like a ship when she walked, engaged a small group of us, five or six students.

We did a lot of unstructured projects in which Mrs. Lambert gave us a few objects—Popsicle sticks, pine cones, pieces of cloth—and we made art. Or she'd give us a small written passage and instruct us to craft our own stories. There were few white students at Fair Park Elementary and it seems most of them were in TAG. I was the only black boy in class. And maybe because of that, Mrs. Lambert took a special interest in me. She noticed my flair for writing.

She called me to her desk one day. "You ever heard of the great black poet Langston Hughes?" She whispered the question while the other TAG students were busy with their art projects.

I was confused. Was I supposed to know who Langston Hughes was? Mrs. Lambert was whispering, so was he a secret?

Looking into her wide face, I whispered back. "No."

She reached into a brown floral-print bag under her desk and handed me a small, fat book: *Collected Poems*.

"Read some of those and tell me what you think," she said, smiling and still whispering. "Take good care of the book because I want it back, OK?"

On the bus ride home I leafed through the pages and was immediately struck by the music, which drowned out the noise around me. His lines were like trumpet solos or sax obbligatos, and the voice was always vivid and familiar.

Langston painted pictures that reminded me of the blues women—Aunt Kay, Miss Beadie and her daughter Linda—who strolled up and down the roads of Malvern empty-handed, whose words were edged with salt. Their manner was often rough but underneath, hidden below the layers of heartbreak, sweetness still flowed.

After I returned the Langston Hughes book, Mrs. Lambert passed others to me: the poetry of Maya Angelou, Nikki Giovanni, Paul Laurence Dunbar, and Eloise Greenfield. Mrs. Lambert was friends with Mrs. Isom, the school's librarian, another cosmetics-free black woman at Fair Park who carried herself like a Baptist church mother. She allowed me to spend my recess time in the library, sometimes shelving books and magazines. A few other TAG students were there, too. We escaped into our books, our classmates at a safe distance.

I read Beverly Cleary novels and encyclopedias; illustrated biographies written for elementary school kids on James Baldwin, Zora Neale Hurston, and Martin Luther King Jr. Each book carried an uplifting message about great people who dared to dream, and said I could, too. What would I be? Where would I go? I hadn't a clue.

But a door inside had been blown open. My imagination started to expand and grow; possibilities abounded. I studied color-coded maps and wondered what it was like in those countries so far away. What did the people eat? What did the air smell like?

A giraffe silhouetted against a cherry sunset; crystal bodies of water encircled by jade-green hills; a bare-breasted ebony woman in Africa kneeling in dust the color of saffron—the images in *National Geographic* magazines swept me away. My mouth hung open until I flipped the last page. It was around this time that I began to figure that books and good music were perhaps my keys to soul liberation.

At Fair Park I felt protected by the matronly teachers, and I was always encouraged. I eventually became something of a teacher's pet, and the other kids didn't tease me much anymore. They ignored me as I did them. The library was my private Eden as my mind sailed to colorful places until the bell rang. For fifteen minutes in the middle of the day, I was nothing, serenely invisible.

There, I wasn't worried about boys with dewy hoop dreams calling me a faggot.

The summer of 1988, Dusa was pregnant and close to delivery, which meant she had been carrying the child when she and Mama fought. I wondered if she knew that as she ran out of the house and through all that windswept snow. Mama acted as though she didn't care. But it was all a front. Her mood was more mercurial than it had ever been. She wasn't sleeping well. No matter how unaffected she tried to be, she was just as concerned, surely more so, about Dusa's whereabouts than Reagan and I were. But we knew better than to ask her anything or to mention Dusa's name because we'd get cussed out.

Then out of the blue one evening, Mama Teacake called. I answered the phone.

"Dusty?"

"Yes. Hey, Mama Teacake."

"Where Dianne?"

"She in her room."

"Put her ass on the phone."

I ran upstairs and into Mama's room, where she lay on the bed reading a *National Enquirer*.

"Who is it?" she whispered. Mama didn't like answering the phone for fear of bill collectors.

"Mama Teacake."

I stood in the doorway as she picked up the phone on her nightstand.

"Go hang up the other line."

I went into the kitchen and placed the phone on the receiver. Remembering a trick I saw Dusa do once, I carefully lifted it while covering the mouthpiece and listened.

"You oughta be 'shamed, Dianne."

"'Shamed of what?"

"Puttin' that girl out like you did."

"That *girl* stood up in my house and fought me." Mama's voice had thorns.

"Well, you knew she was pregnant."

"No, I didn't know that."

"Stop lyin', Dianne."

"Well, that's not my problem, Mama. Dusa had been on birth control since she was fourteen. If she got pregnant, she wanted to be. And I wasn't takin' care of no babies. I still got Dusty and Reagan here."

"Nobody put you outdoors when you come up pregnant with Dusa."

"And I didn't stand up in your house and call you no bitch and fight you, either."

"Dusa say you beat her and kicked her outdoors."

"Mama, she's lyin'. If she was grown enough to stand up and fight me in my own house, then she's grown enough to fend for herself."

"That's cold, Dianne. Nobody did you like that."

"Mama, I really ain't got time for this."

"Well, she'd been stayin' over in Hot Springs with Phyl; then she was over there with them Hunters. That's the daddy, Felix, that Hunter boy."

"Mama, is there something you wanted?"

"Dianne, you oughta quit. Dusa s'posed to have that baby next week some time. You don't think she scared? Don't think she been scared?"

"Dusa's grown. That's her baby."

"Then you gon' carry yo' ass up there to Little Rock. Ain't check to see whether that girl had a pot to pee, coulda been livin' in the gutter somewhere. You always have had ugly ways like that, Dianne."

"Mama, I'm tellin' you: I ain't got time for this."

"And I'm tellin' you: That's still yo' damn child and nobody did you like that when you come up pregnant, after all that money we spent to send yo' ass to school. You knew damn well yo' ass was pregnant 'fore you left here, like folks had money to just throw away. You was the brain of the family, thought you was so god-damn high-class and ended up doin' just what Phyl did: got pregnant. Hell, least Phyl took her black ass to nursin' school. You flew off in behind Raymond, that sorry, slew-foot mutha . . ."

"Mama, I'm about to hang the hell up."

"You bet' not! Listen, Dianne: Dusa needs you and you need to quit with all that damn attitude and be there for her, call, see what she needs. Ain't nobody throw yo' ass outdoors. Hell, pro'ly needed to now that I think about it."

"Bye, Mama."

"Fine, then, be hateful. But ain't nothin' good gon' come to you actin' like that."

"Oh, you one to talk."

"What?"

"I'm hangin' up this phone."

"Bye, Dianne. Hateful ass."

"Bye, Mama."

On Sunday morning, August 7, Phyl called Mama to let her know that Dusa had been admitted into AMI Hospital, where Mama used to work. Felix, his sisters, and his parents were there. Dusa had a girl: Brandi Dannese Hunter. Reagan and I sat at the foot of Mama's bed as she lay under the covers relaying the news. We were excited.

"When we gon' see the baby?" Reagan asked.

Mama looked at the window. "I don't know."

"Where she stayin'?" I asked.

"Think she gon' be over to Mama's. I don't know."

"I'm a auntie!" Reagan said. "But I ain't old."

"You don't have to be old to be somebody's auntie," I said.

Reagan ignored me. "I wanna see the baby."

Mama's eyes were distant and still focused on the sunlight filtering through the curtains. "Me too."

Dusa's eyes weren't cold but they didn't welcome us either.

We went to Malvern about a week after Brandi was born. Dusa was staying at Mama Teacake's. When we walked in, she was sitting on the couch, her breasts swollen, her hair pulled back into a ponytail. She wore no makeup; her eyes held no cheer. Her greeting was lifeless, as though she'd seen us just the day before. "Hey."

The baby lay curled on a small pink blanket next to Dusa. Reagan and I hovered over her, astonished. Brandi was a beauty. And although she was lying on her side asleep and we couldn't fully see her face, there was no denying who she looked like. The pug nose gave it away. She was definitely Felix Hunter's daughter.

Mama Teacake appeared in the kitchen entrance, wiping her hands on a dish towel. "Where Dianne? I know she just didn't drop y'all asses off here."

"She's outside," I said.

Just then, Mama appeared at the front door holding a large Wal-Mart bag stuffed with new baby clothes and other things she'd picked up before we left Little Rock. Mama placed her large sunglasses on top of her head.

She and Dusa exchanged guarded looks. Mama glanced at the baby and back at Dusa. She seemed relieved to see her on Mama Teacake's couch, sitting there in a loose, powder-blue housedress, her feet nestled in soft matching slippers. Something in Mama's eyes melted, and it seemed for a moment that her sunshine smile would appear to complement the sweet relief in her eyes. But instead she cleared her throat and remembered the bag in her hand.

"Hey, uh, I got some things for Brandi," she said, reaching over the coffee table. "Here, Dusty, hand that to Dusa."

Dusa retrieved the bag and reached inside. Softly, she said, "Thank you."

"Dusty, Reagan, y'all move," Mama said as she made her way to the baby.

Brandi started to stretch and whine. Her moon-shaped eyes popped open.

"Oh, we done woke you up?" Mama said, sitting next to her.

"Think it's time for her to eat again," Mama Teacake said, hanging the dish towel on her shoulder.

Mama scooped up Brandi. "Ooo, looka there, looka there. If this ain't Felix's baby."

"I know," Dusa said, smirking.

"Dusa, she looks nothing like you," Mama said.

"Dusa was longer than that," Mama Teacake added.

"Sho was," Mama nodded. "And this is a Hunter nose."

"That's what Felix's mama said." Dusa's eyes and voice were warm now. "When I had my ultrasound, that's all you could see was that nose. Miss Hunter said, 'Uh-huh. That's a Hunter.'"

Mama chuckled. "She ain't lied about that."

"I wanna hold her," Reagan whined.

Mama ignored her and looked into Brandi's face. "Look at you. Ain't you cute?"

Brandi cooed and Mama smiled at last. Dusa examined the baby clothes from the Wal-Mart bag. Reagan and I waited our turn to hold the baby.

"I'm gon' get her bottle," Mama Teacake said and went back into the kitchen.

Soon afterward, things between Mama and Dusa got better—at least they were talking semiregularly. Dusa moved around Hot Springs often when Brandi was an infant. At one point, she lived with Phyl; later she had a place of her own; she and our cousin Kim, Phyl's oldest daughter, briefly shared a place; then Dusa was back on her own again—all within a matter of months.

Brandi was usually with Felix's family. And although he didn't pay child support or spend much time with her, his parents and sisters took up the slack. Dusa worked long hours at Taco Bell. When she wasn't working, she tripped in and out of toxic relationships.

Brandi wasn't even toddling when Dusa became pregnant again. The father, a tall dark-skinned man named Frank, was several years older and already had two preteen kids with a woman he had been with for years. They were a common-law couple and lived together in a big rambling house on a hill. Dusa was in a sparsely furnished apartment a few miles away. It was an ideal setup for Frank: wife on the hill, side chick across town.

Dusa had a son barely a year after Brandi was born. She boldly named him Frank Jr., partly out of her almost obsessive love for

Frank Sr. and also because the baby was born on his father's birthday.

Reagan, Mama, and I saw the baby only once, about a week or so after Dusa gave birth to him. At that point, Dusa was living in Malvern with our Aunt Stephanie, Mama's youngest sister. Dusa was deeply depressed, close to a nervous breakdown, Stephanie later told Mama. About a month after the baby was born, Frank Sr., came to Malvern to get him. He and his common-law wife raised him in that rambling house on the hill near downtown Hot Springs. Although the baby boy was barely an hour away, we never saw him. Dusa got a job at a Styrofoam plant in Malvern and went on about her life, remaining uninvolved with Frank Jr. Meanwhile, Brandi floated between Malvern and Felix's family in Hot Springs.

If Mama had any opinions about Dusa's raggedy personal life, I never heard her say anything. When Brandi visited us for the first time in Little Rock, we had moved again. Rent at Chateau Deville had gotten too high. We were living in a brown-brick duplex on Tanya Street on the periphery of Twin Lakes, a subdivision filled with immaculately kept Colonial and split-level homes mostly owned by solidly middle-class blacks: educators, post office workers, and other government employees. Brick duplexes lined either side of Tanya Street and were mostly rented by single mothers or working-class families with middle-class aspirations.

Our duplex was as big as a house, with two large bedrooms and two full baths. Mama's master suite had one bathroom, and Reagan and I shared the one right outside our bedroom. Covered with seventies-era, paisley, marigold-print wallpaper, the dining area adjacent to the kitchen and divided by a bar was spacious enough for the oak dining set plus a couch and chair. The old Magnavox console TV fit in there, too, and this was the family room.

Slide the patio door open and there was a grassy backyard boxed in by a chain-link fence and shaded by towering pine trees. Mama's shiny, two-year-old 1988 Nissan Sentra sat under the carport in the front near the brick steps. She was now working as a nutritionist at St. Vincent Hospital, no longer doing two full-time gigs. At last, it felt as though we were stable with the child support coming regularly. No shutoff notices in the mail. No repo guys from rent-to-own joints pulling up and knocking on the door to reclaim a stereo or living room set that Mama knew damn well she couldn't afford in the first place. No more lying to the impatient man at the door asking about her whereabouts.

Once, when we were living at our last house in Hot Springs, not long after Mama beat Dusa and sent her running through the snow, Mama embarrassed me as I was trying to cover for her.

"Where's Miss Ollison?" asked the repo man, a tall black guy with a high-top fade.

"She's not here."

"When will she be home?"

"I don't know."

"You don't know when your mother's coming home?"

"She workin' overtime. I guess you'll have to come back."

"She's three months late."

"Well, she ain't here, though."

He huffed. "When will she be home, young blood?"

Just then, Mama's bug-eyed Chevette crept toward the house, and my attention was diverted beyond the repo man. He turned around. When Mama saw the yellow rent-to-own van parked out front and the two of us standing on the porch, she zoomed past the house and made a sharp right turn. The repo guy recognized Mama, chuckled, and shook his head.

He tore off a pink slip from his clipboard. "Give this to your mama after she makes a few blocks."

He was still laughing as he sauntered to the van and pulled away.

When Mama walked through the door about half an hour later, she acted as though nothing had happened.

"You didn't see the repo man when you passed the house?" I handed her the slip he'd left behind.

"What? What you talking about?" she said, snatching it from my hand and sashaying to the kitchen, raising her nose to smell the food I'd been preparing. "What you cook?"

I was becoming a better cook by the day. I'd long perfected the spaghetti recipe Mama taught me. I also fried chicken and pork chops better than she did. I was thirteen years old and running the kitchen as though I had been a faithful and refined domestic in a previous life.

Big Mama was an inspiration. In the kitchen stirring the pots, she was a culinary sorceress. I watched her thin, elegant hands. Dusted with flour, they gently pressed out dough for cobblers. Under running water, they scooped blackberries picked down the hill near where the McAdoo family lived. With a magician's grace, they pulled pin bones from fish. Grains of salt rained from her fingertips over a pan of gravy or a skillet of freshly shucked corn.

When we visited, I preferred to sit and watch her magic at the stove while Reagan and a few kids on East Section Line played games under the mammoth pecan tree in Big Mama's yard.

As spring burned into summer, children ran up and down Tanya Street screaming and laughing. They jumped rope and Double Dutched in driveways and pop-locked to hip-hop blaring from boomboxes under carports.

The summer before Reagan and I entered the sixth and seventh grades, we were holed up in the house for a month with Brandi. Dusa had dropped her off with just a diaper bag. Mama bought her pastel outfits from Walmart. During the day, Mama called every hour to check on us.

"What Brandi doin? She 'sleep? Y'all bet' not be in there fightin' and carryin' on while that baby's in there."

Reagan took to Brandi more than I did, morphing into a little mother hen. She combed her hair, prepared her bottles, and treated her like a living doll. And Brandi took to her: cooing and grinning in her arms, her moon eyes aglow. Whenever I held her, she whined and squirmed.

"Give her back," Reagan said.

"Here, take her."

Shortly after Dusa finally came to get Brandi, Mama got word that Daddy had moved to Oregon. We were used to never seeing him, even when we occasionally went to Malvern on the weekends. Mama's rule never changed: if Daddy didn't call for us, we weren't allowed to go to East Section Line. We heard about Daddy's whereabouts through Mama's gossip-loving relatives.

Saw Raymond down at Junebug's. He ax 'bout y'all.

Hear Raymond goin' with one of them Tony sisters. You know, the youngest one, what went to school with Kay. They say she on that stuff. Hear Raymond's back smokin' it, too. Wouldn't surprise me none.

Yeah, I saw y'all Daddy. He was drivin' Old Lady Ollison somewhere, pro'ly to the Food Center.

When was the last time y'all seen him?

Even if we didn't see him, there was comfort in knowing he was somewhere around Malvern. Reynolds aluminum transferred him to Portland. He got a raise and our child support started coming regularly, which seemed to be the only concern Mama had regarding Daddy. As was her style, she abruptly announced his move one night as we ate pizza in the living room while watching *In Living Color*.

"Raymond done moved to Oregon."

I swallowed. "Where?"

"Oregon."

"For what?" Reagan asked.

"Work."

"Are we gonna see him before he move up there?" I asked.

Mama reached for another pepperoni slice. "See what? He already gone up there."

I finished my pizza and stood up.

"Where you goin'?" Mama asked.

"I'm done," I said.

"Dusty? There's more pizza here," Mama said.

I ignored her and went to the room Reagan and I shared and lay across my bed. Daddy was always flying off somewhere. Was he ever coming back? Why the hell did it even matter? It was clear the only person he cared about, the only muthafucka he ever cared about, was himself. So why was I longing for him? I made up my mind to try to forget him since he had apparently forgotten me.

Despite her frequent threats to leave work one evening, drive past the house, and never come back, Mama was the only consistent presence in my life. She moved us from neighborhood to neighborhood, always nice ones, so that we could be comfortable. She'd worked herself into bad health to keep us aloft. So why was I always reaching for Daddy in my thoughts and dreams? None of it meant anything. None of it was going to bring him back into my life. He could hang out at Junebug's; he could fuck around with one of those trifling Tony sisters; he could move a thousand miles away and not say good-bye.

Papa was a rolling stone, the Temptations sang. Daddy once owned that record, and it was in one of the stacks he left me. I was always ambivalent about that song but now it started to resonate. Before he died, the father in the lyric had never been part of his son's life.

Daddy had once been the sun in my world but he chose to ride the wind instead. Either he was on his way somewhere or thinking about going somewhere. He never seemed to be fully present. Maybe I was just a diversion, a little nappy-headed distraction with eyes like his.

At the old house on Garden Street, as he spread yellow mustard on a saltine cracker and gingerly placed a sardine on top for me, it seemed a wind would come at any moment and sweep him out of the door. So I was hyperpresent, absorbing every aspect of him—how he lovingly spread the mustard, how beautiful his ebony fingers were holding the white cracker, the way he popped the whole thing in his mouth and squinted when he chewed. I couldn't eat it all the way he did. I realized that only after I once shoved the whole thing in my mouth and nearly choked to death.

"Take your time, Dus-Dus. Chew slow, son. Ain't nobody takin' anything from you. Here, drink some water."

When Daddy laughed and rubbed my head, when "Dus-Dus" slipped off his tongue with a lived-in affection as though it were the name of a blues song he adored, I felt no ground beneath my feet.

But shit was starting to change. I was starting to change. Sprigs of hair were sprouting around my dick, and I seemed to grow out of my shoes and clothes every other Wednesday, which annoyed Mama.

"You sure know how to cook," she said. "Maybe you need to start sewing. Didn't I just buy you those pants, and now they too small?"

My voice started to deepen.

"You tryin' to become a man 'round here?" Mama said, smirking.

And Daddy was nowhere to be found, had run off to Oregon when it seemed I needed his validation the most. He didn't come around and I didn't see him when I was in Malvern. But I always knew he was a phone call away, that he was accessible. Surely one day he'd call or come by, but days melted into months; months hardened into years. Anytime a relative said, "Oh, yeah, I seen yo' daddy," I was relieved. At least he was around somewhere. Safe. Alive. Now he was off to Oregon. And for how long?

Papa was a rolling stone. And maybe Mama had been right all along: "Raymond Ollison Jr. ain't worth a damn."

That summer we moved to Tanya Street, Mama thought it was a good idea to join a church.

Wendell Griffen, a distant cousin, was pastor of Emmanuel Baptist over on Twelfth Street, a once-comfortable neighborhood with old, stately houses that were near dilapidation in the early nineties. Folks were always getting shot, robbed, and fucked up on and around Twelfth Street, a long stretch through central Little Rock.

Emmanuel was low-key. Retired professionals made up most of the congregation: educators, nurses, postal workers—black folks who had migrated decades ago from sharecropping towns in southern and eastern Arkansas. They had gone to segregated schools and Negro colleges where they learned to do the white man's work with a chest-swelling sense of pride and accomplishment.

They were longtime members of sororities and fraternities, and the Greek letters—Alpha Kappa Alpha, Delta Sigma Theta, Omega Psi Phi, Alpha Phi Alpha, Zeta Phi Beta—emblazoned license-plate frames on their gleaming Cadillacs, Buicks, and Lincoln town cars.

They sat straight-backed in the pews and never turned around when folks snuck in late. There was no shouting at Emmanuel. No tambourine shaking. No stomping. No running up and down the aisles. No need for "church nurses" alert in starched white uniforms and thick white stockings with fans ready to help revive a Holy Ghost–stricken congregant. At Emmanuel, nobody ever got slain in the spirit.

The hymns and spirituals, which the choir sang in billowy maroon robes, were usually led by Helen Cyrus, an imposing woman whose magnolia-white curls framed a forbidding bronze face. Her piercing mezzo-soprano rang through the venerable old building on "Nearer, My God, to Thee" and "How Great Thou Art."

The modest-sized congregation listened intently to Pastor Griffen, a tall, handsome man who was in his mid-thirties but carried himself with a varnished dignity from another era. With his eyeglasses, dark suits, and tasteful ties, he reminded me of sepia pictures of a young James Weldon Johnson or Thurgood Marshall.

Well-respected in political and elite social circles around Little Rock, Pastor Griffen was also an accomplished attorney and one of the few black judges in the city. His sermons were free of histrionics and typical black-preacher theatrics—no flash, no pomposity. He didn't wear a robe, flail his arms, or even raise his voice much. Seasoned with a slight Southern twang, his baritone seemed to soothe the congregation as he delivered his sermons as though he were teaching a class on the Constitution.

He was keen on how the young men at Emmanuel carried themselves. Reverend Griffen and the deacons of the church formed "The Shepherds' Club," where the boys of the congregation met monthly with the men, usually over a breakfast of doughnuts, coffee, and juice, and talked about what it meant to be a man. Well, mostly the men talked and we listened. Mama made sure I made every meeting in the church basement where the deacons and Reverend Griffen shared stories about the trials of growing up during segregation and what it meant to maintain your dignity and integrity in the hostile face of racism.

"Nothing much has changed," said Brother Cyrus, the oldest deacon present and husband of Emmanuel's standout soprano. "Just because you don't see 'Colored Only' signs don't mean the lines still ain't there. Am I right?"

The men nodded and said, "Amen," as I sat wide-eyed, wolfing down a bear claw.

After benediction each Sunday, as congregants filed by to greet him, Reverend Griffen gave a brief tutorial to the boys on how to shake a man's hand.

"Rashod, look me in the eye," he'd say. "Grip my hand, son. Always stand straight and look a man in his eye, and always give a firm handshake. There, like that. Let them know who you are."

His wife, Pat, had grown up in Malvern with Mama. They attended Wilson High School. Pat, who was a few years older than Reverend Griffen, was a successful clinical psychologist, quiet and unassuming. She made many of her own dresses and suits, had round glasses, wore very little makeup, and although she was just forty, her sensible bob haircut was streaked with gray.

Pat was well-established in her career and marriage before she gave birth to the couple's two sons, Martyn and Elliott, when she was in her mid-thirties. They were well-behaved boys with appraising eyes. They were still as mannequins in the front pew just behind their mother as she played piano for the dignified choir.

I felt welcomed at Emmanuel. The congregants became a surrogate family and seemed sincerely interested in us—not just nosy.

How are you doing in school, Rashod? And, Reagan, how are you?

Sister Ollison, you're looking well. Thank God.

Emmanuel was a good resource for Mama. She befriended older members: Jean Cross, a nurse with a voice so warm and spring-like it evoked images of country streams, lilac and willow trees; and Gertrude Gardner, who had grown up with Mrs. Cross. She taught the teens' Sunday school class, talked with a lisp, and covered her mouth when she laughed. She took to Reagan immediately. "This is my little sister," she'd say, hugging Reagan's shoulders. The "little sister" tag was amusing given that Mrs. Gardner was old enough to be our grandmother.

Betty Mitchell, who presided over the youth ministry (meaning she was a glorified babysitter, coordinating activities for the young folks), reminded me of the matronly teachers at Fair Park. She was irrepressibly cheery, her round face always brightened by a generous smile.

Her husband, Reverend William Mitchell, was the assistant pastor. His long-winded sermons filled with rambling stories about growing up in the country induced sleep throughout the congregation. But his singing voice—powerful and rugged—was always a treat. His leathery baritone complemented Mrs. Mitchell's silvery soprano, and they often fronted the choir. At home, Mama referred to them as "Emmanuel's Peaches & Herb."

Mrs. Mitchell took a special interest in me. "You're such an exceptional young man," she'd say. I wondered what she saw that I didn't see. At Bible study on Wednesday nights, which was basically a study hall for the kids and teenagers who showed up at Emmanuel while our parents were upstairs in their Bible study classes, Mrs. Mitchell oversaw the activities in the large recreation room in the church's basement.

One Wednesday night as I did my homework in a corner, Mrs. Mitchell pulled up a chair beside me.

"And what are we working on, Mr. Rashod?"

"My English homework."

"I loved English in school."

"Really?"

"That's right."

"I'm not really all that good with math, but I read a lot."

"Oh, that's good. You don't find too many boys who like to read."

"I write—well, I try to."

"Write what?"

"Poems." My face felt flushed. I hadn't told anybody that I wrote poems, something I had just started doing to music. I don't know why I blurted that out.

"Is that right?" Mrs. Mitchell's fleshy face lit up. "You got any?"

"Well, I, uh, I keep 'em in my notebook here," I said, stammering and reaching into my backpack beside me.

I handed Mrs. Mitchell my red spiral notebook, which she retrieved with wide eyes, as though I had just handed her an envelope stuffed with cash. She scanned the pages, squinting here and there.

"You have some pretty handwriting, Rashod."

"Thank you."

She flipped through the pages. "You should be a teacher one day. You should think about that. What do you want to be?"

"I don't know," I shrugged. "My teachers like my writing in class."

Mrs. Mitchell's eyes brightened. "Be a writer!"

I wondered if her perpetual, almost theatrical enthusiasm was a put-on. Was she on some happy pill or something? Because she was always like that, ecstatic about any major or minor achievement the young folks at Emmanuel made, I eventually decided it couldn't be an act. I just wasn't used to grown folks taking anything I did seriously. Their faces never lit up when I entered a room, not until we joined Emmanuel.

"You know what you ought to do, Rashod? You should read something in church next Sunday. It's children's Sunday. I have to make up the program. You can read one of these poems." Mrs. Mitchell flipped through the pages. "How about this one?"

She paused for a moment and read a few lines aloud.

They say I come from kings and queens
But what does it all mean?
The answer to me is clear and loud
I must always be black and proud

The words sounded almost musical in Mrs. Mitchell's lilting, flutelike voice. I blushed.

"You're so talented, Rashod. Why don't you read this one in church next Sunday? That's it. You're gonna read this next Sunday in church."

"I ain't never read anything in front of folks before."

Mrs. Mitchell raised her eyebrows. "Oh, Rashod, I just read this beautiful poem you wrote. With your way with words, don't say 'ain't,' honey. And don't worry, you'll do fine. I'll put you on the program."

And with that, Mrs. Mitchell closed my notebook and slid it next to my books. "You'll do fine," she repeated before leaving her chair and crossing the room. I didn't know how to feel. I was going to stand before the self-serious congregation and recite my poem? I'd never even had an Easter speech. What would I do with my hands? I didn't want to embarrass myself—or Mama. Would the congregation think I was a faggot? I didn't know how to feel—whether to be excited or horrified. I felt a mix of both.

"Betty Mitchell come tellin' me you reading a poem in church next Sunday?" Mama said, pulling out of the church's parking lot.

It was Reagan's turn to ride shotgun, and I was in the back-seat. After the adults finished with Bible study, they came downstairs for butter cookies, fruit punch, and stiff small talk. I saw Mrs. Mitchell chatting with Mama across the room. Her Bible clutched to her chest, Mama nodded and smiled politely as Mrs. Mitchell flailed her arms and shook her head. Apparently, she was sharing her excitement about reading one of my poems.

"She said you wrote some poem she wants you to read," Mama said, eyeing me in the rearview mirror.

"Yeah."

"Well. You're gonna have to learn to read it right."

I rolled my eyes.

"Don't cut your eyes at me, Dusty. I saw that."

"Aren't you supposed to be driving?"

Reagan chuckled.

"I know you ain't back there gettin' smart. Keep that up and you won't be readin' poems, 'cause you won't have eyes to read 'em with after I slap 'em out'cha face."

Reagan cracked up.

"Shut up, Reagan." Mama said, stopping at a red light.

"I didn't ask her if I could read my poem in church. I don't wanna do it anyway."

"Well, you're gonna do it. You need to learn how get up in front of folks."

I sighed. "I really don't want to."

"Dusty, you need to. You need to come out that shell you're in. I did drama in school, you know."

Reagan and I groaned; we knew where this was going. Whenever Mama got the chance to bring up her theater days in high school, she launched into a coon speech she gave in a production, one filled with so much exaggerated Southern dialect it would have put Hattie McDaniel to shame.

"Please, Mama, don't," I said.

Reagan chimed in. "Yeah, nobody wanna hear . . ."

"Who dat knockin' at dat doh?" Mama shouted. "Why, Ike Johnson, yes fa sho'! I'se mighty glad you's come down."

Reagan covered her ears.

"Mama!" I pleaded.

"I put on my calico."

"Mama! Please, I'll do it. Just stop with Ike Johnson already."

"Y'all oughta be 'shamed," Mama said, chuckling. "I could've had Oscar and Tony awards by now."

"Not even," Reagan said.

"See there? You and Dusty are haters."

"Nobody's hating on you and Ike Johnson, whoever that is," I said.

"You just worry about getting up in that church next Sunday and reciting that poem, which I need to see first. Ain't no tellin' what you might get up there and say."

"It's about being black and proud, Mama."

"Oh, Lord, I surely need to see it then. Don't need you standin' up there offendin' those Negroes up in Emmanuel."

The next day after she came home from work, Mama called me into her bedroom to recite my poem. She lay across the bed as I stood at the foot holding the folder containing the poem.

"You haven't memorized it yet, Dusty?"

"Memorize it? No."

"You should. It would be more convincing to stand up there and recite it from memory."

"I'm not gonna be able to memorize it, Mama."

"Have you tried?"

"No."

"Then how you know?"

"Because I'll get up there and I'll miss a word or something and it'll throw me off."

"You should at least try to memorize it."

"I don't wanna try to memorize it, Mama."

She rolled over on her back and bucked her eyes at the ceiling fan. "Boy, I'm not gonna argue with you about this. Fine! Don't memorize it. Come pull me up."

I grabbed her hand and tugged.

"Damn, Dusty, don't pull my arm off."

Once Mama was upright, she faced me. "Read."

They say I come from kings and queens
But what does it all mean?

"You're looking down, Dusty. You have to look up at the people."

I huffed. "Then how am I supposed to read the poem if I'm not looking at it, Mama?"

"If you'd memorize it, you wouldn't have this problem."

"OK, Mama."

"Read."

The answer to me is clear and loud
I must always be black and proud

"Sound stern. You don't sound sure of yourself."

"I wrote the poem, though."

"Make me believe it, then."

White folks have shamed us. White folks have maimed us . . .

"You might wanna cut that, Dusty."

"What?"

"Don't 'what' me."

"What's wrong with it?"

"Why you gotta say 'white folks'? If you say 'they,' wouldn't that be understood? Hell, Negroes have done enough shamin' and maimin' to themselves."

"But wouldn't it be clearer to say 'white folks' since I mean white folks?"

"'They' is better, sounds less angry—you know, like you accusing somebody. Ain't nobody shamed and maimed you, Dusty. You're speaking at Emmanuel Baptist Church, not the Nation of Islam."

I was getting irritated. "Mrs. Mitchell didn't say anything about it."

"Mrs. Mitchell isn't your mama."

I huffed. "Can I just keep going here?"

"I don't know. Can you, Mr. Poet?" Mama smirked.

Yet we created math and blazed a path toward brilliance. Martin said let freedom ring. Aretha told us all to sing r-e-s-p-e-c-t . . .

"What the hell you know 'bout Aretha spelling 'respect,' boy?"

"Mama!"

"Should you even say that in church? This is a church."

"I'm not cussin' or nothin'."

"You better not!"

"Mama, please!"

"Stand up straight, Dusty. Project your voice more."

. . .

*Others may never know my beauty or my wonder, but in my heart
rolling like thunder is a pride I won't ever deny. I'll believe it 'til
the day I die. Saying it so clear and loud: I must always be black
and proud.*

Mama nodded. "When you go up there, address the congregation,
say, 'Giving honor to God and acknowledge Reverend Griffen
and Reverend Mitchell."

"Why I gotta do all that?"

"Stop being so difficult and do it, Dusty. Damn! Stand with your
back straight, look at the audience and project your voice more."

"There's gonna be a microphone, Mama."

"You still need to project your voice, smart-ass. And if you're so
damn black and proud, make us believe it."

My short-sleeved shirt matched my pleated slacks; both were lilac. Mama liked to color-coordinate our clothes for church, something she did when we were babies. We were extensions of her
after all. Even our initials, R.D.O, matched her name, Royce Dianne Ollison. Dusa was Roycelyn Dannette; I, Rashod Dustin;
and Reagan Danielle. Dusa's last name was the only exception.
Mama and Dusa's father were long done with each other before
Dusa was born, and Daddy never officially adopted her. So Dusa
wore Mama's maiden name: Smith.

The morning I read my poem, "To Be Black and Proud," in
church, Mama laid out our clothes. My lilac complemented her
royal-purple skirt suit and rose-pink blouse, which matched the
color of Reagan's jacket and pleated skirt. On the ride to church,
I looked out of the window, my folder and Bible in my lap.

"You in deep thought or somethin'?" Mama asked.

"No."

"Must be nervous," Reagan said from the backseat.

"I'm not, since you know so much."

"Whatever."

"Yeah, whatever."

"Hope you get up there and mess up."

"Shut up!"

"Hey, both of y'all shut up," Mama said. "Don't start with that this mornin'."

"She always got something to say." I sulked, wanting to open the car door and hurl myself out onto the street. Yes, I was nervous, and I guess I was doing a terrible job at hiding it.

"Dusty, get yourself together," Mama said.

My nerves didn't settle much as we entered the church and were handed programs. There was my name. I'd go up in front of the congregation after the morning announcements were read.

Mrs. Mitchell spotted me as she entered the sanctuary, her choir robe draped over her arm. I was about to sit in the fourth center pew but remained standing when I saw Mrs. Mitchell beam her radiant smile and make her way over to me.

"Good morning, Rashod."

"Mornin,' Mrs. Mitchell."

"You look so handsome in your purple. Love that."

"Thank you."

"You bring your poem? You see your name in the program, didn't you?"

"Yes, I saw it. I have it here." I held the black folder aloft.

"Good, good! I know you're gonna do well."

"I'm really kinda nervous."

Mrs. Mitchell rubbed my arm. "Oh, sugar, don't be. You'll be fine. Didn't I tell you that you'll be fine?"

Mrs. Griffen started playing the opening chords to a hymn, a signal that service was about to begin.

"Oh! I better get this robe on," Mrs. Mitchell said, rushing away.

Sunlight streamed through the tall stained glass windows, cutting across the maroon robes of the sopranos in the choir's front row. Congregants filled the pews, the air fragrant with pungent colognes and floral perfumes. Smiles fixed and backs erect, women were queens in their down-home crowns, elaborate angular hats—some punctuated with glittery blossoms. Deacons looked serious and proud, distinguished in dark suits.

Pastor Griffen stepped into the pulpit, trailed by Reverend Mitchell. After he greeted the congregation and opened with scripture, he asked that we remain standing.

"For this is a day that the Lord has made," he said, his baritone soothing and affirming.

Dignified "amens" rippled through the congregation.

"Let us rejoice," Reverend Griffen said with a pause, letting the command hang in the air for a moment, to which a few sisters answered with "Yes, Lord!"

"Let us rejoice and be glad in it."

The church sang "This Is the Day That the Lord Has Made." I sat behind Mama. Reagan sat in the pew across from me with her friend Tamara, a boisterous girl who looked much older than she was.

After Miss Hill, a petite junior high school teacher, read the morning announcements and various cards sent to the church, it was my turn to go up to the microphone.

A mix of soft and robust "amens" trailed me as I made my way to the front. I stood before the congregation, just below the pulpit and near the choir stand, and placed my folder on the podium. I looked at Mama whose eyes quickly swept the stained glass windows to her right then fell to her lap. She seemed nervous, which strangely made me calm. At the back of the church floating against the wall, Daddy stood holding a cigarette. He brought it to his lips before dissipating like a mist.

I cleared my throat.

"Giving honor to God," I said, taken aback a little by my newly deepened voice booming through the sanctuary. "Uh, giving honor to God, Pastor Griffen, and Reverend Mitchell. I'm going to read a poem I wrote, uh, it's called 'To Be Black and Proud.'"

Brother Cyrus said loudly, "Amen, young brother," from his corner seat in the second pew. Chuckles rippled through the congregation, and I felt myself smiling.

As I read the poem, a warm sensation, almost erotic it felt so good, radiated through me and I felt taller. My back straightened.

These folks, the proud Negroes of Emmanuel, were listening to me—and responding.

When I remembered to look up from the page, I saw sisters nodding in their wide-brimmed hats. The men smiled. I heard Pastor Griffen behind laugh and say, "Amen, now," when I got to the r-e-s-p-e-c-t line.

Others may never know my beauty or my wonder,
but in my heart rolling like thunder is a pride I won't ever deny.
I'll believe it 'til the day I die. Saying it so clear and loud:
I must always be black and proud.

"Thank you," I said. And the congregation clapped. As I walked back to my seat, Mama's arms were folded as she slowly nodded as if to say, "Good job, good job."

After church was over, congregants filed by Pastor Griffen and greeted him with wide smiles and throaty laughs. I stopped at the door.

"Brother Rashod."

"Hey, Pastor Griffen."

He held out his broad hand. I gripped it.

"That poem was wonderful, young man. You have a gift."

"Thank you."

His grip tightened.

"Firmer, son."

I squeezed his hand.

"Look me in the eye, son."

I looked up and smiled.

"Let them know who you are."

Mama talked of Sylvan Hills as though it were an exclusive private school. The name suggested a lush campus crawling with rich kids in designer gear from head to toe.

The year I entered the seventh grade and junior high school, she signed me up for the M to M Transfer, an acronym for Minority to Majority. In other words, it was a busing program for black kids in central Little Rock. Instead of attending the schools nearby, several of which had problems with violence and student truancy, kids in M to M Transfer were bused some twenty-five to thirty miles away to schools out in the 'burbs. I was assigned Sylvan Hills Junior High in Sherwood, a comfortable suburb just outside of North Little Rock.

"Yeah, girl, Dusty gonna be goin' out to Sylvan Hills," Mama said on the phone to one of her friends. "They don't even have a free-lunch program out there. Ain't that somethin'?"

She was bragging, but I was worried. If it were true that Sylvan Hills had no free-lunch program, I was going to starve to death depending on Mama for lunch money every day. She was forever squeezing a nickel 'til the eagle grinned, as the blues song said. Ask Mama for a dollar to get a pack of Jackson lemon cookies at the corner store or for an orange push-up pop from the ice cream man and you'd get cussed out.

A dollar? Are you serious? I ain't got no dollar. I gotta pay the light bill and buy your ass some new pants. Look at 'em, already floodin' 'round the ankles, lookin' like you live in the lowlands or somethin'. You don't need no cookies anyhow. You clean that kitchen up?

As the beginning of school drew near, my sleep became more fragmented and I could get no rest. I was worried about being ostracized for what some deemed effeminate behavior. Even with the protection of the matronly teachers at Fair Park, there was the occasional whispered insult: "Rashod, he acts like a girl."

I ignored it. If they had to whisper it behind my back—and I heard everything—I figured they must have been intimidated. My name was always on the honor roll, printed in a bold font, all caps, on the bulletin board near the principal's office. For a school that was predominantly black, the honor roll list was overwhelmingly white, dominated by the kids I sat among in TAG classes. I was one of few black males on the list; some semesters I was the only one.

With teachers often calling on me and praising my poems, which they occasionally let me read aloud in class, I figured the nappy heads around me were jealous. I began to think my bookishness and smarts were a good defense, a protective shield from the quick-tempered boys and razor-tongued girls. School for them seemed like a holding pen; for me it was a haven.

When I wasn't called a "girl" or a "faggot," they whispered, "Rashod think he white." In my prepubescent mind, I reasoned that to rise above them, cruel folks who looked as though they could have been my cousins, I had to posture behind my smarts, continue to seek refuge there, all of which was validated by teachers who acted like church mothers, who patted my shoulder and said, "Good job, Rashod, keep it up," who told me, "Don't pay those kids any attention. You are a brilliant young man. They're gonna read about you one day."

Those teachers at Fair Park provided a soul validation that Mama was too busy or unable to give. As long as my immediate needs were met, and they were, she seemed to consider her job done. And there would be no moping around Mama about having no friends.

Well, you have to be a friend to have a friend, Dusty.

But I try to make friends and speak and all that, and they still talk 'bout me.

Folks gon' always talk about you, Dusty, so you better get used to that.

I don't have no friends.

Any friends, Mr. Poet. And, look, people gonna either accept you or reject you, and you don't have anything to do with either choice. If they talked about Jesus, what makes you so special? Now, did you put those towels in the dryer? Make sure they get real dry; can't stand damp towels. And be a friend to that trash can and take it to the curb.

That was Mama's way. She was very annoyed or irritated whenever we went to her seeking emotional comfort. We received the same curtness when we were sick.

"Dusty, how many times do I have to tell you to put on an undershirt? Go lay down. Let me see what medicine I got in here."

And I'd drag myself to the bedroom and pull the sheets over my head, wanting to disappear. Wavers in our self-esteem or any illness enraged her. Between maintaining a semblance of a comfortable life and meeting our essential needs, she just didn't have energy for anything else. Self-doubt, anxiety, depression, a cold, the flu, diarrhea—those were evils to fight and kill immediately. She needed us to be like her: indomitable towers of persistence and responsibility. She had no sugar-dusted words of encouragement, no open arms to enfold you. Any abrasions on the heart you had better pray away or seek an outlet that wouldn't get you killed.

Fair Park had been a reassuring place for me with Mrs. James, Mrs. Lambert, Mrs. Isom, and other teachers who pushed and encouraged me. I wasn't sure if I would get that loving support from teachers at Sylvan Hills; didn't know if the teachers were going to look and act like respectable aunts, who often mixed lessons on black figures like Booker T. Washington and George Washington Carver with requisite American history on Abraham Lincoln and Thomas Jefferson. I didn't know what to expect at a school with a name that evoked thick handsome trees and spoiled rich kids. But I knew my cocoon was always a safe place, and inside of it was always music.

Mama bought my new outfit for the first day of school without taking me with her. So my navy-blue slacks, into which she had ironed a crease sharp enough to cut a ham, were too roomy in the waist.

"Mama! These too big."

"No, they're not. By the end of next week, they'll be too tight, the way you're growing. Put on a belt."

My shirt was white with a V-neck collar and navy-blue short sleeves. All of my supplies weighed down the flimsy red backpack Mama had bought, and I knew it would fray and rip by mid-semester.

Reagan was entering the sixth grade and ecstatic about the fact that I would not be at Fair Park with her. While the teachers thought of me as an exceptional student, they didn't quite get why Reagan was just average. She scored well on standardized tests but brought home C's and D's regularly. Being the gruff tomboy she was, she got into fights with boys and girls. Reagan and I reached puberty around the same time. She'd gotten her period in the fourth grade, on a summer day when we had briefly visited Dusa at her place in Hot Springs.

"I feel something wet in my pants," she whispered to me while we watched TV in the living room. Brandi was just crawling then, and she was asleep with Dusa in the next room.

"You pee on yourself? That's nasty."

"It's not pee, though."

Reagan looked scared.

"Tell Dusa."

"She 'sleep."

"Wake her up then."

"You do it."

"Why me? My pants ain't wet."

"Do it, Dusty."

"Reagan, go in there and tell Dusa what's goin' on."

"I'm scared."

"So."

"Come with me."

"Ain't."

"I hate you."

"Hate you too."

Reagan tiptoed into Dusa's room and woke her up. Early in her pregnancy with Frank Jr., Dusa got up and went to the store to buy Reagan a box of sanitary napkins. When she returned, she and Reagan went into the bathroom and stayed in there for a while. When Reagan came back to the living room, showered and in a roomy pair of Dusa's pajama bottoms and a T-shirt, I asked what the deal was.

"I got my period," Reagan said, looking a bit confused.

"Your period? Did it hurt?"

"No. Dusa said it means I can have babies now."

I was shocked. "You want babies now?"

"No, dumb ass. Ain't nobody tryin' to be like Dusa."

On Reagan's first day at Fair Park without me, her style was much hipper than mine. Mama let her wear a bouncy clip-on ponytail, tight black pants, and a tight white T-shirt. She wore shiny patent-leather lace-up shoes with thick soles, the kind popularized by MC Hammer. She wore round glasses, nonprescription, with a flip-top shade, a cheap version of the ones worn by Kadeem Hardison's character Dwayne Wayne on the TV show *A Different World*.

Reagan was the little fly girl and I was the nerd. That Saturday before, Mama had dropped me off at the Barrow Road barbershop to get my hair cut—close to the scalp with what she called a "respectable preacher boy part" on the side. I hated it.

Reagan was also ecstatic about the idea of catching the bus alone. We often got into fights at the bus stop. But because she had to be at her stop, which was just around the corner, about an hour before I was due at mine, Mama insisted that I still walk with her and wait until the bus came.

For some reason on the first day of school—a mix-up with the routing or something, I'm not sure—I had to catch the bus way over on Lehigh Street, about three long blocks west of Tanya and at the bottom of a steep hill that, of course, I'd have to climb in the blazing Arkansas sun on my way back home.

That morning, it was already hot as I stood on the shady side of the street facing the stop sign. I waited with a girl who must've lived in the banana-yellow Colonial just two doors down, because I saw her leave the steps when I walked up to the stop.

I could tell she was older, maybe in high school. She had an asymmetrical haircut, short on one side, long on the other, like the style Salt-N-Pepa wore. And her lipstick was Kool-Aid red. Her skin was a smooth nutmeg brown; she was pretty, with the sullen attitudinal face that was common among girls in Little Rock.

She gave me a half-smirk, half-smile before dropping her backpack and purse on the ground near the stop sign. As she stood directly across the street from me, she put her hand on her hip and leaned back, stretching, her belly protruding under her billowy, sky-blue top. She looked to be about four or five months pregnant.

I didn't mean to stare. When she noticed, she cocked an eyebrow.

"Can I help you?"

I averted my eyes and said nothing.

"What's your name?" Her tone was still edgy but a touch friendly.

"Rashod."

"What grade you in?"

"Seventh."

She rolled her eyes and waved her hand as if shooing away fly. "Just a baby."

"What grade you in?"

"I'm a senior, be graduating this year. Will be so glad. What school you going to?"

"Sylvan Hills."

"Oh, the junior high."

"Yeah. What's your name?"

"Erica."

"You pregnant?"

Erica chuckled and shook her head. "Boy, you sure are smart. No, I'm pregnant."

"I just asked."

"It's cool. I mean, you just a baby yo'self, prob'ly don't even know where babies even come from."

She reminded me of Dusa's friends back in Hot Springs, girls who rushed into womanhood. They were awkward, strutting around in a grown woman's mask, affecting the mannerisms of blues women around the neighborhood who had been there and done that; women who weren't necessarily wise, just hardened by a chain of fools, a culmination of shitty decisions that led them time and time again down roads full of potholes and detours they often willfully ignored.

Their natural beauty had been obscured by and eventually faded under such a mask, this devil-may-care, ain't-no-big-thang attitude. But underneath all of that was still the honey-sweet girl who peeked out every now and then, the pink-bows-and-lace girl who wanted Daddy or anybody to validate her prettiness. Oftentimes, though, that meant opening her legs to a half-witted knucklehead or a jive pimp wannabe who saw nothing of value, just a hot and waiting thing, something to do.

"Do you know if you havin' a girl or a boy?" I asked.

"I don't know. I think it's a boy. I mean, I'm hoping it's a boy."

She smiled, rubbing her stomach, the honey-sweet girl peeking out.

"Why you hopin' it's a boy?"

"'Cause I don't want no girl," Erica said, frowning. "Girls, bitches—they just too much trouble."

"But you a girl, though," I said, smiling.

Her face dropped as though I had said something offensive. "I ain't no girl."

I was confused. "But you in high school."

"I ain't no girl, though. I'm a young woman 'bout to be a mama, so . . ."

She trailed off and made a visor out of her hand as she peered down the street. "That's the bus."

She grabbed her things. The bus pulled up, and I followed Erica onto it. There were no other passengers. Erica sat near the front and I slid into a seat near the middle. As the bus made its way down Barrow Road and onto the interstate, I figured Erica and I would be the only passengers.

I looked out at the glass buildings bright in sunlight and inhaled the sugar air rushing through the windows as we crossed the bridge into North Little Rock and rode past the Jackson's cookie company.

My mind floated above the morning traffic and the tops of trees and houses in the distance. I heard a mournful saxophone winding through my head that echoed how I felt all of a sudden: alone. It was a soulful moan that transported me back to Garden Street.

My lips parted at the memory of Daddy's defeated-looking shoulders every time he walked away. It was funny how he looked confident entering a room yet seemed broken as he left. I straightened my back against the hard, frog-green seat. I didn't want to look defeated coming or going. The serpentine saxophone lines soared and spiraled, and I heard Reverend Griffen's warm baritone and felt his hand grip mine: "Let them know who you are."

As the saxophone squealed, I saw Mama Teacake's cold, appraising eyes and saw her mouth curl. "He ain't gon' be nothin' but another Raymond," her words darting at me. "That's all. Ain't gon' be nothin' but another Raymond."

Who was he anyway?

Sometimes when relatives talked about him, there was almost a sense of pride, their sly smiles and laughter suggesting a private joke. Uncle Henry, Aunt Nita's husband, used to run around with Daddy, smoking weed and riding on Henry's motorcycle soon after Mama and Daddy were married.

Raymond, man, that nigga was a trip. Funny as all get-out. A shame him and Dianne didn't make it. You know, but your daddy, he didn't give a fuck. I mean, ain't that the way to live? Just do yo' thang, don't give a shit about what another nigga think? That was Raymond.

But, you know, there is a thang called consequences. Raymond, man, he was makin' all that money down at Reynolds. Dianne over there, with the lights off and shit, while Raymond laid up with some bitch somewhere. Y'all was babies then; don't have no memory of that.

And then them Ollisons—Old Lady Ollison and Mr. Ollison would go get Raymond out of one thing or the next. He'd run out on Dianne. They didn't go see whether she had enough food for y'all or if the lights was on. They'd go get him out of jail or drag him outta some juke joint or outta some bitch's house, and he'd go over there to East Section Line, back home to his mama and daddy and stay there for days. Guess he didn't wanna go home to Dianne and y'all, while she over there tryin' to make ends meet. You and Reagan was in diapers. Then she had Dusa over there, who was just a baby herself, really. Ain't that somethin'? Married but strugglin' by yo'self anyhow.

See, me and Raymond, we used to sit up, smoke weed, listen to Bobby Womack or whoever, hang out. But after me and Nita had the kids, you know, I had to stop all that runnin' 'round, be a man, and get a stable job. Had to handle my responsibilities, so I stopped hangin' out and smokin' and shit with Raymond. But, you know, Raymond always took it another further. See, weed wasn't enough. It was liquor, then weed, then he'd do a lit' heroin, whatever he felt like doin,' and the nigga be fucked up. That's the problem with Raymond; he never did grow up.

And a man gotta grow up.

The bus made its way down a narrow two-lane street shaded by trees and veered left. Three blocky red-and-gray brick buildings—the Sylvan Hills educational compound, as it were; the elementary, junior, and high schools—all sat on a hill encircled by trees, hence the name. The bus rode past the elementary school and stopped at the high school.

On her way off the bus, Erica stopped by my seat: "Welcome to junior high. You the next stop."

"Thanks."

She waddled off and I never saw her again after that day. I stepped off in front of the junior high, walking underneath a long, rusty pavilion that led to the open hallways. Most of the school was out in the open with ugly, slightly rusted lockers, blue like a robin's egg.

The halls teemed with noisy teenagers; most towered over me. Some guys, many of the black ones, already had facial hair and lumbered around with regal high-top fades. The black girls' breasts threatened to bust through their tops, their defiant mouths glossed in various shades of red.

Burly and rakish white boys walked around dressed in cowboy boots, dark Wrangler jeans, and rodeo shirts. The white girls sauntered by with big Aqua Netted bangs. Pimple-faced fat kids and pencil-thin short ones. Kids who looked as old as the teachers. And awkward, cherub-faced nerds like me, looking scared.

This was not the school I had imagined, sitting atop a hill with moneyed preppy whites and pristine halls.

My first semester, I was placed in regular classes and was bored out of my mind. The teachers spent less time actually teaching and more time disciplining the hardheaded students, most of whom came from the predominantly black and poor McAlmount community nearby.

When I turned in my papers in English, Mrs. Oliver, a thin brunette, always remarked on how well I wrote.

"Another 'A,' Rashod," she'd say, as though I'd done some kind of magic trick. I sat near the front of each class, always quiet and doodling, sometimes invisible—or so I thought. It didn't take long for the whispers to start. I heard them as I made my way to class.

He a fag, ain't he?

He walk like a fag.

Look at how he carry his books.

I avoided eye contact and ate alone at lunch.

"School is like your job," Mama told me once. "You go and do your job and you come right on home. You don't live there."

I remembered that whenever I was in the courtyard in between classes. Keep focused; concentrate on your work. Fortunately for me, I was able to sit in the library during lunchtime, like I did at Fair Park. The one at Sylvan Hills was much bigger, but it wasn't as brightly lit and had few windows.

Often, others like me were in there, too—loners afraid of the loud courtyard, outcasts who much preferred the imaginative escape of books to the cold appraisal and rejection of classmates.

There, we understood each other without saying a word. We didn't make eye contact. But we seemed to feel comforted knowing that other scared and awkward souls were nearby doing the same thing, trying to disappear into a book.

If I wasn't doing my homework during the lunch period, I flipped through the magazines and perused the shelves. Low on a shelf one day, I found a small, thick book with a white cover and an illustration of four black birds flying toward the sun, broken chains around their tail feathers: *The Black Poets*, an anthology edited by Dudley Randall.

The volume was new; the spine hadn't even been cracked. Flipping through it, I caught a whiff of that woodsy paper smell I always loved. I was pulled into some of the most beautiful language I'd read—poems by Claude McKay, Countee Cullen, Sterling Brown, Langston Hughes, my favorite, and others. I checked that book out multiple times and savored the words and the rhythms. Although I barely understood the meanings of many of the poems, I absorbed the music on the pages.

When I made straight A's my first semester, I was called to the guidance counselor's office, where I was given a test for advance placement for the next semester.

"I'm not sure why you were put there in the first place—and for this long," my guidance counselor said, looking genuinely shocked. She was an older white woman whom I saw only that one time when I had to take the advance placement test.

She carried herself with a dignified, entitled air and wore a large diamond ring. I was fixated on her delicate hands as she turned the pages in my folder, her long, manicured nails red as valentines.

"You are an exceptional young man, Rashod," she said, a smile creeping across her face. "And straight A's. I'm so pleased."

Mama was, too—so much so that she insisted I take a copy of my report card on one of our weekend trips to Malvern so that I could show Mama Teacake.

"Why? She could care less," I said.

"Don't be like that, Dusty. She does care," Mama said. "She might even give you some money."

"She's so not gonna do that."

"She might. Mama knows how important getting an education is."

Who in the hell was she talking about?

This was the same woman who read mostly tabloids and believed every word, including ridiculous stories about Elvis returning on a spaceship, or a woman having a cocker spaniel's baby.

It irritated me whenever she talked about Mama Teacake as though she were a warm, loving, crocheting, biscuit-making, cake-baking Sadie figure who doted on her grandkids. She was none of that, especially to me. I'd hear her on the phone telling her friends about Mama Teacake, attributing wise, elegant quotes to her that I knew damn well the bootlegger on Happy Street in Malvern would never say.

I could only guess this was Mama's way of mentally refashioning the woman who, in an argument with her live-in boyfriend, pulled a gun out in front of four girls—her girls—and carelessly, stupidly shot one in the neck.

Maybe talking about her in such an endearing way made her forget about the nights she cried for her grandmother, Miss Elesta, who smelled of Jergens lotion and turned ordinary dinners into classy affairs, the one who loved her creamy skin and outfitted her in dainty dresses and lace-trimmed skirts as though she were a living doll.

Perhaps talking about her blues-loving, bootleg liquor–peddling, pistol-packing mother in such a precious way made her forget about Mama Teacake's eyes cutting her down when she returned from Henderson State University before the end of her freshman year. She had dropped out and moved back home to Third Street to await the birth of Dusa, having hidden the pregnancy with girdles until she no longer could.

Maybe never speaking ill of Mama Teacake despite the woman's meanness made her feel a love that probably didn't exist. Or maybe it did exist: a cold love, a no-bullshit love, a love redolent of vinegar without the slightest hint of sweetness. Whatever kind of love it was, and however it came, Mama took it. Always.

Mama Teacake was tolerable only after she'd had a taste of Seagram's VO, which mellowed her out somewhat.

But if brown liquor didn't warm her up, Mama Teacake stayed cold. It seemed as though she only tolerated her eldest daughter.

Maybe in her own way, she loved her but didn't seem to like her all that much.

Her manner was often abrupt.

I don't know, Dianne. Shit, why you asking me?

And she was critical, stingingly so.

Look at yo' ass, Dianne. Good God! I can't get that much meat in my deep freezer. How you s'posed to get a daddy fa them kids and yo' ass is big as Texas?

Mama would say nothing. Her eyes would become vacant as she looked off in the distance, or she'd furrow her eyebrows as she leafed through a *Jet* magazine. Ever the thoughtful daughter, she sometimes brought Mama Teacake small gifts—cassettes of Al Green's or B. B. King's greatest hits, a pair of slippers or a floral cotton housedress—and all she got was a barely audible "thank you," if that.

Still, Mama insisted that my permanently scowling grandmother, who'd never had anything remotely cheerful to say to me, would be absolutely delighted by my report card.

"Do you always have to be so damn pessimistic, Dusty?"

"Your mama does not like me."

"Hey, that's my mama you're talkin' about."

"That's what I said."

"I don't like how you said 'your mama,' with all that damn attitude. That's your grandmother."

"And?"

"That's enough, Dusty. Bring your ass and that report card."

When we got to Malvern, Mama Teacake was seated in her usual place at the head of the kitchen table, peeling potatoes. She looked up over her glasses at us and muttered a dry hello.

Reagan and I sat in the living room after we spoke, where Ollie was in his easy chair, halfway drunk on an early Saturday afternoon and watching TV. Aunt Kay, who lived across the street, was cleaning. She turned away from dusting a side table.

"Hey there, Dusty and Reagan."

Sassy and down to earth, Kay was a bright spot. And she was helpful, acting as Mama Teacake's personal maid sometimes. She'd clean her own house then cross the street to clean her mother's. The only time anything close to a smile registered across Ollie's face was when Kay sashayed through the room.

Mama Teacake knew this and maybe she was jealous. When company was around—and Mama Teacake loved an audience—she'd often say something snide or downright mean about Kay, making sure Ollie heard every word.

It was usually something about her on-again, off-again drug habit. "Uh-huh, they say Kay goin' 'round here smokin' that crack," Mama Teacake said once during a family barbecue that Kay didn't attend. "She's a rock star without a guitar."

Ollie turned away, grimaced into his cup of whiskey, and took a swig. Such comments stung him into silence as Mama Teacake rolled her eyes.

If Kay were smoking crack, you never knew it by her appearance. She was fastidious about how she carried herself and proud of her petite, shapely figure. Her hair was always neat, her hands beautifully manicured. I stared at them as she made circles with a gray rag around the black bubble base of one of the lamps in the living room, rubbing it as though a genie would escape.

"What you lookin' at, Dusty? You wanna help?"

I chuckled. "No."

"Well, the way you sittin' there starin' it looks like you wanna help."

Mama, who was seated at the kitchen table opposite her mother, shouted from her seat. "Hey, Kay, girl. I thought I heard you in there."

"Hey, Dianne. What you know good?"

"Girl, nothin'. You know Dusty got straight A's."

Kay, who was bent over arranging the *Jet* magazines on the coffee table, shot up dramatically and put her hands on her hips. "Is that right, Dusty?"

I blushed.

"Go 'head then! Reagan, what you get?"

Reagan, who was sitting on the couch with me, smirked. "Not straight A's."

Kay laughed. "Girl, I know that's right."

"Dusty, you bring your report card in here?" Mama shouted.

"No, I didn't."

"Well, go get it out the car and bring it in here so Mama can see it."

I sighed and went out to the car. I returned through the side door that opened to the kitchen, report card in hand. Standing at the stove stirring greens, Mama Teacake put the lid on and wiped her hands on the ever-present towel slung over her shoulder.

I handed her the report card, which she held low and away, the better to read it through her bifocals.

"Hmph!" she said, handing it back to me.

"They gon' put him in all advance classes," Mama said, a smile in her voice.

Mama Teacake returned to her place at the table. "Advance classes? Is that for niggas that think they shit don't stink?"

"The classes where they put, you know, smart kids," Mama said.

Mama Teacake glanced at me as I stood near the stove holding my report card, not knowing how to feel. "I guess you s'posed to be smart, huh?"

I straightened my back. "I am. Got the grades to prove it."

Mama Teacake frowned. "Oh. Is that right? Ya daddy never was that smart in school. Shit, didn't he flunk a grade and ended up graduatin' with Stella? Graduatin' with his little sister. He damn sho wasn't smart."

I looked at the round red clock hanging high on the wood-paneled wall, the hands frozen at 3:15 because the batteries in it were dead. I wanted to be as still as the clock and suddenly crumble into a pile of dust as my report card settled on top of what used to be me.

"I'm not my daddy, though," I said, lips tightening. "Did you see his name on my report card?"

"Dusty, watch your mouth," Mama said.

"Don't tell him nothin'," Mama Teacake said, picking up a knife with one hand and a potato in the other. "Just 'cause he got straight A's don't make him all that smart. Keep sassin' me and he'll get peeled like this here potato."

I turned to Mama, whose manner had noticeably cooled. "Go'n, Dusty," she said, picking up a section of the newspaper nearby. "Put the report card back in the car."

They stared and stared—not in that passive way that white kids did at schools in Hot Springs, a kind of extended glance then a quick turn of the head once my gaze met theirs. These kids stared at me as though they could see every muscle, bone, and vein in my body. I stared back determined to see through them, too.

"This is Rashod, everyone," Mrs. Baugh said. She was a blond woman with a feathered hairstyle that was dated in the early nineties. A Southern drawl thickened her sentences, and a no-nonsense edge kindled in her voice. "Y'all make him feel welcomed."

Then she turned to me and flashed a quick smile. "Welcome, Rashod."

The twenty white students and I sat at desks inside a trailer in the middle of campus. I passed it every day on my way to class and never paid much attention to it or to the white students filing out of it.

Well, that's not entirely true.

I would from time to time notice the students streaming in and out of the trailer. They weren't like the dingy yokels or rough ghetto kids who yelled, fought, and lumbered through the hallways. You could tell they were from solidly middle-class homes, with their erect posture and name-brand clothes. They looked clean and sat with one another at lunch and were never loud and obnoxious. I'd spot them in the crowded hallways, then they'd disappear. But when I passed the mysterious trailer in the middle of campus, which had no windows, I'd sometimes see those same pristine kids walking calmly in and out.

When I was moved to advance classes, I was assigned a Talented and Gifted coordinator, Mrs. Baugh, whose trailer we reported to twice a day—first thing in the morning and later in the afternoon. In the sparsely decorated room, we worked on artsy projects and assignments from other classes, and we talked about current events, like the Gulf War, to which I paid no attention.

After hearing tales of how Vietnam had warped Daddy and knowing only the soul-depleted time bomb of a man who had returned, I figured the only purpose of any war was to destroy lives. So I pursed my lips at the tales the TAG students shared about parents who were deployed or how proud they were to be Americans.

It took a while for me to open up in these classes, surrounded by white kids with preppy clothes and conservative views about the government. They stared at me. I stared at them. They didn't speak to me for a long time. I didn't speak to them. Strangely, I felt right at home.

But the teachers took to me, writing encouraging marginal notes on my papers. I enjoyed the advanced English classes, where we read and had lively discussions about *To Kill a Mockingbird*, *Animal Farm*, and *Great Expectations*. My eighth-grade English teacher, Mrs. Carpenter, was like a white version of Mrs. Lambert at Fair Park—a large, matronly woman who didn't wear makeup, seemed older than what she was, and had a quiet but affirming way about her.

During the spring semester, she assigned a research paper focused on an author of our choice. The only black boy in the class, I was the only one who chose a black writer: Nikki Giovanni. I got an A, one of the few Mrs. Carpenter gave in the class. "Impressive," she wrote in the margins in red ink.

Toward the end of class on the Friday before winter break, she called me to her desk and explained that she was taking a course in African American literature.

"I have a few books here I think you'd like, Rashod."

There on her desk was a small stack of paperbacks: a slim short-story collection by Alice Walker, *The Women of Brewster Place* by Gloria Naylor, and a dog-eared copy of *The Bluest Eye* by Toni Morrison.

"It's not homework," she said, smiling. "But I think you'd like these books."

During the time off I devoured all three, but *The Bluest Eye* left the deepest impression. The story of Pecola Breedlove, a girl nobody validated and who ultimately surrendered to insanity because of a woeful lack of affirming love, wasn't my story. But I was able to engage it—the pain of isolation, of loneliness, of longing for a parent to shine a light your way.

Pecola had no one, and I often felt that I had no one, but music was always a harbor. And there was music in the way Morrison wrote—a prose suffused with a blues impulse, beautiful lines weaving an ugly tale. The oppressive funkiness of the people in the novel's Ohio city reminded me of Happy Street and all the sad-eyed neighbors who streamed in and out of Mama Teacake's. What she sold helped them get from day to day—a fifth of brown liquor in which to down their sorrows and fried pork skins drenched with her homemade barbecue sauce, among the many salty and fatty foods that pacified them.

After reading *The Bluest Eye*, I knew what I was going to do one day: tell stories. In the meantime, I continued writing poems and reciting them in front of the dignified congregation at Emmanuel Baptist. But after running into Mrs. Lambert while out with Mama one afternoon, it wasn't long before I started reciting my poems in other places.

Reagan was getting her hair braided, which took hours at the beautician's house. Mama and I went out to pick up a few things at Mega Market, where I spotted Mrs. Lambert, who looked younger and refreshingly less stately in a powder-blue windbreaker and sneakers.

"Mama, that's Mrs. Lambert," I said, waving at her. "Mrs. Lambert!"

"Dusty, stop yellin' in this store."

Mrs. Lambert turned her head, saw me waving like a maniac, and smiled. She pushed her cart down the aisle.

"Rashod! And how are you?" she said, beaming.

I hugged her and she returned the embrace. "Hi, Mrs. Lambert."

I stepped back. "This my mama."

"Oh, Mrs. Ollison, I remember you came to one of our programs," Mrs. Lambert said. Mama had dropped by a TAG arts and craft show in the conference room of the expansive lobby of St. Vincent Hospital, which was convenient for Mama because she worked there. I remember the excitement that surged through me when she stepped inside the room, beautiful in her white lab coat.

Mama returned Mrs. Lambert's smile. "How are you, Mrs. Lambert?"

"I'm well, thank God." She turned to me. "So you're in the eighth grade now, right? Where are you?"

"Sylvan Hills."

"Way out there?"

Mama interjected. "We did the M to M Transfer program."

Mrs. Lambert nodded. "I see. Are you still writing, Rashod?"

"Yes."

"Yes, ma'am," Mama said.

I mumbled, "Yes, ma'am."

"That's good to hear. That's your gift. You know, it's a good thing I ran into you, Mrs. Ollison, there's a woman, a nice sister at Southwest Branch Library—"

"Over off Baseline, right?" Mama asked.

"Yes. She puts together this Black History Month program at the library, very nice. She has poets and speakers. I still have some of Rashod's poems he wrote in my class. I can tell Melrita—Melrita Bonner is her name—about Rashod."

Mama glanced at me and smiled. "You know, he's been reading his poems at church."

"Is that right? Which church do you attend?"

"Emmanuel Baptist, where attorney Wendell Griffen is pastor," Mama said, sounding as though she'd rehearsed that line dozens of times.

"Oh, over on Twelfth Street?"

"Yes, very good church."

"Uh-huh. Well, Melrita's program is a few weeks away. In fact . . ." Mrs. Lambert grabbed her purse out of the cart and fidgeted around inside for a pen. "You mind if I get your number, Mrs. Ollison, so that I can call you with more of the details?"

I felt myself smiling; my favorite teacher was being so friendly with Mama, who gave her our phone number, which Mrs. Lambert scribbled on the back of a card she stuck back inside her wallet.

"Good. I will give you a call this week after I see Melrita and give you all the details. This will be so good for Rashod. We need to see more of our young boys reading and writing and encouraging their gifts, you know, especially with all this gang violence going on. Seems like every time you turn on the TV, there's some black child getting shot in these streets."

Mama nodded. "I know."

"Well," Mrs. Lambert smiled at me and rubbed my shoulder. "Rashod was always one of my good students. You keep writing."

"I will."

Mrs. Lambert waved an elegant hand at Mama. "It was nice seeing you again, Mrs. Ollison, and I'll be calling you about Melrita's program."

"Thank you," Mama said. "Good seeing you, too."

As Mrs. Lambert pushed her cart away from us, I beamed. "Can I do this program?"

"I don't know," Mama said. "Can you?"

"May I?"

"Don't get to worryin' me before Mrs. Lambert can even tell us when it is."

Mrs. Lambert called a few evenings later as promised. She gave Mama Mrs. Bonner's number. "Here, Dusty, you call this woman and introduce yourself. And remember your manners."

Mrs. Bonner's voice was a warm earthy breeze on the other end. "Edith told me a lot about you," she said. "I can't wait to hear what you have."

Mama made me wear a tie and Reagan a dress, which she absolutely hated. The evening we arrived at the library, I was a bundle of nerves. I had imagined for weeks a standing-room-only crowd, folks lined up waiting to hear my words. I shared this thought with Reagan a few nights before that Friday evening.

"You think it's gonna be a lot of people there?"

"People where?"

"Up in the library."

"Ain't nobody gonna be there. I wouldn't be if Mama wasn't makin' me go. Don't nobody care."

I looked at Reagan's Cleopatra braids and frowned. "Fuck you, Reagan."

"Fuck you, too."

The large meeting room was to the left after we entered through the automated sliding doors of the Southwest Branch Library. We were early. No one had arrived yet. Mrs. Bonner was putting the finishing touches on a book display on one of the tables lining the far-right wall. When she turned her head, the toss of her full thick mane made the gesture seem movie-star dramatic. Her smile was wide.

"The Ollisons, right?" she said, crossing the room to greet us.

"Yes. Mrs. Bonner?" Mama said.

"Yes! Yes! Welcome. Thanks so much for coming. What a beautiful family. And you must be Rashod?"

Before I could answer, she gave me a warm hug. Her scent reminded me of a musky version of the honeysuckle that thickened the air in Big Mama's backyard. "Thanks so much for your participation."

After Mrs. Bonner hugged Reagan and complimented her braids, she breezed back to the table where she'd set up the book display and returned with programs. I was the third one up. Several rows of chairs faced a long conference table, in the center of which stood a portable oak lectern.

Soon, the two other guests on the program arrived—a good-looking bald man in a dark suit who recited Martin Luther King Jr.'s "I Have a Dream" speech, imitating the civil rights martyr's measured, thunderous style; and an older woman with a silver natural who told Negro folktales during which she affected antiquated Southern dialect—lettuce, for instance, became "lettish" as she spun the story of Brer Rabbit.

The audience that arrived by the time the program started was decent, filling about three rows near the middle—nothing like the standing-room-only crowd my ego had imagined. Mrs. Lambert came and sat near the back. I was in the front row with the other participants and felt more encouraged when I noticed her after I made my way to the lectern with my folder of poems. Daddy hovered by the door, the spook he had become, his feet floating off the floor, his eyes smiling at me. The tip of his ever-present cigarette glowed as he took a drag then disappeared.

I tried to remember the points on elocution Mama had told me, to look up here and there from the page and into the eyes of the audience, something I often forgot to do. It made me nervous. "You're not reading to yourself, Dusty," Mama said. And I tried to remember which lines to emphasize. Looking up from the pages, I caught Mrs. Bonner deep in concentration and slowly nodding her head as she listened, her eyes on me. Mrs. Lambert beamed from her seat in the back. Mama stared past me, her face intense as though listening carefully, probably to catch something wrong. But her laser gaze fixed on me when I introduced the last poem, a piece I had written in Mrs. Carpenter's class, "The Ballad of Johnnie Mae Fay."

Desolate she stood
And desolate were her children too
She lived an absent and weary life
And pain was all she knew
She developed from the fruit of a flower
But that flower had to die
Her soul has now been emptied; she hangs her head to cry
Life for her has not been easy; in and out of love she keeps falling
And now in the corners of these old backrooms she sits alone
Waiting for her calling.

I received warm applause and Mrs. Bonner concluded the program. Afterward, Mrs. Lambert gave me a hug. Mrs. Bonner thanked me and told me she'd be in touch for other programs. Reagan seemed relieved that it was all over and that she could go and get out of the plain black dress Mama had made her wear. On the ride home, Mama said nothing as we listened to the radio. When we got home and after Mama had returned a phone call, I entered her bedroom to get her appraisal.

"What you think?"

"About what?"

"The program."

Looking at the evening news on the TV near her dresser, Mama adjusted her pillow and pulled the comforter over her legs. She grabbed the remote and turned the volume down. "Who's Johnnie Mae Fay?"

"Huh?"

"That poem you read—" Mama's voice was prickly. "Johnnie Mae Fay, who's that?"

"A character I made up."

"And she's all alone with three desolate kids?"

"Yeah."

"Who were you up there talking about?"

"Uh, Johnnie Mae Fay."

"Is Johnnie Mae Fay supposed to be me?"

"No."

Mama cocked an eyebrow. "Uh-huh."

"Why you think it's about you? You the only woman with three kids?"

"You getting smart?"

"No."

"'Cause if you standing here tryin' to get smart, you won't be readin' no damn poems."

I looked at the carpet and mumbled, "Not everything's about you."

"What?"

I looked at Mama, the hardworking queen in her queen-sized bed. "I said not everything's about you. It's a character."

The air chilled for a moment. Mama grabbed the remote and turned her attention back to the news. I stood there looking at her. After she pressed the volume up, she said without looking in my direction, "I'm done, Dusty. Go'n."

I went across the hall to the room Reagan and I shared, thankful that Reagan was in the den watching TV and I had the space to myself for a moment. I didn't know how to feel. I thought maybe I was supposed to be upset. But then I felt almost giddy. Mama was not Johnnie Mae Fay. The image I had in my mind when I wrote the poem looked more like Aunt Kay than Mama. But she saw herself in my words. And she felt something. I lay back on my bed and stared at the ceiling in the dark, my smile widening.

Mama's middle-class aspirations in comfortable West Little Rock were stifled once again by her perpetual lack of funds. So she came home from work one day and said, "Y'all get to throwin' shit away y'all don't need and start cleaning up."

"We movin'?" Reagan asked.

"What you think?" I said, rolling my eyes.

"Shoot!" Reagan crossed her arms.

"Well, the rent done got too high over here," Mama said, crashing on the couch and kicking off her shoes.

"I like it over here, though," Reagan said, pouting.

"Yeah, I do, too." I pushed my glasses up on the bridge of my nose.

"If y'all got some money to pay this high-ass rent then we can stay. But since neither of you pay for anything around here, well, I guess we'll be moving."

I looked around our family room and at the marigold wallpaper. The duplex on Tanya Street, which had a fenced-in backyard, felt like a roomy house, and we were right on the periphery of Twin Lakes, where respectable blacks with respectable jobs lived, where folks with immaculate yards where robotic Santa Clauses waved during the holidays, where proud Negroes with vivid memories of civil rights marches washed and shined their Cadillacs and Buicks in the driveway on sunny Saturdays.

And for a time, it seemed as though we were one of those middle-class families with extra resources. Mama started entertaining soon after we moved into the impressive brown-brick duplex. She and her good girlfriend Glenda decorated the place with black and gold streamers and balloons for Mama's fortieth birthday party, during which Mama entertained a houseful of her close friends and associates, all of whom got dressed up that September evening in cocktail dresses and heels and buffed loafers and slacks. A DJ stationed himself in the living room and spun all the Motown and Stax hits of Mama's teenage years, and the counters in the kitchen teemed with cakes, pies, fried chicken, cold and warm dips, chips, beer, and liquor. That evening, Reagan and I stayed at Glenda's place with her daughters, Adrian and Winta, over on W. Capitol Street in central Little Rock, where we watched videos on BET and ate Doritos with Rotel dip.

When Mama Teacake turned sixty in March 1991, six months after Mama's fortieth birthday party, we hosted her party on a beautiful Sunday afternoon. Aunt Stephanie and Dusa had come up the day before from Malvern to help cook pots of collard greens, make bowls of potato salad, and bake various pies. Mama bought two ten-pound bags of chicken quarters, which I cut up, fried, and kept warm in the oven while Mama and Reagan went to church that morning. Mama Teacake, Ollie, Aunt Stephanie and her husband, Jerry, and several cousins filled the house as we all ate, laughed, and talked shit aplenty.

A cup or two of Seagram's VO had mellowed Mama Teacake before she'd arrived and she didn't have an acidic word for anyone as she sat on the sky-blue sectional in the living room, wearing the whorish red lipstick she always wore when she got dolled up, and ate a slice of her birthday cake. She even smiled at her ever-dutiful eldest daughter, who floated through the house in pearls and a teal-green dress, her hair in a bun, the elegant hostess.

The family came up for Christmas dinner once—the year Mama bought me a new component stereo set housed in a wood cabinet and Reagan got her own telephone line. Mama made a rum cake in which she'd put too much rum, but Ollie, who had arrived half drunk, loved it, and ate two big slices. Mama later wrapped up the cake, which nobody else ate, and sent it back with Ollie.

Reminiscent of the warm funkiness of Omega Street in Hot Springs, Tanya Street buzzed with music during the summer—the blues booming next door or hip-hop bumping from a car a few doors down. The street had character, and it seemed we were living the comfortable middle-class life Mama always wanted for us.

But I guess I should have figured that the end was near when, during our last year on Tanya Street, Reagan and I came home one afternoon from school and the electricity was off. We looked at each other as if to say, "Damn. This shit again?" I called Mama at work and she said it'd be back on first thing in the morning, that she'd forgotten to send the payment. We did our homework by candlelight in the den until Mama came home that night, looking tired and carrying a big box of pepperoni pizza, which made everything all right. And sure enough, the lights were on the next morning as we got ready for school.

But Mama stopped hosting weekend card parties, and she no longer bought the name-brand grocery items we loved at Mega Market. A box of macaroni with powdered cheese, a can of tuna, and a can of cream of mushroom soup became a quick casserole. Cheap fatty cuts of beef, a generic bag of frozen veggies, a potato or two, and a can of tomatoes became a greasy stew, stretched a few days by adding more water.

And now where were we moving?

"We moving out in Southwest," Mama said.

"What's in Southwest?" Reagan asked.

"Our new address," Mama said with a chuckle.

Southwest Little Rock in the early nineties was hit or miss. Some neighborhoods were rough and shitty, others neat and clean. It was still a mostly working-class part of town, not nearly as pristine or inviting as West Little Rock. But knowing Mama, we weren't going to end up anywhere unsafe. Our bus ride to Sylvan Hills wasn't going to be as long since Southwest was closer to the end of the interstate that took you into North Little Rock and on into Sherwood.

A few weeks later, we moved into a boxy house on Arapaho Trail that sat on the edge of a cul-de-sac. Although there were three small bedrooms—and I was grateful to finally have my own space—the house wasn't bigger than the duplex on Tanya. There was a nice-sized backyard with a privacy fence and the garage had been converted into a den, though the work was incomplete. In the winter, no heat from the house reached the room. So when the weather chilled, we pushed the old Magnavox TV into the small living room. The kitchen was roomy and bright; the bathroom just the opposite, tight and dark. In fact, the entire house seemed dark because of the blueberry-colored walls in the living room and down the hall. Mama dug it because the color matched the living room furniture.

I loved having my own room—even with its ugly wood-paneled walls. Reagan and I didn't fight as much after getting our own spaces. We definitely needed it as we became teenagers and evolved into two very different and often-conflicting personalities. Reagan joined the Drill Team at school, something of a dance-oriented cheerleading squad, and tried to fit in. I delved inward, as I always did, spending my nights adrift in music when I wasn't lost in a book or in my frequent fantasies of flight.

The pain was alive in her voice—careening and simmering, sometimes flat and off-pitch but affecting nonetheless.

Its ugliness was its beauty, evoking images of the urban life she'd known, of cracked concrete and battleship-gray skies. There was a hunger, too, invigorating the yearning lyrics delivered in an alto full of flaws, all buttressed by hard-knocking beats.

Her attitude reflected the armor Reagan and other black girls in the neighborhood and at school wore with pride. She didn't smile and her female fans didn't, either. Mary J. Blige seemed to carry a boulder on her shoulder and her voice conveyed all the heartbreak and frustration of a generation of girls who grew up with a mother's indifference and without a father's loving praises.

Reagan had gotten a cassette of Mary's debut, *What's the 411?*, and played it incessantly around the house, which drove Mama and me crazy. And songs such as "You Remind Me" and "Love No Limit" were inescapable on the radio. Here was a chick, heralded as the "Queen of Hip-Hop Soul," singing of pain and desire as old as human blood. But the age-old cry for love and acceptance was embodied by a woman-child who could have been any of the girls on the block, lips curled in defiance under eyes daring you to love them.

From her videos in constant rotation on BET, Reagan started affecting Mary's flavor. The scowl, which she'd always worn, was beautified by dark-red lipstick that she put on while we waited in the morning for the bus and wiped off before Mama came home. Reagan and the other wannabe fly girls at Sylvan Hill Junior High wore Mary's chameleonic hairdos—asymmetrical cuts, puffy blond ponytails, and bangs that swooped over one eye.

They glowered and stood against lockers and brick walls with books held against high breasts, looking as though they were ready to fight. And indeed they fought—each other, boys, or monsters if they had to. Like Mary, these girls didn't seem to be afraid of anything.

But a closer look, or listen, revealed that they were absolutely afraid, just as Mary was—afraid of not being loved, of not being understood, of being cut down by someone's razor eyes, or someone's actual razor. So they put on their armor and listened to Mary's keloid-scarred tales of betrayal and unrequited love and found an altar at which to pray, just as Mama had done with Aretha. Just as I had done with Daddy's soul records, from which I continued to draw strength and through which I always found a portal for escape, especially as boys started invading my private thoughts.

And the boys were beautiful—not their attitudes but their bodies, the way they sauntered and strutted through the halls; the tall, athletic ones, with broad shoulders and stalk-like legs, distracted me. I had no idea what to do with those feelings, and I had no one with whom I could share them. At thirteen I sensed that it might be true, but at fourteen I had concluded without a doubt what perhaps everyone had known all along: I was a faggot.

And I was deeply disappointed by that.

I had never had much of a connection with other boys and always felt that I was an alien among them. So why was I daydreaming about what it would be like to kiss one or to have one kiss me? I was repulsed by how brutish boys could be. Yet that very thing sent a jolt through me, from the pit of my stomach up through my chest and to my head, quickening my heart rate. What was lying there beneath the brutishness, the rudeness, the aggression? Was there a tender spot? What did it taste like, smell like? What would it feel like to have all that hardness pressed against me, to wrestle it and pin it down into submission, or the other way around?

Such thoughts swirled in my head and threatened to consume me, especially in the summertime when the boys on the block went shirtless, with chests as flat as their backs. The boldness of their skin in the sun—sleek and shining—unsettled me.

I had no interest in sports and that debacle on the basketball court in the fourth grade had sealed it for me: I would not have any male friends. In fact, I didn't have any friends. That first year or two at Sylvan Hills was socially what I had always known, that I existed somewhere in my own universe and that others seemed to have no problem connecting with one another. I wasn't rough around the edges; I was sensitive. I read a lot. I hid inside myself and lived there. Excursions outside of my shell often proved disastrous or too traumatic.

Yet I yearned to be like them. Then I didn't. I wanted to be the center of attention. Then I'd hate myself for even entertaining the thought. I was too awkward, too chunky and bookish. I didn't swagger through life as the other boys did. Even in their awkwardness, they seemed more confident than I ever was, especially those who played sports and had fathers who were active in their lives, which were few, I knew. But they seemed protected in some way.

I was not protected in that way, not by a man. All of my life, the women—Mama, Big Mama, Dusa to a certain extent, Mrs. Wyrick, and the project divas over on Omega Street—were the soldiers and protectors, their love fierce, abiding, mean sometimes but steadfast always. The men were holograms. Many of the other boys around my way weren't protected by men, either. But unlike me, they found, or at least seemed to find, validation in each other—and in their music.

In the early nineties, they found on MTV and BET what they assumed a man was supposed to be: insensitive, menacing, and brooding in oversized clothes. Like the Mary J. Blige disciples, they were afraid, too—of being misunderstood and unloved. And given the gang violence erupting throughout Little Rock, especially in the eastern part of the city where poor blacks had long been concentrated, they were also afraid of the very real possibility of being gunned down.

So as the laconic rhymes of Snoop Dogg flowed over the funk-fortified beats of Dr. Dre, the boys found an altar at which to pray—a music bristling with stories of justified gun violence, glorified tales of divide-and-conquer in the streets, exaggerated and juvenile sexual exploits of the warrior girls around the way who, like them, were in desperate need of a hug.

NWA, Too $hort, Tupac, Biggie Smalls—they all embodied a manhood that didn't necessarily empower or rebuild. If anything, it did the opposite and encouraged in the boys around the way a sense of entitlement that mirrored what I saw in the arrogant preppy white boys who stared at me in TAG classes and the poor disaffected white boys who hung in packs.

Entitled to what, though?

Like the so-called white heroes of American history, the gangsta rappers extolled taking from those whom they deemed weak: I got mine. Fuck you. What you got ain't shit. You ain't shit. For me to stand tall, you, sucka MC, got to live on your knees. I figured that was what Daddy called "blackfaced white supremacy," something I once heard him say during a beer-fueled conversation with one of his running buddies.

Man, black folks don't know shit 'bout themselves

Aw, Raymond, don't go talkin' all that black is where it's at shit, man.

Black is always where it's at. Niggas done forgot that shit, don't respect themselves.

Man . . .

Look at how these youngbloods go 'round with no pride in them-
selves, busy tryin' to be like the white man. White man's water
is wetter; white man's fire is hotter. Let a white man say, "Jump,
nigga!" Nigga be like, "How high deah, boss?"
Raymond, man, you a trip.
Blackfaced white supremacy.
Black what, muthafucka?
Blackfaced white supremacy—when a nigga do the white man's
work and destroy his own people by any means necessary.
We got Malcolm X over here.
You know I'm tellin' the truth, man.
Shut the fuck up and pass me another beer out that cooler.

There were messages in hip-hop that pushed for uplift, extensions
of the "we shall overcome" outlook in the O'Jays, Curtis May-
field, and Staple Singers records Daddy had. Keep ya head, Tupac
said. Public Enemy rapped about the fear of a black planet, but
mostly it was rebellious white boys who bought those cassettes.
Hiding behind their invisible armor, the black boys and girls up
and down the block subscribed to the pain and malice in the hard-
core urban sounds of Mary J. and gangsta rap, music that illuminated the darkness they knew so well.

As for me, I still preferred a more ingratiating place, shep-
herded by a voice steeped in wisdom and experience, nurtured by
a sound born out of the visceral emotionality of sanctified church
singing.

And there were the warm spaces in the music I loved the most,
openings through which I could enter and lay my burdens down.
There, behind the groove and riding on the melody, I was complete and free.

I could be vulnerable because the men were.

Shamelessly, Marvin Gaye pleaded for his distant lover to
come back home, all while remaining regal. Al Green could moan
and squeal about the glory of love with his manhood and pride in-
tact. Like jagged blades cutting through the speakers, the primal
wails of James Brown and Bobby Womack lacerated the soul and

splayed it open. But as the song faded to a close, something inside had been affirmed and, at last, had started to heal.

To fully engage hip-hop, I felt I needed to be a member of an exclusive club, and I'd never belong. I understood the nuances of the music, its angst and its drive, but inside of it I felt neither welcomed nor authenticated.

We were in the drab house with the blueberry walls and drafty, unfinished den for just a year before we moved again during the fall I entered the ninth grade. This time, we were farther out in southwest Little Rock in Deer Meadows, a quiet subdivision of mostly middle-class blacks. It was reminiscent of Twin Lakes but not quite as polished. The rental property we lived in was managed by the second pianist at Emmanuel Baptist, a stylish woman named Becky Finney. Mama had known her mother when we lived in Hot Springs.

The house, like our previous address, sat in a cul-de-sac but was much nicer. A long foyer led into a living room dominated by a stone fireplace. Through the patio doors to the right of the fireplace was a spacious deck and a large backyard shaded by pine trees. A one-car garage. Wall-to-wall sand-colored carpet. Three large bedrooms. Mama had her own bath in her master bedroom, and Reagan and I shared the one across the hall from our rooms. A few doors down, we caught the bus to school, where socially I gradually opened up.

I was becoming more comfortable around my TAG classmates and friendly with a girl named Missy, who had large eyes and an ingratiating smile, which she flashed often. She was in my advanced English and science classes, but her friendliness sometimes felt like an obligation. After all, we were the only black students in class, though Missy seemed more comfortable with the white girls, a few of whom were on Drill Team with her. We talked music sometimes. She was a big Prince fan and didn't understand my fascination with music that her parents listened to. She laughed at my jokes; I laughed at her cluelessness.

Around this time, I was also experimenting with my personal style. Brothers wore natural crowns, high-top fades that reached toward the sky, with lines and zigzags etched on the sides by skilled barbers. Some wore a blond streak in the front, like the rapper Kwame. While gangsta rap had eclipsed the militant "Black CNN" style of Public Enemy and the bohemian black nerd approach of A Tribe Called Quest and De La Soul, an aggressively romanticized Afrocentricity still informed styles around school and in the neighborhood. We wore "It's a Black Thang. You Wouldn't Understand" T-shirts and leather Africa medallions.

Inspired by the poetry I read after lunch in the library and at home holed up in my room—exclamatory works by Amiri Baraka, Haki Madhubuti, Sonia Sanchez, and others—I wanted my look to reflect what I thought was a "real" black consciousness. I grew out my hair and begged Reagan to twist it up so that I could start dreadlocks, but that look lasted only a month or two before Mama made me shave it off. I didn't protest much after my hair started looking like a mass of nappy worms, and I had terrible dandruff. I went to the barber one Saturday and was relieved as the hair fell in clumps around the chair. From the ninth grade on, I wore a bald head, inspired by those iconic Isaac Hayes album covers.

Mama had befriended a seamstress named Daisy, who lived nearby. She was a wonder with a sewing machine and made several dresses and skirt suits for Mama and a dress or two for Reagan. Daisy also made me outfits in African patterns; one in particular was aqua blue and ruby red, a long dashiki with matching pants. I felt regal in it and I was so thankful for Daisy's clothes. She'd saved me from the embarrassment of the jive outfits Mama bought without ever taking me along to try them on. She'd bring home corny sweaters, old man–looking slacks, and lame button-down shirts that never fit—too short, too long, too loose, too tight. I'd bitch and moan and Mama would just wave her hand. "Looks fine to me."

Daisy's Afrocentric getups, which I wore to school and to poetry readings I did at local libraries during Black History Month, clicked with the image I wanted to convey, that I was some regal

Nubian prince, that I communed with the ancestors and shit, and that I deeply believed Daddy's "Black is where it's at" ideology he adopted after returning from Vietnam.

But I couldn't reconcile that image of black militancy, as hollow as it was, with my desire for the same sex, which seemed to become more intense by the day. No set of broad shoulders, strong hands, big feet, full lips, or round ass went unnoticed by my lusty fourteen-year-old eyes.

The historical figures I idolized, Martin Luther King Jr. and Malcolm X chief among them, embodied an idealized sense of strong black manhood, but they were straight. The love poems I absorbed in dog-eared black poetry anthologies were clearly written from a heterosexual point of view. This burning curiosity about other boys, I figured, would pass. Maybe it was because Daddy wasn't around to help me through this phase. Maybe this longing to be affectionate and sexual with other boys was all about missing him. Whatever it was, I didn't know what to do with it, and I told myself that the feelings would all fade away. The dashikis and clumsy Afrocentric rhetoric would disguise the desire, distract me from it, or maybe erase it altogether.

Then he came in spring.

He arrived in the middle of my ninth grade year, a new student wearing a hoodie with black and white horizontal stripes. His high-top fade was a perfect box atop his head, his skin maple syrup brown. He entered first period science class just after the morning announcements and the pledge of allegiance. The teacher introduced him: Andre. He sat in a row over near Missy. So now there were three blacks in class—and another boy. A gorgeous one. I averted eye contact. Part of me was excited to see another black boy in TAG, but another part of me wanted to be sure to avoid him. Black boys were usually the meanest. The white boys in TAG occasionally spoke to me outside of class after they became comfortable with me. It was understood, though, that I wasn't invited to join them at lunch or hang out or anything.

My luck with befriending black boys had always been shoddy. I guess I was off-putting to them with my aloof, quiet ways and disinterest in sports and rowdiness. And I'm sure the fact that my head was always in a book, even on the bus, didn't make me seem like the most hip and happening guy around.

Still, that didn't change my attraction to them. I just admired them from afar and had grown used to being mostly ignored by them, especially as I strolled around in my Afrocentric outfits. They still snickered at me, but at least they stopped whispering "faggot" as I passed through the halls dressed like an extra from the movie *Coming to America*.

"Got any bean pies," some smart-ass would say, a chorus of giggles following.

Later in the week after Andre came to Sylvan Hills, he did something not too many had done before: He sauntered into the cafeteria and plopped down across from me. Missy would occasionally eat with me, but I'd gotten used to eating by myself before heading to the library while everybody else congregated in the courtyard.

"You're in my class," he said, unpacking his lunch.

I looked up at him and was startled by the fact that he took the seat across from me as though he had done it countless times before, and that he was cuter up close than he was from a distance, disarmingly so.

I put on my invisible armor. "Yeah."

His smile was wide, his teeth Colgate-perfect. He looked as though he could have been a token black kid on one of those corny ABC Afterschool Specials.

"I'm Andre." He sounded hopelessly cheery.

"Rashod."

He bit into his sandwich and looked around the room then back at me. "You like it here?"

"It's school. Who likes it at school?"

He chuckled. "That's true, though. You funny."

The armor started to melt. "You like it here?"

"I mean, it's OK."

"Where you come from?"

"We moved from West Memphis."

"Oh."

"What you think about science class?"

"I don't."

"Yeah, it's boring."

"I know."

"Teacher's weird."

"He is."

"Kinda creepy."

"And ugly. He looks like the inside of a frog's ass."

Andre dropped his head on his arm and his shoulders shook as he laughed. When he lifted his head, tears were in his eyes.

"What does that even look like?"

"His face."

Andre cracked up again. When he laughed, he made a high wheezing sound. His raven-dark hair looked soft, his face a camera's dream. I smiled.

Andre and I became fast friends. He was soon transferred to advanced English, where he rarely added anything to the class discussions. After lunch he often joined me in the library, where we talked in low voices, but Mrs. Monk, the librarian, often told us to "quiet down" anyway, because Andre always cracked up at something I said. Sometimes we just sat at the table and read across from one another—my head in a black poetry book, his in a Stephen King novel he'd brought from home.

The rest of Sylvan Hills seemed to disappear. I didn't feel the need to edit myself or police my mannerisms around him. I never noticed a judgmental glance from him. Andre always dressed as though he'd stepped out of the junior section of a JC Penney catalog—his jeans and Polo shirts always crisp. He dug my Afrocentric gear.

"Mama ain't letting me wear anything like that," he said. "But it's cool on you, though."

We talked on the phone almost every night—sometimes doing our homework but often making fun of teachers and classmates. Andre egged me on, asking me what I thought about this person or that one, all so he could crack up at one of my profane zingers. He seemed amused by my gift for cussing, something I'd picked

up early on from hanging with Daddy and his foul-mouthed running buddies. Reagan was also Tabasco-tongued, and the air between us was often hot with profanity when Mama wasn't around.

One Monday night on the phone, Andre invited me over for
the weekend.

"You think your mama will let you catch the bus over after
school Friday? The pool down the street just opened."

"Really? It has been hot as fuck."

Andre snickered. "Boy, you cussin' at home? Yo mama there?"

"Nah, she at work, stay at work."

"You and your sister be home by yourself?"

"Yeah. Who else gon' be here? We can take care of ourselves."

"Oh."

"Right."

"You think your mama will let you come over? My mama said
it was cool. I be tellin' her some of the things you say—without the
cuss words, though. She thinks you sound funny. Oh, if you come
over, you can't cuss."

"I wouldn't cuss in front of your mama, Andre, damn."

He laughed that wheezing laugh. "I don't know, Rashod. You
don't care sometimes."

"Don't give a shit."

He laughed harder. "That's you."

I went into Mama's room the next evening soon after she'd
gotten home from work.

"Mama, can I go over Andre's house this weekend?"

She turned away from *Jeopardy!* on TV. "What?"

"Can I go over Andre's this weekend?"

"Who the hell is Andre?"

"My friend."

She bucked her eyes in mock surprise. "You have friends?"

I chuckled. "Yes, I do."

"I've never known you to have friends, Mr. Poet. You're actually talking to people? What an improvement."

"C'mon, Mama."

"Who's Andre?"

"He's in my science and English classes. We talk on the phone."

"You talk on the phone? To people?"

"Mama, stop playin'."

"I have to speak with Andre's mother first."

"Why?"

"Because I don't know shit about her. You're not going over to somebody else's house to stay and I don't know the people, Dusty. She says it's OK for you to go over there?"

"Andre said she said it was OK."

"Well, Andre isn't his mama, now is he?"

"Do I need to get a permission slip, like it's a field trip or somethin'?"

"Are you getting smart?"

I huffed. "No."

"I need to speak to Andre's mama before you go taking your ass over to that woman's house. And even if she says it's OK, you still not going over there 'til this house is cleaned up."

"The house is cleaned up?"

"Yeah, and your room is cleaned up, and that floor is mopped in that kitchen and in that bathroom, the vacuum run over the floor and down that hall. And do I smell those neck bones you put on? You need to go in there and check on 'em."

Mama spoke briefly to Andre's mother over the phone later in the week, talking in her clipped professional voice, enunciating every word. I was shocked when she gave me twenty dollars for the weekend.

"There's your spending money," she said, tucking the bill into my hand the night before school.

"You won't need this back for a bill or something?"

"Dusty, I think I can spare twenty dollars."

"Just sayin'."

I kept my overnight bag in my locker and caught the bus home with Andre that Friday after school. He lived in Sherwood, not far from Sylvan Hills, in a boxy, brown-brick house that sat on the corner in a quiet neighborhood with immaculate lawns. The house was small inside but tastefully decorated and very clean.

Andre's mother was there when we arrived—a gorgeous woman with the same maple syrup skin Andre had and thick, coal-black hair that rained down her back. She looked as though she could have been Andre's older sister. He had told me once that she'd had him young. Andre's stepfather, a light-skinned man with freckles, arrived soon afterward with Andre's younger sister in tow, a sprightly girl in elementary school with hair like her mother's.

Later that evening, Andre's mother dropped us off at the movies nearby, where we saw Mario Van Peebles in *Posse*, which we didn't like. We crossed the street to McCain Mall and walked around, eating bags of candy and laughing at people.

"Look at the busted bitch over there. That weave looks like a bath rug. Damn."

Andre elbowed me. "Rashod, dude, you loud."

I slept on the pullout bed in Andre's room, which was low to the floor next to his twin bed. Andre rolled over on his side and looked down at me.

"You havin' fun?"

"Yeah."

"I'm glad you came."

"Really?"

"Yeah. You make me laugh."

"Y'all gotta nice house."

"It's OK. Why y'all live way out in southwest?"

"I don't know. Mama moved us out there. Wish we could live out here, though."

"Where's your father? You never talk about him."

"Nothin' to talk about really." My stomach sank a little.

"He still alive?"

"Guess so," I tried to sound nonchalant. "He up in Oregon somewhere."

I glanced around Andre's room, the faint light of the street lamp just outside his window streaming into the darkness. I could make out his cartoon drawings pinned on the walls.

"You miss him?"

"Who?"

"Your daddy."

"Sometimes. I guess. You like your stepdaddy?"

"Craig? He OK. I don't pay attention to him. He stupid."
We chuckled.

"I wanna be a father one day," Andre said.

"You do?"

"Yeah. You want kids?"

"I don't know."

"I can see you with kids, cussin' 'em out."

"I'd kick their ass."

"You remember to bring your swimming trunks?"

"Yeah."

"Do you know how to swim?"

"I told you I didn't. Gonna get out in that water and drown."

Andre chuckled. "I won't let you."

The sun drenched the neighborhood with blinding light as we walked to the pool early that Saturday afternoon. We squinted and made visors with our hands. A white woman and her two children were there when Andre and I arrived. As we set our towels down and took off our shirts, she gathered her things and sweetly told her little blond kids to exit the pool.

I whispered to Andre. "You think she's leavin' because we black?"

He shrugged. "I don't know. Who cares? We got the pool to ourselves then."

Andre dove in and showed off his moves, his lean body graceful under the water. He jumped up and wiped his eyes. "You just gon' sit there?"

I sat on the edge, my feet in the water, trying not to feel too self-conscious about my little potbelly. "I told you I don't know how to swim."

"You have to get in the water to learn."

"This is cool. Do your thing."

"C'mon, Rashod." He flashed his beautiful teeth.

If he had said come to Jupiter, I would have gone. I eased in. Andre waded to the deepest part as I walked out until the water kissed my chest.

"C'mon," Andre said.

"This is far enough."

He grinned and went under. When he came back up, he was standing directly in front of me. "You can back-float, can you?"

"I can what?"

"C'mon." He moved to my side. When his hand touched the middle of my back, I stood straight up and felt myself stiffening in my swimming trunks.

"Lay back," he said.

"I can't."

"Yeah, you can. Fall back. Relax, though."

My feet left the bottom of the pool, and Andre instructed me to kick my legs a little. One of his hands gently pressed my lower back, the other behind my neck. The smell of chlorine filled my nostrils as the water circled my face. I looked up at Andre's smile and loved that it was often there when I was around.

"See there? You floatin'," he said.

"I am? Don't move."

"You won't drown, boy."

Just beyond the wooden fence, birds chirped in the sycamores. I wanted Andre's hands to stay where they were. When I closed my eyes, I could still see the sun.

That Sunday evening as I lay in my own bed in the darkness, I could still see his face.

But I didn't want to feel what I felt—a desire that excited and saddened me all at once. The radio on my mini boombox played low in my headboard bookcase.

"It's the Quiet Storm mix," the DJ purred in his mahogany baritone. "And Minnie Riperton wants to take you inside her love."

She crooned about two people just meeting and barely touching each other. As the strings swelled at the chorus, I surrendered to the song, remembering the hands touching me underwater, imagining the kiss I'd never receive. The music was seductive, heightening the memory and the yearning.

I turned on my stomach and pressed my body against the mattress. I didn't want to feel what I felt, but the feeling wasn't going anywhere as it coursed through every vein and charged every nerve.

I had to set it free.

I kicked off my underwear and moved my hips against the sheet. Burying my face into the pillow, I saw not only his face but others that passed me in the halls at school and on the street.

Images flashed in a steady stream—what their thighs did to dress slacks, the bold beauty of their skin in summer as they strolled and bopped through the neighborhood, their shirts slung over their shoulders, beads of sweat gliding down their backs. The rich funk that trailed them. The beautiful lips that curled around an insult, then the flash of gorgeous teeth. The threat glinting in their eyes; the vulnerability they could never disguise no matter how steely the posture or fearsome the mask. Their hardness pressed against the world was the same hardness I imagined pressed against me.

Do you wanna ride inside my love?

The pressure gathering between me and the sheet, the question sung so sweetly on the radio . . .

Do you wanna ride inside my love?

The invitation I thought I saw in his eyes as he beckoned me into the water, his hands . . . don't move . . . right there . . .

The intense tingling and the gooey wetness all over stomach startled me.

I crept past Mama's room where she snored loudly with the TV on and past Reagan's door, which was closed. I cleaned up in the bathroom and pulled a new sheet from the linen closet. After I changed my bed, I turned off the radio, lay on my side, and stared at the wall. I loved what I felt.

But it scared me, too.

Andre and I were so close that spring that going to school to see him in class and hang out at lunch had become the highlight of my so-called life.

As the school year came to a close, we had planned on hanging out all summer. I had been recommended for the AEGIS (Academic Enrichment for the Gifted/Talented in Summer) program, where kids with various interests in the arts and sciences congregated in remote parts of the state during the early weeks of summer. I was accepted in a creative and performing arts camp in Mena, a town surrounded by the stunning Ouachita National Forest, about three hours from our home in Little Rock. Andre was excited for me.

"This is great, Rashod. You're smart. You deserve to go."

"Why didn't you apply?"

Andre shrugged; he didn't care. His enthusiasm for me, though, made it feel as though the camp was a really big deal. But Mama worried not only about the cost of everything I needed—toiletries, clothes, snacks, spending money—but also because Mena long had a reputation for being hostile toward blacks.

"Don't they still lynch niggas up there?"

"Uh, wasn't that a long time ago, Mama?"

"And?"

"I was accepted, so I don't think I'm gonna get lynched."

"Lord, I hope not."

I shared the news with Mrs. Mitchell at Emmanuel, and in her typical overjoyed way, her face lit up and she flailed her arms. "This is so exciting, Rashod!"

She announced it in church one Sunday morning: "One of our own, Rashod, will be attending an AEGIS program this summer. Look at God!" Mama didn't have to worry much after that. The church gave some money to help defray the costs. While we couldn't depend on relatives in Malvern to help with shit, various members of Emmanuel always stepped in.

In the two weeks or so between the last day of school and when I had to go to Mena, Andre and I had planned to hang out as much as we could. I preferred going to his house. Mama was always reticent about Reagan and I having visitors. Except for

Winta, the youngest daughter of Mama's good friend Glenda, no one was ever allowed to stay over—and Winta only spent the night maybe once or twice.

I had gotten permission to stay at Andre's house the weekend after school let out, but I never heard from him. I called several times and there was no answer. The last time I tried, the phone had been disconnected.

I asked Mama if we could go by the house.

"Drive all the way out there to Sherwood? Hell, no."

"But he hasn't called me back, and the phone is disconnected." I was trying not to sound too worried, but Mama heard it in my voice anyway.

"Oh? Listen at you."

"Well, I was supposed to go over there."

"Uh-huh." She cocked an eyebrow. What did that look mean? "You really trying to go over there, ain't you?"

I huffed and looked away.

"Well, if the phone's turned off, Dusty, seems like the last thing they need is you over there. Sounds like they've fallen on hard times. Lord knows it happens."

Late that Friday night, Andre finally called.

"Where are you?" I heard noise in the background.

The lilt in his voice wasn't the same; he sounded down. "We in West Memphis."

"For the summer?"

"I guess. Mama left Craig. We at my grandma's right now."

"So, what? Y'all not coming back to Sherwood?"

Andre sighed heavily into the phone. "Probably not."

I had no idea his mother and stepdad were having issues. Andre never said anything. I had noticed how flirty they were with each other when I visited.

"I was waiting for you to come back. You know I go to AEGIS this summer and I thought . . ."

"Yeah, I know, man. That's good."

Someone in the background called Andre's name. "Hey, I gotta go."

"Oh."

"Yeah."

"Well, you, uh . . ." I was trying to suck it up so that my voice wouldn't break. Good thing I was on the phone; he couldn't see the tears. "Have fun down there."

"Yeah. I know you gonna like that camp—sounds like fun, you know. You the smartest dude I know, Rashod." The sunny lilt in his voice momentarily returned.

"Keep drawing, though. I wish I could draw like that."

"Yeah."

The same person in the background called his name again.

"You gotta go."

"Yeah, I do."

"See you later then."

"Have fun next year—and at AEGIS."

"Cool. I will."

"Bye, Rashod. Take care."

"Bye."

I hung up. Reagan peeked into my bedroom where I had taken the phone.

"You off? I wanna use it."

"Yeah." I looked away and wiped my eyes.

"What's wrong with you?"

"Nothin'. Here." I handed her the phone.

"You been cryin'?"

"No. I'm off. Here."

"'Scuse me. Damn, nigga made you cry?"

"Reagan, get the fuck out."

"I'm goin', bitch."

She slammed the door behind her, and I sat on my bed staring at the window, hating that I felt anything.

During my weeks in Mena, Reagan was in Malvern hanging with our cousin Wee Wee, who was her age. A friend from Mama's job, a tall, lanky man whose wide face and stringy mustache reminded me of a catfish, drove us to the quaint town. In the driveway, he greeted me with a poetically ugly grin as he opened the trunk to his clean, sky-blue sedan. I gave him a limp dishrag of a greeting, "Hey," as I started loading my things in the trunk.

"Let me help you, lit' man," he said.

"I got it."

On the way up, I sat in the back reading a short-story anthology as Mama and her friend gossiped about folks at work. We arrived at the camp high in the hills, surrounded by trees that rolled on forever. The tops looked like rows and rows of deeply green Afros. Down the hill from the rambling gray-brick camp house—one side for the boys, the other for the girls—a gorgeous lake made a fanlike shape.

Mama didn't stick around for the orientation like the other parents. She wanted to get back to Little Rock before dark. Soon after her friend and I unpacked the car, she was gone. She stuffed forty dollars into my hand and told me to "be good." No hugs, no kisses—that wasn't Mama's style. I watched the powdery, cinnamon-colored dust on the road rise and fall as she and her friend zoomed out of sight.

Back at the camp house, the place teemed with teens and their parents. I chose a bunk bed near the back of the large room where we boys, about twenty of us, slept and shared the showers and toilets. All white boys. I was used to this. There were about four blacks out of the twenty-five girls.

AEGIS felt like an extended stay at Sylvan Hills, where I didn't easily warm to the other kids. Small groups of us met for sessions in creative writing under the trees. We shared poems and talked about style, all of which I liked. A gawky girl named Sarah had a gift for imagery. She once read a three-part poem about her mother's recent miscarriage that moved some to tears. After reading it, she excused herself from the group. I watched her slim back and the flow of her chestnut hair as she held her head down under a towering oak tree.

I was lonely. I wondered what Andre was doing. I wondered if I was as good as the other young writers at the camp. I shared my poems and character sketches, all written from an irrevocable Afrocentric point of view, which garnered quizzical looks from my peers, most of whom had come from little Arkansas towns where the only black faces they saw were on TV. Our instructor, a birdlike white woman with a tentative energy, nodded every time I shared a piece, squinted, and said, "You're so vivid, just vivid."

By the end of the first week, I was ready to leave. The loneliness became more intense at night as the boys talked and laughed while I lay on my bunk bed, missing my own bed and thinking about how disappointed Mama and the folks at Emmanuel would be if I called and begged to come home.

Mama had told me to be sure to write a letter to Emmanuel to let them know how I was doing and to formally thank the church for the check it had written to send me. At the end of the first week, I wrote a flowery note in which I thanked the church for praying for me, and said that I missed home and that I often felt alone in the rolling Ouachita hills.

"Keep me lifted," I wrote.

Toward the end of the second week at AEGIS, as I had resigned myself to being invisible at camp, eating at the end of a table, and watching others interact, I received a letter. I ripped it open immediately after the resident assistant, a fleshy-faced redhead in his early twenties who smiled at me as though he pitied me, dropped it on my bed. The handwriting was sharp and slanting, the stationery from Hyatt Hotels & Resorts.

July 23, 1992

Hello Rashod,

I hope that you receive this letter in good health and spirit as you continue the wonderful adventure afforded you to participate in the creative writing program. I'm writing from Minneapolis, where I am attending a meeting of federal judges, so I know how being away from home and familiar sights and sounds can tear at the heart. In fact, I have known that experience for quite a while now having experienced my first such trip when I was 8 years old. I still get homesick, believe it or not. And of the several hundred people here I am one of less than 5 Black lawyers. Yes, I know very well how tough it is to be away from home in your situation.

Please let me share some Bible truths that sustain and strengthen me in any way of faith. I do so hoping that you will be strengthened and comforted.

1. *God knows how you feel! Your anxieties, fears, and home-sickness are well-known to Him. Since Adam and Eve had to face the alien world outside the Garden of Eden, God has sustained and guided humanity.*
2. *Your experience is part of God's mission for your life. God's plan for your life includes granting you the insight to write as well as giving you opportunities to grow as a writer and person. As painful as this may seem now, God intends for you to grow as a person and writer in many ways that cannot happen if you never leave home and family. You must accept the challenge of confront-ing homesickness and its load of anxieties as part of the pilgrimage you take with God in faith.*
3. *You can trust God's presence and power in every set-ting—even in Mena! After Moses died, God called Joshua to lead Israel. God's words to Joshua at Joshua 1:1–9 have comforted me many times. At Joshua 1:5–6 God is quoted: "Just as I have been with Moses, I will be with you; I will not fail you or forsake you. Be strong and courageous . . ." And at Joshua 1:9, God said to Joshua: "Have I not commanded you? Be strong and courageous! Do not tremble or be dismayed, for the Lord your God is with you wherever you go." Rashod, you are not alone. You are not abandoned. Trust God's presence and power for strength to grow in this adventure of faith.*

I am convinced that your writing ability and spiritual insight are God-given gifts. I believe that God is using you and those gifts to bless people. I believe that you can not only grow as a person and writer through attending this writer's retreat, but that God will also use you to bless others in the process.

Will you trust God to empower you to receive that growth and to be that blessing?

I will close this letter now before I bore you too much. Before I do, let me thank you for sharing your anxiety and home-sickness with me and with your family at Emmanuel. Let me encourage you to follow Jesus' example at Gethsemane when he prayed and was strengthened.

Trust God's mission. Trust His promise to be present and powerful with you. And expect His loving strength as you continue this adventure in your pilgrimage.

My prayer for you is that God will give you His peace and the assurance of His presence in this experience, and always, and that you will someday recall this experience with great joy! May God strengthen you!

Your pastor and friend,
Wendell L. Griffen
Ephesians 3:20–21

I folded the letter, returned it to the envelope, and felt a wave of comfort, a kind of metaphysical hug. The loneliness melted away right there on the bed as I remembered Reverend Griffen's broad hand tightening around mine in the vestibule at Emmanuel.

Let them know who you are.

For the rest of my time in Mena, I stepped out of my shell and showed that I had a sense of humor. I spoke up more in the writing sessions, freely explaining nuances in my work that the other young writers didn't seem to understand—references to soul lyrics and to famous black writers they'd never heard of. I soon realized I was at a retreat full of introverts, most of us outcasts at school. And we were all serious about wanting to be good writers, which bonded us.

The food at the camp was also great. The main cook, a gregarious, stout white woman, made homemade spaghetti one evening that was better than what Mama had taught me. I went into the kitchen after dinner that night and asked her about the recipe.

She seemed thrilled to know that I cooked. "Tomato paste," she said. "Add tomato paste, dear, and let it simmer."

At the end of my few weeks in Mena, I felt more invigorated about my writing and confident about connecting with my peers. I didn't feel so ostracized the way I did at Sylvan Hills, where the black kids didn't quite know what to make of me and the white ones knew me as the only black boy in TAG who took every opportunity to bring up something about black history and black people. In Mena, we got each other's senses of humor, and I didn't feel the need to rearrange myself, something I could never do very well anyway.

I called Mama the night before she was due to pick me up. "What time you comin'?"

"Huh?"

I became nervous. Whenever Mama answered a question with a delayed "Huh?" I knew I was about to be pissed off.

"What time you comin' to get me, Mama?"

"I was gonna call up there. You can't catch a ride with somebody?"

"Catch a ride?"

"Yeah, can somebody bring you into Little Rock somewhere and I can meet you? I'll pay for the gas."

My stomach roiled. "What's wrong with your car? Where's that man, whoever he was?"

"I'm not puttin' my car on the road that far. I need to get tires."

I huffed—didn't know whether to throw the phone or slump against the wall and cry.

"Dusty?"

"So I'm just left up here, I guess."

"Stop being dramatic. See if you can catch a ride with somebody. Damn! Somebody gotta be comin' this way."

I hated that whenever it seemed I felt secure and could breathe, whenever I got the notion that my life wasn't one big inconvenience, the proverbial rug was pulled and I was right back on my ass, looking up and feeling stupid for thinking that everything was really OK.

"I don't know, Mama. I guess I'll go around this camp and beg these white folks to take me and all my stuff back to Little Rock."

"There's got to be somebody comin' back this way. Who's there?"

"Folks are leaving tonight." My voice was tense.

"You up there crying?"

"I gotta get off the phone. Folks need to use it—and I need to go around camp and beg some good white folks for a ride all the way back to Little Rock. Or, you know, I could just live here in Mena. Hope I don't get lynched."

Mama either missed or chose to ignore my sarcasm. "Call me back and let me know."

"Bye." I hung up, completely pissed with her.

I walked out onto the porch of the camp house, where folks were hugging and saying good-bye in the humid evening air. Martha, a friendly blond who was always nice, stopped to say good-bye and noticed the tears in my eyes.

"Are you OK?"

"I'll be fine."

"You're leaving tonight?"

"Not exactly."

Just then, Martha's mother, a smiling woman in shades with a sensible blond bob, sauntered over. She rubbed Martha's shoulder and greeted me with a warm hello.

"Who's your friend?"

"This is Rashod, Mama, a really good writer."

"Oh! Nice to meet you. You're on your way home, too?"

"My mother . . ." My voice broke. I was so embarrassed.

Martha's mother rubbed my arm. "Everything's OK?"

I pulled it together. "My mother can't come get me."

"Where do you live?" Something in the woman's voice was reassuring.

"In Little Rock."

"That's not a problem. We'll take you home, but we'll have to come back in the morning. The car is loaded. I can come back around nine. Just be ready then."

"You don't have to do that, ma'am."

The woman waved her hand. "It's not a problem. We'll get you home."

She patted my arm, Martha waved good-bye, and they were gone.

That night, the room where all the boys had been was empty, save for the resident assistant and me.

"I can't leave until you do," he said, standing over me. "You sure you got a ride home?"

"Yeah, I do."

He flashed his smile of pity, which made me feel even more like a loser, and turned away. When he clicked off the light, I curled up in my bunk in the darkness and tried to forget the knots in my stomach. I thought about floating in cool water under a blinding sun and Andre's assured instructions to "fall back." I thought about Minnie Riperton crooning a seductive invitation, her voice a crystalline elixir, and sleep came at last.

I woke up about an hour before Martha's mama was due at the camp. I was worried that she wouldn't return to pick up a sad-eyed black boy whom she'd met just hours before under the piss-yellow glow of the camp house porch light. I was the only kid left. My things were packed and I was waiting on the porch when Martha and her mom pulled up in a hatchback Volvo at nine on the dot.

During the ride, they talked to each other in cheerful voices about relatives, Martha's friends, and projects at home while I rode silently in the back. A Jimmy Buffett greatest hits cassette played over and over for the nearly three-hour ride, and sometimes Martha and her mom would sing along. As we arrived inside the city limits of Little Rock, I vowed to avoid the corny music of Jimmy Buffett for the rest of my life.

Martha's mom asked which exit to take, and we made the long trek down Baseline Road, the main drag in southwest Little Rock, and on to the Deer Meadows subdivision. When we pulled up to the house, no one was there. I was glad I had thought to take my house key. Martha and her mom helped me unload my trunk and bags onto the porch.

"Doesn't look like my mama's home, but I have a key, so I'm good."

Martha's mother smiled behind her shades and rubbed my arm. "Well, I told ya we'll get you home. Take care, Rashod."

I was glad to inhale the familiar homey scent of Carpet Fresh and Pine-Sol. After I took my stuff into my room, I went into the kitchen to find something to eat. I had warmed-up leftover pot roast and swallowed the last few bites at the table when I heard Mama pull up. Although I was glad to see her, I didn't have much to say to her.

"Dusty, you home?"

"In the kitchen."

Mama came in with a Walmart bag in hand.

"Well, welcome home." There was a smile in her voice. "See you found you something to eat. Any more of that roast left?"

"Yeah."

Mama put the bag on the counter and opened the fridge. "How'd you get home? I was waiting for you to call and let me know how you were getting back. Had me up in here worried."

"I got back."

"How?"

"Magic carpet."

"Look, don't come up in here with no damn attitude. You coulda stayed your ass in Mena with all that."

I mumbled, "Maybe I should have."

"What?"

"Nothin'."

"Boy . . ."

Mama put her food in the microwave as I sipped my lemonade. I wanted to abruptly excuse myself to my room, but I was upset and felt the need to give Mama more attitude. I knew how far to take it, though, or else a plate of hot roast beef and collard greens would have been flying toward my face.

"So how was Mena?"

"Good."

"Oh, well, I see you get up there with those artsy white folks in the woods and come back not knowing how to act."

"Well, you left me up there."

"Dusty, I told you I gotta get new tires."

"Where's Reagan?"

"Still in Malvern."

"How she getting home?"

"Nita's gonna bring her back."

Mama took her food out of the microwave and sat opposite me at the table. "So who brought you home?"

"A white woman and her daughter."

"They have names, don't they? Gonna have to send a thank-you card or something. That's what you supposed to do."

"Well, I thought you were comin' to get me, so . . ."

Mama clanked her fork against the plate. "I told you I have to get some damn tires, and I wasn't gonna drive all that way needing new tires. I knew nobody was just gonna leave you up there."

"How'd you know that? I could've been left up there forever."

"Dusty, I'm your mama, but I ain't got time for all that drama, OK? Save it. Who the hell brought you back?"

"A girl named Martha and her mama."

"What's the last name?"

"Brantley, or something like that."

Mama stopped chewing. "Her daddy Max Brantley?"

"Am I supposed to know who that is?"

"You know everything else. He runs the *Arkansas Times*."

That was the liberal newspaper in town Mama loved reading. "I don't know."

"I think Max's wife is a judge." Mama's face lit up. She loved close proximity to people who did well, especially if they were comfortably middle class. "You should have gotten a phone number or something, Dusty. I think that's his daughter, though. Pretty sure it is."

"Well, I don't know."

"I'll find out."

And she did. Two days later, Mama bought a thank-you card and made me sign it. After she sealed the envelope to drop in the mail later that morning, she said, "Whenever somebody goes out of their way, or even if it's not out of their way, you always say, 'Thank you,' 'cause I'm tellin' you: Nobody has to do shit for you."

The year we lived in the Deer Meadows subdivision mostly felt as comfortable as our time on Tanya Street. Mama and her good friend Glenda hosted a family barbecue after I returned from AE-GIS camp, and relatives from Malvern filled the house again with their rowdiness months later at Christmas. The utilities stayed on, and we were at Emmanuel Baptist every Sunday praising God along with the dignified congregation.

We spent a lot of time in front of the Magnavox in the living room, laughing until we cried at *Def Comedy Jam*, which premiered on HBO that year. We sat with our mouths open as we watched the L.A. riots on the news following the Rodney King beating.

I was still doing poetry readings during Black History Month as part of a small, vibrant collective of local artists who recited poems and sang original songs once a month at Pyramid art gallery and bookstore on Main Street in downtown Little Rock, which was owned and operated by Garbo Hearne, the aloof wife of a well-known black doctor in town. I was one of the youngest members of the group of seven or eight budding musicians and writers who regularly participated. My connection came through Mrs. Mitchell, who knew one of the members.

Mama never showed up. She was always at work during the spoken-word nights at Pyramid, which were usually spirited and well attended. Reagan begrudgingly came with me only because Mama made her. Mama didn't like the idea of Reagan being home alone—or rather she didn't trust Reagan in the house by

herself. The older artists in the collective warmly encouraged me.
The more assured I became, Daddy, his vaporous representative
with his ever-present cigarette, hovered in corners less and less.
Though part of me always looked for him, I was relieved when he
didn't appear.

Our sense of stability at home started fading toward the end
of my ninth-grade year as I was about to enter Sylvan Hills High
School. Reagan was the first to notice. She came into my room
one night while Mama was still at work.

"I knew there was something I meant to tell you."

I put my book down. "What?"

"Yesterday, Mama got something in the mail."

"And?"

"I don't know what it was, but she got real pissed."

"Probably some bill. She's always pissed at bills."

"Uh-uh. It was something in a long envelope. Then she went
out in the garage and starting beating the top of the car."

"Damn. And I missed this?"

"I went out there when I heard her fussin' and shit and asked
her what was wrong with her."

"What she say?"

"Nothin'. Told me it was none of my business. But she looked
real mad. You know Mama don't act a fool like that."

"No, that's usually how *you* roll."

"Whatever, Dusty. You just a damn hater, I swear."

"I wonder what it was, though. You come in here to ask me to
ask her? You know she not gon' say shit."

"I think it's got something to do with the car. I heard her on
the phone the other night, and I think she said somethin' 'bout
her being behind on the payments."

"Wouldn't surprise me. But she never tells us shit."

"Nope. And you bet' not ask."

"Or you'll get cussed out."

"You know how she do."

Shortly after Mama pounded her fists on the top of the Nissan Sentra, she lost her job at St. Vincent. She came home early

one evening and abruptly gave us the news. She never divulged the details to us about what had happened. But as usual, Reagan and I picked up pieces from what we overheard from her phone conversations.

She had been fired for leaving her desk and using her boss's private bathroom. The one she and the other women in the office typically used was being cleaned at the time. Her supervisor, an older white woman, had been oppressive. Mama said the woman was intimidated by her because she spoke well and didn't carry herself in a subservient, ass-kissing way like the other black women in the office. Mama was planning to take the matter to the Equal Employment Opportunity Commission and she sounded confident on the phone.

In the meantime I was worried, so much so that my sleep was fitful and I woke up tired. I had never known Mama not to work. And what did this mean for us? Mama started playing Aretha's *Amazing Grace* cassette often, which gave me a feeling of relief and fear—relieved by the sanctified fieriness of the music, feeling that all would be well because Aretha said so. But I was afraid because I had no real idea of what was going to happen. Also, the last time *Amazing Grace* had been so prominent around the house was when Daddy left us on Garden Street and at age six my heart broke for the first time.

Ever resourceful, Mama kept things afloat for as long as she could. She temporarily received food stamps and managed to secure a temp job as a secretary at a telecommunications firm in West Little Rock. But it was a deep cut in pay. The car was soon repossessed. That same week, we were packing up the house. Neither Reagan nor I had the nerve to ask where we were moving this time. Part of me didn't want to know. Movers came one Saturday and took away the furniture and other large items.

That night, we all slept on pallets in Mama's room. I didn't sleep much at all and neither did Mama. From where I lay I could see her eyes fixed on the bare window across the room. Her face was drained and vacant—similar to what happened to her eyes when Mama Teacake said something nasty to her. She didn't seem to be in deep thought, just gone for the moment. She must not have felt me staring at her in the dark; if she did, she didn't care. Mama was not in the room, in the house, or in the world.

The next morning, a gracious woman from Emmanuel, Tonya Springer, came over to help with the rest of the move. A tall, full-figured woman who was seldom without a welcoming smile, she sang in the choir and carried herself with a self-possession that made her seem older than her thirtysomething years. When Mama and I were alone in the kitchen as Reagan and Tonya loaded Tonya's car, I finally asked, "Where we goin'?"

Mama kept wiping the counter, ignoring me. I asked again, "Mama, where we going?"

She turned around in a huff. "Tonya's, Dusty."

"Tonya's? Where does she even stay? We start school on Monday."

"I know that. It's only temporary, Dusty. Don't start trippin'." Mama was irritated, as though she'd already told me all of this.

We put everything in storage and headed over to West Little Rock, where Tonya lived in a sprawling apartment complex. Her one-bedroom apartment was well appointed but not roomy enough for two adults and two teenagers who could pass for adults. Tonya seemed genuinely happy to have us there and went out of her way to make it all feel like one big sleepover with movies and snacks galore. She gave Mama her bed and she camped out on the couch while Reagan and I slept on the floor. I was so uneasy about our displacement that I got sick right away. My stomach was unsettled and I couldn't keep much down our first night there. It was all nerves. School started that Monday, and Mama and Tonya thought it a good idea for me to stay home.

They went to work, and Tonya's mother, Linda, took Reagan to school. I was alone in Tonya's apartment, where she had a beautiful stereo she had inherited from an uncle who had recently died. A trunk of his old albums was in the bedroom—all pristine copies of soul, pop, and jazz, most from the seventies.

Apparently he had a thing for Natalie Cole because several of her albums were in there. I placed the headphones on and sipped ginger ale as Natalie crooned about passionate kisses on the sandy shores of "La Costa." I escaped with her, floating beyond Tonya's living room crowded with our bags and beyond Little Rock to where the air was thin and I was weightless. Most important, as I was adrift on the music, I didn't feel the shame and embarrassment of our displacement.

We were at Tonya's for about a month and during that time we had no contact with family in Malvern. We could never depend on them for anything anyway. Mama never divulged hardships to Mama Teacake or her sisters. There was no loving "Girl, we got your back" camaraderie among them, at least none I ever saw. Venomous gossip often dominated family conversations, and I was always dismayed by how unsupportive and downright nasty Mama's folks could be, getting that last kick in when you were already down. Nobody knew that better than Mama, which is why they didn't know about our temporary homelessness.

If Mama was despondent about our situation, she never showed it at Tonya's, where she seemed less lonely. They got along well, and their conversations, even serious ones, were usually filled with loud, head-thrown-back laughter. But we never forgot we were guests, and we made sure not to become more of an inconvenience than we already were. Reagan, Mama, and I were fastidious about keeping Tonya's place clean, and I cooked most nights after school.

In the meantime, Mama got a full-time position at the telecommunications firm, and she had applied for Section 8 housing at Terrace Green, a well-kept, cream-colored apartment complex in southwest Little Rock. Years before, it had been a haven for lowlifes until new property management took it over, adding a black, wrought-iron security gate and lush landscaping that gave the place an almost bucolic look. When Mama found out she had been approved for a three-bedroom apartment, she ordered celebratory rib dinners from Sims barbecue.

Deacons from Emmanuel helped us move our things from storage into our new place. My room was down a narrow hall; it was small and isolated, which I didn't mind. Our neighbors were diverse, almost evenly white and black. A white couple across the parking lot from us homeschooled their three small boys. It was the mid-nineties but they seemed snatched from another era. The mother wore a mushroom-shaped, Dorothy Hamill–like bob and big round glasses; her husband, also bespectacled, sported a handlebar mustache, and they all piled into a beat-up old powder-blue station wagon to make weekly shopping trips.

Squeaky, a short, dark-skinned woman who lived next door with her two sons and never smiled, reminded me of the projects divas on Omega Street with her gloriously profane mouth and gruff way of being neighborly. She never formally introduced herself—just knocked on the door one day and said, "Y'all want some fuckin' hot dogs or somethin'? I'm grillin'." Squeaky often sat in a Queen Anne chair near her front door smoking cigarettes, watching neighbors and soap operas. She and Mama became fast friends.

Soon after we were settled into our new place, Uncle Henry helped Mama get a car, a 1978 Chrysler Newport that an old man in Malvern owned and barely drove. It was lemon yellow and the seats felt like couches. Reagan called it the "The Pimp Dog." After the ugly car had been parked outside our new place for a few months, Mama called Reagan and me into the living room and told us we needed jobs.

"Y'all sixteen and fifteen years old now, and y'all need to start working," she said.

Mama's tone was prickly, as though she'd already dropped this bit of news on us and was annoyed with having to repeat it.

"So we supposed to leave now and go find jobs?" I asked.

Mama rolled her eyes. "No, smart-ass, but y'all need to start looking. Y'all old enough to work now. My money's only stretching so far."

I thought to myself, "When has that not ever been the case?" But I didn't dare say it. I glanced at Reagan, who smirked and looked away. I could tell she was thinking the same thing.

"For real," Mama continued. "Y'all have to start pulling some weight around here, because we got nobody to turn to like Tonya. She was a blessing."

Mama had a point. I had long grown tired of asking her for money for anything other than the bare essentials. She never had extra cash. Although Tonya had made things comfortable, the idea of being displaced sharpened something in me. I felt like a charity case, sleeping on the floor of her one-bedroom apartment. And I was nobody's charity case. I was ready to assume more responsibility in taking care of myself.

I felt awful about it but I resented Mama for not having enough of anything. She worked harder than anyone I knew, and everybody who knew her knew that about her. But I was tired—sick and tired—of the constant struggle. I wanted my own money, and maybe with my own money I could assert myself and feel more like a man, whatever that meant.

But the one who should have taught me something about what that meant had been for several years a cigarette-smoking figment of my imagination. I started to feel something like hate toward Daddy, broiling whenever I thought about him—how he must've been in Portland living his life without a passing thought of us, because we never heard from him.

Shortly before Mama told us we needed jobs, we had gotten word that Daddy was moving back to Malvern, that he was taking an early retirement from Reynolds. Nothing inside leapt or shifted when I heard the news. I don't believe I cared. Besides, I had a new focus.

I had to get a job.

I responded to an ad in the paper about a position at Central Arkansas Library downtown on Louisiana Street, which reeked of pissy homeless people and old musty books. I wore one of the dashikis Daisy had made for me, an orange one, with black slacks. Mama dropped me off that Saturday and fussed for the entire ride about my choice of clothes.

"I should've made you go back in the house and change."

"Nothing's wrong with what I got on, Mama."

"It's a job interview and you're going in a damn dashiki?"

"What am I supposed to wear?"

"A shirt, a tie, a jacket—not walkin' in there lookin' like somethin' outta the Black Panthers history book."

My look didn't seem to bother Tracey, the gregarious, chunky white woman who briefly interviewed me on the second floor of the library. Her smile was wide when I walked through the door. "Welcome," she said, slowly rising from the chair behind her desk. "You must be Rashod."

The position was for a book processor—the person responsible for wrapping new books in plastic, gluing the checkout card pockets inside, and stamping the tops of the books with the address of the library branch. Seemed easy enough. The work station was in a corner of the large office with Tracey and two other librarians—Jeff, a hippie-looking guy with auburn hair that dusted his shoulders, and Amy, an old woman with a silver crew cut, ever-present suspenders, and a large hump in her back.

The hours were between four thirty and until the library closed, at eight. The pay: five dollars an hour, a dollar and a half above minimum wage.

"If you have headphones, you can wear those, as long as they're not too loud," Tracey said. "It helps pass the time because, honestly, the work can get a little monotonous."

When she said I could wear my headphones, I was sold.

"Well, Rashod, if you want the job, it's yours."

"And I'll take it."

Sylvan Hill High School sat atop a hill behind the junior high, and like most American public high schools for poor and middle-class students it had the dismal, industrial look of a prison complex, with harsh lighting and ugly concrete walls. The wooden lockers were forest green. Unlike the drafty junior high where the lockers were outside, the high school was enclosed, with two levels.

The TAG classes were upstairs, and most of my classmates were the same ones I'd had since seventh grade. By this time I had become friendlier with them—though we still weren't close. They all lived in Sherwood and hung out after school. Some were already driving and chatted on and on before class about joyriding and going to the mall.

My tenth-grade year, as the rest of high school would be for me, was all about focus. The brief homeless spell made me seriously consider what I wanted for myself and what my life would be after high school. College was definitely in the plan, and while many of my classmates were busy affecting the self-conscious gangsta posturing seen in Dr. Dre and Snoop Dogg videos; the disaffected, brooding look of grunge superstar Kurt Cobain; and the sleek cowboy style of Garth Brooks, I was thinking about a career. Several of my TAG peers seemed to be, too; some already knew they were going into medicine or education. So I didn't feel alone in that respect.

Reading *The Bluest Eye* had sealed it for me. I knew I would write, but it was my creative writing teacher, Mrs. Martin, whose refined mannerisms gave her something of an aristocratic air, who suggested journalism. In addition to teaching regular English classes and the morning course in creative writing, Mrs. Martin also oversaw the *Banner*, the high school newspaper, and she usually recruited its writers from her classes.

After I turned in an assignment one day, Mrs. Martin asked if I'd ever considered journalism.

"Like, writing about all the black folks getting shot over in East Little Rock? Not really."

Mrs. Martin grinned. "No, no. There are other forms of journalism. You're good at writing. Journalism is a practical way to use those skills. You get to travel."

"Oh."

"Consider it. In the meantime, you can start writing for the *Banner*."

During my first-period creative writing class, Mrs. Martin allowed me to work on music reviews for the paper. The first was on Mary J. Blige's second album, *My Life*, which had come out that year and solidified her place as the wounded warrior voice of my generation. Her aching alto and pain-suffused lyrics were enfolded by the vintage soul samples her producer, Sean "Puffy" Combs, used, music I recognized from my records at home.

Music to which Mary J. apparently felt a visceral connection, releasing an unvarnished soul testimony for the gangsta rap era, a cynical period when so many of us tried to harden ourselves, not wanting to feel anything.

At sixteen, I figured I'd never have sex.

It surely wasn't because I didn't want it. In between school and working at the library, fantasies of fucking consumed my mind. At night before starting my homework, I masturbated. Before school, I masturbated. I was always sure to lock the door because Mama and Reagan had a habit of barging in.

"You in there playin' with yourself?" Reagan would ask, banging on the door.

At the library, I came across a copy of *The Joy of Gay Sex*, an illustrated book, and managed to sneak it out. I studied the explicit pictures and imagined what it would feel like to be inside a guy. But the sensual parts detailed in the early chapters were more appealing, the kissing, caressing, and expressions of tenderness I never saw outside of movies—straight movies, of course—and only imagined when I played music, especially the love songs of Marvin Gaye.

At sixteen, I looked in the mirror and assessed the dull round face, the straggly mustache above the thick lips, the slightly pudgy stomach and figured that maybe I wasn't attractive enough to fuck. Beyond that, I didn't have the swagger that other boys seemed to just step into.

Even some of the girls had it.

I wasn't sure if Reagan was fucking. She was annoyingly private, though I don't know when she would have had the time to sneak around between school and her job at the Athlete's Foot. Boys were calling the house and asking for her, so she was certainly courting. She seemed assured in her body, which had blossomed into the Coke-bottle figure that women in the family inherited.

My older male cousins sauntered down the narrow country roads of Malvern, like the city boys on the avenues in Little Rock,

looking confident even if they weren't, bragging about sexual con-
quests they may or may not have had. But they could talk freely
about getting pussy or skipping school with their homeboys to
"run a train" on some unsuspecting girl, which seemed to be a
favorite pastime for the overgrown and overheated boys around
the way. What was I going to talk about, wanting to spoon in bed
with another boy? I'd long learned to keep those fantasies inside
my head. It wasn't as though I was ever getting ribbed for being
a budding lady's man.

Got his head in them books again.

*Rashod is a straight-up nerd. Ain't seen pussy since pussy
seen him.*

Boy's smart, though. Go'n be somebody. Ain't that right, Dusty?

*Good you stayin' outta trouble. Lord knows there's enough nig-
gas 'round here ain't doin' shit. You just keep doin' what you doin';
don't get sidetracked by all that nonsense and all that riffraff.*

I listened to the boys' sexed-up conversations at the bus stop,
before and after gym class in the locker room, where I kept my
eyes to the floor, and in the hallways. I feigned ignorance but vi-
sualized their tall tales with an almost cinematic sweep—his back
arching and beautiful buttocks clenching as long, shapely legs
wrapped themselves around an athletic waist. The sweat on his
brow. The jerk of his body. The cocky grin across his face. Her
confused expression. The awkward silence as they hurriedly dress,
acting as though nothing had ever happened.

But there I was at sixteen, convinced nothing sexual would
happen for me, looking in the mirror and hating what I saw.

In my eleventh-grade year, I found a safe harbor outside of music
and books in the familiar warmth of female company.

They were funny, plain brown girls with wise ways: Tasha, Tiffany, and Erica. They were a grade ahead of me, already seniors,
and nothing like the hard-shelled Mary J. Blige wannabes or the
despondent ones who had already given birth to a child or two
before senior year. They were "good girls" who did well in class

and never got into trouble or talked loudly in the halls. Tiffany and Tasha had a few TAG classes.

They let me sit with them in the cafeteria and for a while I didn't say much. As I did when I sat around Mama and her friends or around my aunts in Malvern, I listened to the ebb and flow of their conversations, the way their words dipped, leapt, and pirouetted—a kind of elaborate linguistic dance that black girls seemed to master early in life.

Whenever I spoke, their heads all turned like the proverbial deer in headlights. They laughed at my jokes; they chided me when I opposed their opinions about certain pop stars or songs on the radio. But I never sensed any venom. They didn't flirt with me. Although it was never discussed, and I certainly didn't make it known to them or anybody else, I believe they knew I was gay. They didn't have boyfriends, either. So we never talked about crushes we may have had.

We all had after-school jobs and sometimes we hung out on weekends. Tiffany, the most solidly middle class among us, had a car. Erica lived in Tiffany's neighborhood over in Twin Lakes, and they didn't mind driving out to southwest Little Rock to pick me up.

We mostly went to the movies, to the mall, or to Tiffany's house, where we talked and laughed for hours while watching videos on BET. Her mother, Mrs. Armstrong, was a French and social studies teacher at Sylvan Hills Junior High School and always welcomed us. She'd cook for us or allow me to cook in her kitchen.

Mama loved that I hung out with the girls, especially Tiffany, whose family's status she respected and admired. My brief friendship with Andre a few years before had made her uneasy. I could tell she didn't like my closeness to him, especially the way my mood darkened when Andre abruptly moved to West Memphis.

She noticed that I had crawled into myself.

"You still thinkin' about that boy?"

"What boy?"

A smirk crept across her face, a look I couldn't discern. "You know what boy."

"No."

"Uh-huh."

But she always asked about Tiffany, Tasha, and Erica. There seemed to be a sense of relief in her voice whenever she answered the phone when one of them called, or whenever I mentioned I was hanging out with them after work. Reagan going on dates and accompanying boys to prom was fine. In fact, I didn't attend any of my proms, opting instead to stay at home and watch *Comic View* on BET or *Def Comedy Jam* on HBO.

I didn't seem to belong at prom, and I never saw the point of acting as though I was interested in any female beyond a platonic relationship.

"How come you not gonna go to prom?" Tiffany asked. "It's just about having fun."

"Sounds like torture to me."

She shook her head. "Whatever, Rashod."

In my wildest dreams, I would go to prom with a beautiful boy and slip my hand around his waist as we posed for pictures in matching tuxes, and hold his hand as we floated around the room, the envy of everyone, and we'd end the night with a kiss so sweet and powerful we'd levitate into the sky.

But I tried not to ever talk about boys. Mama seemed noticeably uncomfortable if I even casually mentioned another boy's name.

"Who you talkin' about?" she'd ask, her trumpet voice sharp and pointed.

In her presence, I was careful not to say anything about other boys. Even an innocuous observation would be misconstrued.

"I think I want some of those pants he got on."

The look in Mama's eyes matched the sharpness of her tone. "And why are you starin' at his pants?"

I'd take a deep breath and wish I could float away somewhere—far, far away somewhere with that beautiful boy in my wildest dreams, our lips locked as we sailed across the sky, the envy of everyone.

Most of us in TAG spent sophomore year filling out applications and writing essays for college admissions, various scholarships, and grants. We studied on weekends for standardized tests: the ACT and SAT. Mama kept a file of my applications in a crate in her room and kept up with the due dates. She'd put them in first-class mail at work, where she didn't have to pay for postage.

I had been inducted into all of the academic clubs: the National Honor Society, the Beta Club, and Mu Alpha Theta, the honor society for mathematics. The inductions were small ceremonies held in the school library, where we received certificates and pendants, and parents applauded and snapped pictures. I was the only black face in the room, as usual, and Mama's pretty face was never there because she couldn't get off work.

But she wasn't going to miss her chance to go to Florida with me.

That spring, I won first place in the Beta Club's regional creative writing competition, which afforded me the opportunity to compete at the national convention in Miami. I was ecstatic about receiving the nice dark-wood trophy, but my English teacher, Mrs. Young, who oversaw the school's chapter of the Beta Club, thought I had a good chance of winning at the nationals.

"We've never had anybody to go," she said. "Oh, we're definitely sending you."

The Beta Club held a few fundraisers, including a Saturday afternoon car wash in Sherwood, to pay for the trip. It would be my first ride on a plane and the farthest I'd ever been from Arkansas.

"Me and Dusty goin' to Miami, girl," Mama told our neighbor Squeaky, who had dropped by one afternoon. I couldn't see her face because I was in the kitchen, which was adjacent to the living room, but I could hear the pride in Mama's voice. She was relaxed, too. The beer she was sipping surely helped with that.

"That's right, girl. You told me 'bout that," Squeaky said. "Hey, Dusty! Dianne told me you won some contest. What was it?"

I gently dropped a few pieces of chicken into a pot of hot grease. "Beta Club."

"Betty who?"

"Beta Club, Squeaky," I shouted and chuckled.

"Oh, I don't know nothin' 'bout that. Must be one of them fancy clubs for you smart muthafuckas."

"Yeah, something like that," I said.

"Well, you go'n 'head with your smart ass," Squeaky said. "If you write as good as you cook, nigga, you gon' go down there and win."

"Don't be blowin' his head up no bigger than it already is, girl," Mama said.

"Dianne, hush. If my boy was doin' half the shit Dusty doin' in school, you wouldn't be able to shut me up. Hey, Dusty! Bring me some of that chicken, smart muthafucka."

Reagan went to Malvern, and she was happy to go, the weekend Mama and I flew to Miami for the National Beta Club convention. Mama gripped the armrest and tightly shut her eyes as the plane took off. I laughed at her.

"What's so funny?"

"You."

"You just hope this plane don't go down."

"Ma, please . . ."

I was glued to the window. Little Rock became a patchwork quilt of green and amber squares. Then the clouds obscured everything and all was white and pristine blue. I felt at home in the sky.

We had a brief layover in Atlanta, and as we made our way to the connecting gate I recognized her profile when she turned to the man next to her. She was hard to miss in her tangerine head wrap.

"Mama, that's Maya Angelou."

"Where?"

"Up there. See? In that head wrap."

"You sure that's Maya Angelou?"

"It is. I'm gonna go up and speak."

Towering in heels, she was a few paces ahead of us. I walked up beside her, my ever-present notebook in hand.

"Miss Angelou?"

She turned to me and gently grabbed my wrist.

"Dear, I'm rushing," she said, her mahogany voice as resonate as it was on TV. "If you'd walk with me to my gate, I'll sign your notebook there."

"Oh. Well, my mother and I, she's right there," I said, nodding in Mama's direction. "We're on our way to a writing competition. I'm competing, and I've read your poems. I love them."

She was a bit winded as she walked. She nodded and smiled. "Thank you, son. I'm sorry I have to rush to make my plane."

Just then, the man with her, who looked to be an assistant, hailed an airport buggy and they climbed on.

"Good luck," she said, smiling widely as the buggy pulled off.

When we settled on the plane, I could still feel myself smiling.

"Mama, that was Maya Angelou!"

"Dusty, you loud."

I lowered my voice. "Oh. Maya Angelou, though!"

"Uh-huh."

"What? It's Maya Angelou—*I Know Why the Caged Bird Sings?*"

"I know who she is."

"And she was just walking through the airport."

"Right. But did you see those ankles?"

"What?"

"Those damn heels in those sling-back shoes. Maya Angelou. Shit, more like Maya Crustylou. All that money she's made and she walkin' 'round with ashy-ass heels like that?"

I eased back into my seat. Only Mama could take a star moment and snatch it back down to Earth.

I noticed the heat first. When we arrived in Miami, the sun was not the blistering demon it was in Arkansas. I loved the balminess and the palm trees—just like what I remembered from *Miami Vice* and *The Golden Girls*. Mama seemed uncomfortable. Our taxi driver—a handsome dark-skinned man who looked as if he could have been a relative back home in Malvern—spoke mostly Spanish but he understood our English well enough to take us to the hotel.

When we got out of the cab and he unloaded our bags, Mama whispered, "That's something. I thought he was black."

"Mama, he is black. Latinos are black people."

"Speaking Spanish, though?"

"Yes, Mama."

"I'll be damned."

Mama hadn't ever gone far from Malvern except for when she and Daddy lived briefly in El Paso, Texas, soon after he returned from Vietnam in the early seventies. He was strung out on heroin then and often in the streets when he wasn't nodding off at home or having nightmares that made him scream and jump in bed.

Mama was miserable there with Dusa, who was two or three years old. She had no friends and most of the neighbors spoke Spanish. The country girl from Malvern felt alienated, all alone with a toddler and a shell-shocked smack addict. When they returned to Arkansas, Mama swore she'd never live far from her people again. I wondered if encountering so many Spanish-speaking folks in the airport brought back memories of El Paso. Mama's ever-cool and assertive façade had cracked a little.

But she seemed restored when we got to the hotel, checked in, and confirmed my Beta Club registration. White parents and their children, fellow Beta Club members, swarmed the lobby. I was wide-eyed at the opulence—the chandelier that looked like an illuminated, mammoth piece of crystal, the gleaming brass railings and flower arrangements as lush and full as the gumdrop-shaped juniper bushes that edged Big Mama's front yard.

The next day, the various competitions were held in conference rooms on the second floor of the hotel. The creative writing portion was similar to the regional contest in Little Rock. We were given a small list of unrelated items that we had an hour to weave into a poem or a piece of prose.

I don't remember exactly what the items were but I clearly remember the short story I wrote about a girl who realized she had magical powers after her mother died. I named the character Maya.

Afterward, Mama and I explored the area immediately around the hotel, which was tourist heavy and lame.

"Let's get in a cab and check out the city," I suggested.

"Boy, we don't know where we goin' 'round here. Better stay 'round this hotel. Don't know shit about these folks in Miami."

"Ain't nothing really around here."

Mama ignored me. We walked across the street to a tacky souvenir shop, where she bought T-shirts for folks back home.

"I think Mama and Ollie would like these."

I rolled my eyes. "They didn't give us any money to come down here, and Mama Teacake ain't never cared about anything I've done. So why should we buy her and drunk Ollie anything?"

Mama glared at me. "Dusty, shut up. You about a selfish ass."

Earlier at the hotel, I had overheard two white women who were with the Beta Club talking about a good seafood restaurant they were going to later.

As we left the souvenir shop, after spending way too much time in there, we were hungry.

"Mama, you remember the name of that seafood place those white ladies were talking to us about in the elevator?"

"You got some seafood money? I don't like seafood."

Mama was getting on my nerves. "Well, we're in a place we haven't been before, we can try something new."

"You got some try-something-new money? Let's go to that Bonanza over there 'cross the street. Maybe they got some seafood on the buffet."

"They got Bonanza back home, Ma."

"They sure do. That's why we goin' over there. C'mon."

The next night was the award ceremony in the hotel's ballroom. Mama and I sat near the front, exchanged glances, and tried to muffle our laughter at a girl who struggled through a ballad she had neither the voice nor charisma to pull off. Mama whispered, "She gets no award for that—no reward, either."

The creative writing category was among the last ones announced. After third place, I thought maybe I didn't win. This was the national convention after all, hundreds of brilliant kids here—and I didn't mingle with a single one. Mama seemed uncomfortable with the surroundings and didn't let me out of her sight.

The two days we were in Miami, we didn't go beyond the souvenir shops across the street and the jive-ass Bonanza buffet a few doors down. We sat around the pool where Mama made small talk with two chatty mothers nearby. I listened to music on my headphones, read my paperback of Toni Morrison's *Sula*, or watched TV in the frigid hotel room while Mama's snoring was loud enough to rival the horns in Tower of Power.

My skin tanned beautifully. Mama bitched about the heat. She couldn't wait to get back to the room to snatch off the tapered wig she'd bought for the trip. Before we left Little Rock, she made Reagan braid her hair into cornrows.

"A wig in Miami, Mama?" I glared at her head on our way to the airport.

"What? It's cute. Shut up, Dusty."

In the ballroom, I was nervous as the National Beta Club president, a broad, conservative-looking man in a dark suit who spoke with the deliberate cadence of a white Southern preacher, read the winning names and school affiliations and handed out the tall, glossy trophies.

"Second place in the National Beta Club creative writing competition goes to"—he flipped the page on the podium—"from Sylvan Hills High School in Sherwood, Arkansas: Rashod Ollison."

Mama tapped my arm. I strolled up to the stage, shook the president's hand—remembering Reverend Griffen's instruction to grip firmly and look directly in the eyes—and retrieved the heavy trophy. On my way back, Daddy's vaporous representative was in my seat next to Mama as she beamed and clapped. His arm snaked around her shoulders, the way it did in that café booth in Mexico. He winked at me, nodded, then vanished. I took my seat and showed the trophy to Mama.

"Look at there. Came all the way down here and won something. Go'n, boy!"

Mama and I had a celebratory dinner in the hotel's restaurant. We shared a gourmet brick-oven pizza under the dim lights. One of the mothers who had been chatty with Mama at the pool earlier stopped by and congratulated me.

"You have to let Mrs. Mitchell and the folks at Emmanuel know soon as you get home," Mama said.

We caught our flight early the next morning, and Mama was glad to be back in Arkansas where the sun was unkind, no palm trees swayed, and folks spoke English in a drawl thick as Alaga syrup. I carried my trophy—a gleaming rectangular piece of dark wood about a foot tall mounted to a gold-trimmed platform—through the airport. During the quick layover in Atlanta, in the same airport where Maya Angelou in a tangerine head wrap had wished me good luck, a few folks asked about the trophy.

"Good for you," an old white woman said.

"Keep on doing your thang," said a black man in a business suit.

It was second place, though. A white girl won the top prize. But Mama beamed and Daddy showed up, winking his approval before he vanished. He was really back in Malvern, and Mama's folks said he was still the same old Raymond, living over on East Section Line with his folks. Not up to shit. Not looking so good.

Heard he got a baby by one of them Thrasher girls. Yeah. Got one of them sorry-ass Thrashers pregnant, what was up in Oregon workin' at Reynolds with him. Think it was that youngest Thrasher girl, the one that wasn't all too bright.

Couldn't been too bright, fuckin' 'round with Raymond.

Ain't it the truth, though?

Yeah, Dusty and Reagan, y'all got a little sister somewhere 'round here. Ain't that nothin'? Raymond's broke-down ass still goin' 'round here gettin' babies and shit.

Heard Old Lady Ollison ain't havin' nothin' to do with this one.

Hell, ain't like she fooled with any of the other strays Raymond got.

She was color-struck. You know, she always did favor Dusty 'cause he light-skinned.

Raymond oughta be 'shamed.

I didn't care. I stayed focused on my books, my academic clubs, hanging out with wise and funny brown girls, and working in the library, when I wasn't indulging silly homosexual fantasies of flying off in the midnight sky with pretty boys. Music remained my cocoon, the place where I found the most coherence and delicious engagement. Each pay period, I bought CD reissues of much of the music Daddy had left behind on vinyl. And I was discovering my own taste for sophisticated fusion soul artists: Randy Crawford, Jean Carne, Roy Ayers, and Leon Ware.

Daddy never called. When we went to Malvern, Mama Teacake often said, "Y'all need to go see 'bout ya daddy." Neither Reagan nor I said anything. We never discussed him, and we were too absorbed in our teenage worlds to rush to a man who didn't seem to care about us. I wanted him to care, of course. I'd long felt something close to hate for him because he didn't seem to care. Yet I still looked for him. But I didn't really know who to look for.

I never knew Raymond Ollison.

The next time I saw him—the man of flesh and bone—he was almost gone for good.

Part Four

· · ·

. . .

I ENTERED MY SENIOR YEAR FOCUSED ON LEAVING MAMA'S HOUSE
for good. College was going to be the exit. I did well on my standardized tests and maintained a 3.5 GPA or better throughout
high school. I did some volunteer work—serving food to the
homeless at a shelter downtown—to satisfy the "community in-
volvement" requirement on a few scholarship applications.

I was editor of the *Banner*, the high school newspaper, whose
stories and headlines I helped choose with Mrs. Martin, my
tenth-grade creative writing teacher, who oversaw the publication. On the evenings the paper went to print, I stayed after school
with two classmates and fellow newspaper writers who also lived
in southwest Little Rock, two chatty white girls named Gigi and
Crystal. Gigi had a car, and she dropped me off after the work was
done and we'd eaten the pizza Mrs. Martin had ordered for us.

I had applied to several colleges, including Howard University
and Morehouse College. But neither offered me a full scholarship, and I refused to take out any loans. With my grades and test
scores, I figured I could get a full ride somewhere. I had thought
long and hard about going to a black college and it seemed like
a logical choice, given how pro-black I had always been. But unlike some of my classmates who had their hearts set on going to
a black school, I wasn't looking for a certain validation. I had
grown up around black folks all of my life. Emmanuel had been
a haven of upstanding blacks who had done well in life and who
had been supportive of me.

I was also used to finding my own way in an environment
where I was rendered invisible, and I wasn't bothered too much
by that. I didn't mind living in my head, something I'd been doing for as long as I could remember. So going to a big university,

surrounded by thousands of folks from all walks of life, didn't intimidate me. I already knew I was going to study journalism and creative writing.

I had visited the University of Arkansas in Fayetteville, about three hours from Little Rock, on a campus tour with a black youth group during the spring of my junior year. The campus was bustling and idyllic and predominately white. The professors we met seemed to be engaging. Plus, the school had a strong, though small, creative writing department. Mama had a friend from Malvern who was an instructor in the journalism school: Gerald Jordan, a respected newspaper journalist who worked as an editor during the summer at the *Philadelphia Inquirer*.

Before the holidays, I received my acceptance letter from the University of Arkansas. Now it was a matter of waiting for the scholarships and grant money to come in.

Then one Saturday in early February, a call came that momentarily knocked me off my cloud of scholastic achievement.

"Cuda's dead?" Reagan had answered the phone. Aunt Nita was on the other end.

Reagan's face dropped. "Mama! Nita on the phone."

She left the receiver on the couch, scurried to her room, and shut the door. I muted whatever Reagan and I had been watching on TV as Mama left the kitchen and rushed to the phone.

"Nita? Cuda's dead?" Mama furrowed her eyebrows. "What happened?"

For years I thought Cuda was Daddy's sister, but she was actually his niece, the daughter of his older sister Charlene, who had died soon after Cuda was born. Daddy was ten years older than Cuda, and they grew up as siblings. Like Daddy, Cuda was back and forth at my grandparents' place on East Section Line, even after she had given birth to her only child, Pat. She'd move into her own place for a spell then was back at Big Mama and Paw Paw's, living what seemed like an extended adolescence.

I remember being fascinated by her—the way she put on her makeup in the bathroom mirror, carefully lining her lips with black eyeliner before filling them in with plum-colored lipstick.

Her smile was bright like her voice, which was high-pitched with a strong timbre. She was always nice.

"Girl, I hate to hear this," Mama said on the phone. "How old was Cuda?"

Thirty-six.

"What was it?"

A heart attack.

I later heard that her drug habit, which had long been whispered about, may have been the cause. I immediately thought about Pat, who had to be about fourteen and had shared a room with his mother all of his life. I thought about Daddy. He and Cuda were close.

Mama hung up the phone. "Y'all gon' have to go over to Mrs. Ollison's," she said. "Nita said she'll call me back when she hears about the funeral arrangements."

I had never gone to a funeral. Going to Cuda's meant I was going to see Daddy, and I wasn't sure how I would feel. It had been years since I'd laid eyes on him. Mama seemed to sense what I was thinking.

"Raymond needs to see y'all anyway," she said, rising from the couch. "He's gonna need y'all there. He and Cuda were always tight. Y'all need to support Raymond."

I glared at Mama. "Support? He ain't never . . ."

"Don't start, Dusty!" she said, her trumpet voice blaring. "This ain't about you."

A week later, early on a Saturday morning, Mama drove us to Malvern. She went alone to Brandon's Funeral Home to view Cuda's body. She wasn't going to the funeral; she'd wait for us at Mama Teacake's.

Dusa, who for a few years had been living in a tiny house with a dusty front yard two streets behind Mama Teacake, dropped us off at East Section Line. Folks hadn't started arriving yet when we strolled onto the porch—I, in a navy-blue suit that didn't quite fit; Reagan, stylish in a knee-length black dress and a black leather coat. After I knocked on the door, we exchanged looks.

We were both nervous and wanted to be there but didn't really want to be there.

A woman whose face I used to study in a sepia eight-by-ten atop Big Mama's console TV opened the door. It was a younger version of Big Mama's face—the high cheekbones, the smooth dark-brown skin, the slight overbite, the same smile that radiated a sense of concern and relief. Only she wasn't sporting the string of pearls and Supremes-like flip hairdo that she wore in the glossy sixties glamour shot.

She was slender in a fitted black dress, her short hair loosely curled: Aunt Theresa, Daddy's baby sister, whom relatives called Ducky. She'd been living in Arizona with her husband, a federal judge, and their son and daughter since the early seventies. I'd only seen pictures of the well-to-do aunt, whom relatives said lived in a big, pretty house out in Arizona.

We stepped inside.

"Dusty and Reagan." Ducky's voice was warm and crisp, a lilting version of Big Mama's. "You know who I am?"

Reagan, who bore a striking resemblance to Ducky, gave her a quizzical look. She never seemed to know anybody.

"You're Aunt Ducky," I said.

She smiled and gave us each a tight hug. "Your daddy is getting dressed."

Big Mama and Paw Paw left their room, both in various stages of getting dressed, to greet us. I was glad to see them. Neither had changed much, but their eyes were understandably sad, especially Paw Paw's. He had spoiled Cuda.

"Y'all want something to eat?" Big Mama asked. The kitchen table I could see was already packed with food, as was the top of the long, deep freezer behind it.

We declined. Big Mama and Paw Paw returned to their room to finish getting dressed. Ducky tapped on Daddy's bedroom door. "Junior, Dusty and Reagan are out here."

The man who entered the living room was not the one who had been haunting my dreams and floating in corners. He was not the handsome guy whose eyes seduced the camera in that café booth snapshot, the dashing protector cuddling a younger, glowing Dianne Smith in Mexico. This was not the self-assured man who stood on Clara Mae's porch, smoothing out his shirt and patting his hair, before she answered the door.

This was not the solidly built, slightly overweight man in a fisherman's cap whose shoulders slumped in that courtroom as the bailiff took him away for failing to pay child support. Shockingly thin and gray, Daddy was swimming in his suit. The eyes that looked through me when I was six years old as he told me to never let anyone turn me into a slave were drained of wonder and vitality. The sadness long calcified in them was magnified now, undoubtedly due to the occasion. But the look in his eyes—so sorrowful, so needful—was almost unbearable.

He mustered a half smile. "My babies. Y'all done got so big."

His voice, which had always carried a slight rasp, was hoarse. He sounded as old as Paw Paw but without the deep resonance. We gave him a hug. Reagan held him longer; there was no meaning, no connection in my embrace. And maybe Daddy sensed my aloofness as he stepped away from me and his eyes fell to the floor. The man who had once seemed tall as a cypress to me was much smaller. I could see over his receding hairline.

"It's good to see y'all," Daddy said. "Hey, y'all come here."

Reagan and I followed him into his bedroom with the pine-green walls and the heavy, dark wooden furniture. He pointed to two framed portraits on the dresser. There was an eight-by-ten of Reagan and me. We're around three and four years old in the picture, the tint on it slightly reddish from age. I'm gloriously Afroed in a black sailor suit and Reagan wears a white sailor dress with red bows in her hair. We're sitting in front of a cheesy backdrop of a Christmas tree and a roaring fireplace, our smiles wide and infectiously happy.

Next to that photograph was a five-by-seven of Mama from the early seventies, with her globular two-toned Afro—streaked blond in the front and black in the back. She's slender and unsmiling, sitting with her legs crossed in a dark turtleneck sweater and a sharp denim pantsuit.

"I bet y'all don't even remember that picture y'all took," Daddy said. "Y'all was just babies then, my babies. Now . . ."

His voice trailed off as he pointed to the picture of Mama. "That's Dianne right there."

"I know," I said.

Reagan cleared her throat. "She can't get into those jeans now."

We all cracked up. Daddy's laughter was interrupted by a hacking cough.

"You OK?" Reagan asked.

He loudly cleared his throat. "Yeah, baby, Daddy's OK. Hey, y'all come on back in the living room."

Daddy's movements were slow and labored. Reagan looked at me, her eyes full of concern, as we followed him back into the living room.

Relatives soon arrived. We sat across from Daddy on the couch as he zoned out into his own world. I tried not to focus on him much while I studied the solemn atmosphere. Cousins, aunts, uncles, and neighbors filled the living room. A woman I didn't recognize in a wide-brimmed black hat sobbed uncontrollably in a corner as Aunt Stella, Daddy's other sister, consoled her. Pat, Cuda's son, was stone-faced standing against a wall.

Daddy rode in the family limo with Big Mama, Paw Paw, and Pat. Reagan and I trailed along in the back seat of a cousin's car. I read the program that had been handed out at the house by the funeral director, a woman with a lovely voice but whose heavy makeup gave her a casket-ready look. Cuda's real name was Valerie Hunter. Valerie? After all those years, I never knew her real name. I guess I never really knew her. I wondered where the name "Cuda" had come from but didn't ask.

Folks wore nicknames born out of old habits, finicky tastes, a deformity, a special talent, a song that moved them, a movie that scared them. People rarely remembered the origin anyway. Dusa, for instance, stuck early on thanks to Phyl. She thought the baby's thick, curly hair resembled the snakes on Medusa's head. Plus, Roycelyn, her birth name, was too hard for some to pronounce. My nickname was an abbreviation of Dustin, my middle name.

The family church was two blocks or so down the street and around the corner. The funeral director lined the family up in pairs as we climbed the steep stairs into the old, packed church. I reached for Reagan's hand and grabbed it. I knew she was going to lose it as we got closer to the casket—and she did.

I thought maybe I would cry but I didn't. The woman in the casket wasn't the one I had known—or thought I had known. I couldn't remember the last time I had seen Cuda, but I didn't remember her looking so bloated. Her reddish, light-brown skin, the same complexion as mine, was now about two shades darker. I felt a deep sadness because I would miss Cuda's kindness and bell-like voice, but no tears ever came.

We sat in the pew with Daddy. Reagan sat between us. I stole glances at him during the service as his beautiful hands rested on his thighs, the same hands that years ago spread yellow mustard and placed a sardine on a saltine for me; the same hands that affectionately rubbed my head when he called me "Dus-Dus." I wanted to cry for that validating touch I'd been missing for years. Instead, I turned away and stared at Cuda's light-pink casket, now closed. About three months later, I'd be back inside that old church, surrounded by many of the same sad faces.

And I'd still long for the touch of those beautiful dark hands.

I knew he'd come.

The night after Cuda's funeral, while I was alone in my room in the dark, staring at the wall and listening to the Isley Brothers on my headphones, the slender, well-dressed man whom I'd long thought was Daddy appeared, floating in a corner. The cigarette glowed between his fingers. I could make out his slippery smile.

I removed my headphones and felt the need to say something, like, "I don't know who you are, but you're not my father." Instead, I said nothing. I didn't return his smile. Annoyed by him, I placed my headphones back on and turned away.

I never saw him again.

By the end of winter, the scholarship notices had started coming in. I had a full academic ride to the University of Arkansas. Mrs. Nichols, the assistant principal at Sylvan Hills and a cane-carrying, no-nonsense black mother figure to the students, stopped me in the hall after school one day to ask me if I'd participate in "Delta Presents." It was akin to a pageant and sponsored by the Delta Sigma Theta sorority, of which Mrs. Nichols had been a longtime member. "Delta Presents" had been something of a big event for the black middle class of Little Rock.

That year, 1996, it was going to be at the swanky Doubletree Hotel downtown. Participants had to fill out an application and write an essay. A week or two after I submitted mine, I found out I had been selected. There were rehearsals for the program, a grand Negro to-do, all for the chance to win a one-thousand-dollar scholarship.

I knew Mama would be excited—and she was. She had called me into her bedroom to massage a cramp in her shoulder.

"Mrs. Nichols said I have a good chance," I said, kneading Mama's tight left shoulder muscle.

"Well, Mrs. Nichols ought to know. That's more money you could get, boy!"

"But this is against every black dude in Little Rock."

"Dusty, have some confidence. Now, I gotta figure out what I'm gonna wear. The Doubletree Hotel? I'll say. Oh, we'll have to get your suit cleaned. Damn! Not so hard, Dusty. Get some more of that Flexall off the dresser."

Between classes and working at the library, there were scholarship luncheons and dinners to attend, senior pictures to take, and lots to buy for the move to Fayetteville, all of which would be covered by scholarships, grants, and money from my after-school gig at the library. Mama wasn't even going to have to buy a tube of toothpaste, and I was exceedingly proud of that. I was proving to myself that I was a man who could take care of himself.

All of the loneliness in TAG classes and escape into my books had culminated into an impressive transcript. I appeared in the *Arkansas Times*, the same publication overseen by journalist Max Brantley, whose wife a few years back had taken me home from the creative arts camp in Mena. Along with other scholastic achievers in central Arkansas, my picture and a small bright story detailing my high school career were featured in the paper's "Academic All-Stars" issue.

I was confident, eager to step into the next chapter and leave home. Leaving also meant I was done with the memory of Daddy. I didn't even speak to him at the gravesite. I stood across from him as they lowered Cuda's casket into the ground. The pitiful sight of him, the vacant look in his eyes, intensified my hate for him.

At eighteen, I didn't have the capacity to empathize with the pain he surely felt as he watched the casket holding his beloved niece enter a hole in the ground. It didn't occur to me to imagine how he may have felt seeing the children he didn't raise—now well-adjusted teenagers—and how the sight of us may have smashed what was left of his heart. There was nothing he could say between processing Cuda's death and seeing for the first time in God knows how long the pie-faced toddlers who grinned at him every day from an eight-by-ten on his bedroom dresser.

The drugs and hard living had finally caught up with Raymond Ollison. That was clear to me as I watched him standing there in the cool February air, looking frail in his dark suit. At age forty-five, he looked as old as his parents. I couldn't reconcile that image with the one I had clung to for years while he was away. And because he didn't appear to be the man I wanted him to be, the man I needed him to be, my hate for him seethed and clarified.

Yet there was still this ache for his approval, for him to say, "I'm sorry, son. I'm here now." But that was never going to happen, and I was pissed at myself for even entertaining those thoughts. Fuck it, Rashod. You're about to go to college, about to start this new chapter of your life. You're about to be your own man.

Do you really need anything from Raymond Ollison?

After Cuda's funeral, I asked a cousin to drop Reagan and me off at Happy Street, where Mama was waiting for us.

"Y'all not coming back to eat with the family?" she asked, dabbing tears.

"No, we have to get back to Little Rock," I said. "Mama's waiting for us. Is that OK?"

"Oh, no, that's fine. Teacake don't live too far from here. I'll drop y'all off right quick. But y'all sure y'all don't wanna come eat with us and sit with ya daddy? I mean, he . . ."

"No."

She lowered her eyes. "OK, Dusty."

In early spring, as the chill in the air started to disappear, we waited for Daddy to die.

In fact, he had already died when he was rushed to the hospital in Malvern, Aunt Stella later said. But he had been revived and was brought to St. Vincent in Little Rock, the same hospital where Mama had worked a few years before.

For nearly two weeks after school and after we got off work, Mama, Reagan, and I sat in the waiting room with the rest of the Ollisons while Daddy lay in a hospital bed a few doors down. He was unresponsive, with tubes in his mouth, hooked up to complicated-looking machines that kept him alive.

The family, some of Daddy's old drinking buddies, and long-time neighbors from East Section Line came to visit him. Aunt Ducky had flown in from Arizona and was ever-present at the hospital when Stella had to go back to Malvern to work. She sometimes stayed with her sister-in-law, who lived in Little Rock, but Ducky was usually at the hospital.

Big Mama and Stella were glad to see us there, especially Mama, whom they introduced to other visiting relatives as "Junior's wife," which didn't seem to bother Mama as she beamed her sunshine smile. Conversations among the grown folks in the waiting room were gossipy and monotonous—who had gotten married or divorced; who had died; whose kids were all grown up now, looking like the spitting image of this person and that one. Remember her? Yeah, she done moved. Gotta nice place out in the country. And on and on.

If Mama hadn't made me go, I would not have been there. I sat among my relatives but I really wasn't there. If I wasn't reading a book or doing homework, I had my headphones on. One evening,

I went across the street to the mall. I had just gotten paid and bought a few things—a new shirt and two new CDs. When I returned to the waiting room, bags in hand, Aunt Ducky looked as though she was irritated.

"Where's Mama and Reagan?" I asked.

"They're in the room with your daddy," Aunt Ducky said. "They didn't know where you went."

"To the mall."

"I see that. Dusty, come with me down to the cafeteria, will you? You can leave your things here; they'll be fine."

Aunt Ducky bought herself a cup of coffee and me a large Sprite. We sat across from each other at a small table in a corner of the large, mostly empty cafeteria.

"We haven't really had a chance to talk; everything's been so crazy," she said. "How are you handling all of this?"

"Handling what?" I purposely tried to sound flippant.

Aunt Ducky offered a tense smile. "Your father."

"I mean, I'm here, you know . . ."

She took a deep breath. "It's been hard for all of us, and I can see you're angry."

"We're talking about a man I haven't seen in years, Ducky."

"Listen, I won't even begin to try to explain my brother's actions. I know he hasn't been the best father or was the best husband. I know this. But what you need to know is that he loves you. He loves all of his children."

"He had a way of showing it, you know—never calling, never showing up."

Aunt Ducky nodded. "Yes, he gets no award for father of the year. But, Dusty, let me tell you this: that anger you're holding on to will turn you bitter, and that bitterness will only hurt you. Your daddy, my brother, has already paid for everything he's done and for what he didn't do. And Dianne knows this. Don't you know that she comes in here before she goes to work in the morning?"

"Really?"

"Yes." She nodded and smiled. "Your mother comes in here and sits in that room with him in the morning, right beside that bed. Your parents had their problems but they loved each other.

They were together for thirteen years, Dusty. Neither of them ever remarried. You don't think this is hard for her, too?"

Aunt Ducky looked away, took a breath, and returned her stern eyes to me. "Dusty, your father was a great example for you."

"A great example?"

"That's right. You're about to start your life and go off to college. Dianne told me all about your scholarships, and she's very proud of you. We're all proud of you. Your father was a great example of what not to be and what not to do. Now, you have no excuse to ever end up like him."

A few days later, Mama's call was transferred to the journalism room at school. I took the call in the teacher's office, a small room adjacent to the class. Mama said the family was going to take Daddy off of life support later that morning.

"I'll be up there to get y'all later on today," Mama said, sounding almost businesslike. "Don't tell Reagan."

"OK."

I hung up and steeled myself for the rest of the day. When Mama came to check us out of school that afternoon, we waited for Reagan to come to the office. I tried not to look at her as Reagan pelted us with questions. The walk from the school office to the front exit seemed especially long.

"Where we going?" Reagan asked. "Mama, why you takin' us out of school? What's going on?"

When we got to the door, Mama stopped and faced Reagan. "Raymond died this morning," she said matter-of-factly. "We're on our way to Malvern."

The change in Reagan's face seemed to happen in slow motion as her light-brown eyes momentarily froze in shock before the pain of the news twisted her face. She dropped her bag and jacket and fell to her knees, her wails echoing in the hall.

Mama held the door open. "Get her, Dusty."

I grabbed her bag and jacket and coaxed Reagan off the floor. "Come on, Reagan. It'll be OK," I said, softening my voice the way I did all those years ago when Cousin Jason woke up in the middle of the night weeping for his mama. "Come on. We got to go now. Come on, Reagan."

She leaned on me as we made our way to the car. I sat in the back with her while she buried her face in the seat and wept. The Fugees' version of Roberta Flack's "Killing Me Softly" was on the radio as Mama drove down the winding road away from Sylvan Hills. The youthful ache in Lauryn Hill's voice complemented Reagan's muffled sobs and moans. I rubbed my sister's back, not knowing what to feel. My eyes were dry and my mind inaccessible for the moment as I looked straight ahead.

I already knew we were going to leave soon after Daddy's funeral. That evening was the "Delta Presents" program. Mrs. Nichols had stopped me in the hall the week before to let me know that she'd heard I had a good chance of winning the scholarship.

"I hear the Deltas were very impressed with your interviews and essay," Mrs. Nichols said, smiling behind her dark-brown glasses.

To make the program, we wouldn't have time to return to the church after the service to eat with the family. This seemed to be something of a relief for all of us. Reagan had been crying all morning and I just wanted to get it over with. Mama's face was an elegant study of unreadable emotion.

"Y'all look nice," she said. "Y'all wait real quick. Let me get a picture."

Neither Reagan nor I smiled as Mama snapped photos of us near the front door. That morning was warm—in fact, it was downright hot, typical Arkansas weather in April. Mama had the air conditioner blasting in the car on the way to Malvern so we wouldn't sweat out our clothes. We were silent for the entire ride and still didn't say a word when we arrived at the white-and-brown house on East Section Line, where Daddy had grown up but didn't grow up.

The small house was already teeming with mourners. Ducky, Big Mama, and Stella gave us all hugs. A tall man, his face, now aged and round, brought to mind gleaming empty beer cans standing like soldiers on a coffee table and Tyrone Davis on the stereo crooning about making a woman melt like ice cream. The conversation about somebody getting killed after returning from Vietnam, Daddy's intense eyes, and how "muthafucka" glinted after the word left his lips—it all came back to me.

"You 'member me, Dusty?" the man said grinning.

"You Daddy's friend?"

"Coleman! I'm Coleman." He extended his hand and I shook it. "Yeah, boy, I 'member you. You was just a lit' boy last time I seen you. Been a long, long time."

His smile was wide, his eyes bloodshot and weary. "Raymond, man . . . Raymond, that was my main man. He was all right with me."

There was an ache in his voice that gave his words heft. He seemed to have intimate knowledge of a man who had been but a vapor in my life, someone who was there but not there; a man I tried to find in the lacerating wails of Bobby Womack and the soulful moans of Johnnie Taylor. A man whose validation I'd longed for but was never going to get, even if he had lived I'm not sure I would have gotten it because Raymond Ollison Jr. never validated himself.

The funeral director with the lovely voice and clownish makeup, the same woman who had overseen Cuda's funeral three months before, called everyone out into the front yard to get their programs and to get ready to head to the church.

Dusa, who was about seven months pregnant, had just pulled up with my aunts Nita and Kay. She was now married and enjoying domestic life with her husband, Ronald, a tall, burly man who adored her. I stood in the sun surrounded by relatives I barely knew, studying the picture of Daddy on the funeral program. It was an old one, his army photo, a picture I hadn't seen before. He's in a sharp green uniform, no facial hair, and his large eyes are unmistakably sad. He had to be about nineteen years old in the photo and already married to a curvy, creamy-skinned girl who lived 'cross town in a rowdy house on Third Street.

Mama, Reagan, and I followed the family limo in the slow procession to the church. I looked out of my window at East Section Line, the houses and folks standing on their porches, the mimosa, maple, and pecan trees, the yards that looked like plush, green carpet squares. Daddy loved this street and it loved him back. He always returned here, where a host of aunts, uncles, and cousins were ready to scold him, chide him, to tell him to "c'mon in and sit'cha self down" while somebody fixed him a plate of something cooked from the garden out back. With all the times we moved because the rent had become too high, I'd never gotten the chance to feel a special allegiance to a neighborhood, save for maybe Omega Street, where music filled the summer air, Mrs. Wyrick fed us neck bones, and projects divas yelled from open windows and doors.

On the same street where the church stood, inside a dingy clapboard house on the corner, Daddy was often found in the living room with his drinking buddies. I had been inside that house with him a few times, where the men sat around talking shit, smoking cigarettes or a joint, and throwing back shots of gin. He was loved there, too. It seemed all of East Section Line was standing on porches or lining the narrow street in front of the church. They had come to say good-bye to Junior. Lowdown Junior. Old Lady Ollison's baby boy, the one who married Dianne, with her pretty self. Ol' Junior. Gone too soon.

We filed into the church. I recognized several members from Emmanuel as I stood in the entrance. Reagan was between Mama and me. We held hands as we made our way to the casket. Reagan was inconsolable and I was hoping she wouldn't collapse the way she had done at school. As we stood at the casket, looking at Daddy one last time, Reagan covered her face and sobbed. I looked down at the man I'd always wanted to know. He looked as though he had been snatched from life, the hard living etched on his face. The imprint from the tubes that had been in his mouth in the hospital was still on his lips. Daddy's gone. I took a deep breath. My anger wasn't going to let me cry.

We sat in the front pew with the family. I watched Big Mama and Paw Paw, the last ones to view him. They were beautiful and dignified in black, Big Mama in a sharp, wide-brimmed hat, Paw Paw in a tailored suit. Big Mama reached out and touched her dear Junior. Paw Paw nodded as though answering a question that only he could hear from his son. Then the casket was closed.

And so was my heart.

I had nothing left for Raymond Ollison. My anger at him felt comfortable and right. I remembered Ducky's words in the hospital, that the anger would only hurt me, not Daddy. He was already dead.

But what would I do with it? There would have to be some way to convert the anger, to turn it into fuel for something progressive, as I had done with the deep loneliness I'd felt most of my life, a loneliness that seeded itself in me when Daddy left.

Your father was a great example of what not be and what not to do.

Those words seared into my brain. The choir sang about a sweet by-and-by. Relatives, including Daddy's cousin Dickie, shared stories about a quiet man who said, "Aw, I'm all right," as his world was crumbling. "And he loved his children," Dickie added. It took everything for me not to laugh out loud. What love?

I loved him.

At the gravesite, Aunt Ducky saw the still-fresh mound of dirt and rocks atop Cuda's grave next to Daddy's and fell to her knees in tears. A solitary tear streaked Mama's makeup as the casket was lowered into the ground. I thought Reagan may not have had any more tears left after crying throughout the service, but she continued to weep. I had no tears. I hugged Big Mama and Paw Paw and several relatives who knew me, though I didn't know them. It was crowded and I was hot. I was ready to go.

After saying our good-byes and explaining to folks why we had to get back to Little Rock, Mama, Reagan, and I returned to the car and pulled away. We were silent as Mama drove through the neighborhood to the highway. There wasn't a cloud in the sky. Reclined in the back seat, I loosened my tie.

"We'll get something to eat when we get to Little Rock," Mama said. "Y'all OK?"

Reagan and I mumbled "yeah" at the same time.

Malvern was miles behind us as my mind raced ahead, trying to figure out what to do with the anger. But there was no time to dwell on it. We'd have to eat and rest and get dressed to go the Doubletree Hotel for "Delta Presents," where I would win the scholarship. A month later, I'd graduate from Sylvan Hills with honors and three months after that move into my own room on the lush green campus of the University of Arkansas. Six months after Daddy's death, on a chilly Saturday morning in October, I'd be on a Greyhound bus on my way back to Malvern for Aunt Kay's funeral. She would be found shot to death in a bootlegger's house.

But on that April afternoon in the car with my mama and sister, I knew that whatever was ahead of me, I'd figure it out. I'd deal with my anger at Daddy some other time.

"It's too quiet in here," Mama said to no one in particular. "Get some music going."

She clicked on the radio.

I waited for the music to take me anywhere.

Acknowledgments

I AM FORTUNATE TO HAVE HAD GREAT SUPPORTERS IN MY LIFE, people who opened professional doors or gave of themselves so lovingly and unselfishly in my personal life. I must thank Amy Alexander for opening the door for me at Beacon Press, where the staff has been so gracious, smart, and sensitive to the birth of this book, especially my editor, Gayatri Patnaik. Thank you for everything.

I must give a big soulful shout-out to the brilliant and wonderful feature staff at the *Virginian-Pilot*, where an excerpt of this book appeared in the *Sunday Magazine* long before I knew it would become a book. It was at the *Pilot* that I blossomed into a more confident writer, thanks to the unwavering support of my editors, Jim Haag and Robert Morast, and the rest of the features staff, including Bill Henry, Michelle Washington, Denise Watson, Patty Jenkins, and Deb Markham. Virginia was a lonely place when I arrived, and I'd be remiss if I didn't thank publicist extraordinaire Ma'rie Hodges for all the thoughtful cards and warm heart-to-heart talks over happy-hour cocktails.

While writing this book, I was also pulling myself out of a serious depression. In addition to hiring a good therapist and fitness trainer, I often leaned on my beautiful friends, who are my family.

For the soul-satisfying laughs and much-needed late-night pep talks, I thank Josette Compton, Tiffany Armstrong-Comeaux, Kayce Ataiyero, Stephanie Arnold, Andre Darey, Tanika Davis, and Kevin and Olivia Dedner. I also thank my "cyber family" on Facebook, way too many to list here, for sending encouraging texts and posts.

I feel the love and absorb every drop.